The Grammar of the Heart

new essays in moral philosophy & theology

edited by Richard H. Bell

1817

Harper & Row, Publishers, San Francisco

Cambridge, Hagerstown, New York, Philadelphia, Washington
London, Mexico City, São Paulo, Singapore, Sydney

5-18-01

FIRST EDITION

Library of Congress Cataloging-in-Publication Data

The Grammar of the heart.

  Includes bibliographical references.
    1. Ethics.   2. Theology.   3. Wittgenstein, Ludwig,
1889–1951. 4. Kierkegaard, Søren, 1813–1855.
I. Bell, Richard H.
BJ1012.G67 1988   200'.1   87–46196
ISBN 0–06–060767–X

88 89 90 91 92 HC 10 9 8 7 6 5 4 3 2 1

For Paul and Phyllis Holmer

Contents

Acknowledgment of Essays

Acknowledgments

Thoughts for this book began about two years ago with an idea to pay tribute to Paul L. Holmer, Noah Porter Professor of Philosophical Theology at Yale University. With the generous support of the Henry Luce III Fund at The College of Wooster, Wooster, Ohio, and the Franklin J. Matchette Foundation, New York, a symposium was organized at The College of Wooster for March 1987: "The Grammar of the Heart: Thinking with Kierkegaard and Wittgenstein." Over one hundred scholars and teachers gathered to honor Paul. Twelve of the sixteen papers presented at the symposium have been revised and are included here. I would like to recognize the excellent contribution made to the symposium by the four scholars whose papers are not included in this book: Professor Niels Thulstrup of the University of Copenhagen, George Lindbeck of Yale University, Andrew Burgess of the University of New Mexico, and James L. Craft of Austin, Texas.

Two previously published essays of Paul Holmer have also been selected to complement central themes of this book. "Making Sense Morally" is reprinted with permission from *Making Christian Sense* by Paul L. Holmer (Philadelphia: Westminster Press, 1984). "The Grammar of Faith" is reprinted with permission from chapter 2 of *The Grammar of Faith* by Paul L. Holmer (San Francisco: Harper & Row, 1978). The previous publishers are gratefully acknowledged.

The assistance of Ms. Amy Patterson, secretary to the philosophy and geology departments of The College of Wooster, enabled the smooth running of the symposium, and Ms. Mimi Moore of the secretarial services, The College of Wooster, supervised the typing of the manuscript.

I am grateful to Henry Copeland, president of The College of Wooster, and to Glenn R. Bucher, dean of the faculty, for their personal support; to Mike Morris, my colleague in philosophy at Wooster, for his very helpful comments on my introductory essay;

and to Clayton E. Carlson, vice president and publisher, Harper & Row, San Francisco, for his trust in the project very early on. Finally, I wish to thank my wife, Barbara L. Bell, my daughter, Rebecca, and my son Jonathan for their kind hospitality to guests of the symposium and their support through the completion of the manuscript.

Richard H. Bell
Wooster, Ohio
June 1987

Introduction
Culture, Morality, and Religious Belief

RICHARD H. BELL

Not since early in this century has there been anything like a "revolution" in philosophy. Various forms of logical empiricism and linguistic analysis spurred a revolution in English-speaking countries.[1] In 1955, a book of philosophical essays was published that grew out of and was a response to this revolution. The book, *New Essays in Philosophical Theology,* gave rise to two decades of lively discussion on the nature of religious and theological language. That discussion is now exhausted—in part because the revolution itself shows few signs of life.

As the last quarter of our century winds down, a new revolutionary mood (if not a fundamentally new revolution) is placing new pressures on the course of philosophy. This latter revolutionary mood has even called for an end to philosophy itself—particularly as it has been practiced for the past fifty years.[2] The criticisms of Richard Rorty and others show the fractured nature of our highly individualized and atomized culture and how very difficult it is for us to get out from under the shadow of positivism. Another critic, Alasdair MacIntyre, focuses on the moral bankruptcy of our culture, calling this a failure of the "enlightenment experiment" of Western culture.[3] Still other voices of this revolutionary mood—largely represented by a group of French and German philosophers who refer to our culture as a "post-modern" one—point a finger at our scientific and technocratic communities, blaming them for the current state of human fragmentation and an oppressive rationalization of human life.[4]

Although these current criticisms are largely diagnostic, some offer clues for the restoration of moral and social wholeness, advocating a more "communitarian" spirit on a small scale to effect better human communication or freer access to information so that a local public can break the tyranny of an overrationalized culture and "narrate" a more just common life for themselves.

To date the constructive efforts within this second revolutionary spirit have focused on change in our moral and social outlooks[5] and few have commented on the role that investigations of theological concepts or religious practice might contribute to a restoration of human spirit and a sense of a common life in the midst of our fragmentation. The essays in this book, subtitled *New Essays in Moral Philosophy and Theology*, offer such a commentary; they are responsive to this second revolutionary mood but offer a decidedly different approach from those mentioned above.

These "new essays" are also decidedly different in how they approach fundamental issues in the philosophy of religion. A close monitoring of standard course texts, journal articles, and various colloquia offered in the philosophy of religion reveals that the majority of literature and discussion still focus on questions of rational justification of religious claims, concern for proof and evidence, and the limits of "epistemic credentials." These concerns are derived from the earlier, more empirically oriented discussions—it is as if the field of philosophy of religion, and consequently some theology, has not really caught up with the rest of philosophy.[6] The essays included in this book break with those "majority" concerns and address more "wholistic" ones—focusing on the integration of language with human life, beliefs with emotions and passions, mind with heart, doubt with faith—without sacrificing a philosophical concern for clarity of thought, certainty, and truth.

In many of the critical views of the new revolutionary mood, particular philosophers are held up as models. These philosophers pointed a way through the difficulties and dilemmas of their own time and still have something fresh to say to our time. Such philosophers become background figures for current investigations. Among those most frequently referred to within our new revolutionary mood are Socrates, Aristotle, Montaigne, Pascal, Kierkegaard, Nietzsche, Simone Weil, and Wittgenstein. This is a curious but quite natural line-up of major thinkers. All of these philosophers give primary attention to the concept of the self as central in the process of understanding; all underscore self-involvement in the moral life and address philosophical problems from a first person perspective (Aristotle is an exception on this point, but his account of the virtues provides us with a framework for first person reflection). All to some degree give importance to language as fundamental to human understanding and human reflection. The pages of this book have two of these philosophers as background figures: Søren Kierkegaard and Ludwig Wittgenstein.

THINKING WITH KIERKEGAARD AND WITTGENSTEIN

In what manner do Kierkegaard and Wittgenstein converge and provide us with a unique mode of investigation? In the midst of the earlier revolution (post–World War II years through the 1950s) Paul L. Holmer[7] began developing a different strategy for understanding the nature of religious language from his British counterparts represented in the 1955 "new essays." The British had little inclination to either read or take seriously Kierkegaard's works.[8] Furthermore, access to Wittgenstein's later thinking was minimal (in the minds only of a few former students and devotees). With the posthumous publication of Wittgenstein's *Philosophical Investigations* in 1953, it was still much too early to see which direction its interpreters would take his thought, especially as it might apply to issues outside of those taken up directly in the *Investigations*.

In this postwar period Anglo-American theology was dominated either by the verificationists'/empiricists' criticism of metaphysics on the one hand or by the "de-mythologizing" activities and "existentialist" critiques of human nature provided by German-speaking philosophers and theologians on the other hand.[9] Concurrent with these dominant views, Paul Holmer began to wed some of the ideas of Kierkegaard and Wittgenstein in ways that gave a new liveliness to their works and suggested some new directions in which moral philosophy and theology might develop. No longer was Kierkegaard just an "existentialist" thinker, nor could Wittgenstein be constrained within narrow "analytic" bounds. They both were seen to address the human heart by their careful analysis of concepts that focused attention on how to understand human subjectivity and how to see our human affections and emotions as part of human life and culture. The logic of the "stages" in Kierkegaard was seen as a way of mapping human emotions to show their place in our existence, and Wittgenstein's concept of "grammar" pointed to the interconnection of our language with our life.

It is only recently that the full corpus of Wittgenstein can be interpreted properly to allow us to see his contribution to moral philosophy and theology. The posthumous literature of Wittgenstein (especially *Culture and Value*, 1980) and recent literature about Wittgenstein (for example, *Recollections of Wittgenstein*, 1984, especially the recollections of M.O'C. Drury) have shown the appreciation Wittgenstein had for Kierkegaard and the knowledge he had of Kierkegaard's religious outlook and also makes clear the deep concerns Wittgenstein had for the personal religious life even though he maintained that he was not himself a religious person. Holmer sensed early the full implications of Wittgenstein's thought, and his immersion in the Kierkegaard literature made the connections with Wittgenstein more self-evident.[10] He turned these new thoughts toward what he called a "morphology of the life of Christian belief, a logic and a grammar that we miss often because a monstrous illusion is fostered by a pattern of thought and speech, wherein objectivity, fact, meaning, truth, and even faith are advertised but never delivered."[11]

This latter point has been brought out very clearly in Fergus Kerr's *Theology After Wittgenstein* (1986). Kerr's book is extremely important in placing Wittgenstein properly in our century. Wittgenstein's links with William James and with Kierkegaard are developed by Kerr, but more important is Kerr's thesis that places Wittgenstein's work as a critique of the 'Cartesian bias' in our modern world. Wittgenstein's originality as a philosopher, says Kerr, "is to have written a text that enables the reader, with patience and luck, to become suspicious of the power the [Cartesian] myth still wields."[12] This in itself is not a new interpretation of Wittgenstein, but Kerr uses it to a particularly important advantage to show how Wittgenstein critiques "modernity" from "a religious point of view."[13] This critique focuses attention on the elementary patterns of our current social and cultural interaction as expressive of our human life with or without God. No longer can we look at our human life in the world as a "detached self, disengaged from personality and historical contingency,"[14] rather, Kerr says, that Wittgenstein moved in the *Philosophical Investigations* to show us that "nothing is more foundational to the whole human enterprise than the community that we create in our natural reactions to one another as they have been cultivated and elaborated in a very contingent historical tradition."[15] All of this, notes Kerr, provides us with "a radical critique of 'the traditional drive to spiritual purity,' " and secures "a focal significance for the human body."[16] What we are is found squarely in what we say and do with and toward others. Thus we must radically reexamine how it is we do these things with or without God and the manner in which God figures into human life. More will be said later about these points as they relate to specific essays in this book.

We are still left with the question of how these two philosophers, Kierkegaard and Wittgenstein, figure into the orientation of the essays in this book. A curious but important feature of these essays is that they cannot be labeled simply "Kierkegaardian" or "Wittgensteinian" in any current sense in which those terms are sometimes used. For example, a common label applied to some who use Wittgenstein to discuss religious belief is to call them "Wittgensteinian fideists."[17] To conceive of Wittgenstein's thought on religious belief in this manner is a very narrow reading of him (it is "one view only" as Jens Glebe-Møller discusses in his essay). The emphasis given to religious practice and the public context of the moral and religious life by most of the authors in this book should clearly separate them from the "fideistic" reading of Wittgenstein. John Whittaker's essay is particularly clear on disassociating Wittgenstein from a "fideistic" bias.

Wittgenstein and Kierkegaard urge their readers to be passionate thinkers. If a reader of these philosophers learns to be such a thinker, if one learns to be attentive to what lays before one's eyes, if one learns to describe aspects of human existence as they unfold, then one has been faithful to their thought. One need not write about either philosopher and ought not try to mimic their styles. Wittgenstein remarked about how one should read his own writings: "I ought to be no more than a mirror, in which my reader can see his own thinking with all its deformities so that, helped in this way, he can put it right."[18] H. A. Nielsen, in his "A Meeting of Minds on Water," provides us with an example of how Kierkegaard and Wittgenstein enable us to see our "own thinking with all its deformities" and how each offers suggestions as to how we might put our own thinking right.

In over thirty years since the publication of the *Philosophical Investigations*, and literally hundreds of essays later on topics related to Wittgenstein and religious belief, Wittgenstein rarely triumphs. He is usually over exposed and dryly used. The goal of each essay here is not exposition or interpretation of either Kierkegaard's or Wittgenstein's thought itself—though in a few essays exposition of texts is important, for example, Kierkegaard texts in Polk and Walsh, and Wittgenstein texts in Whittaker and Glebe-Møller—but rather a creative use of their way of doing philosophy. These essays, I would argue, are genuinely *in the spirit of* both Wittgenstein and Kierkegaard; these philosophers are there "to help us think something through" rather than as authorities to pronounce some forgotten truths.[19] They both have that special gift of making their readers *thinkers*.

Kierkegaard once distinguished two types of authors. Some he said were "essential-thinkers" while others were "premise-thinkers." The former are inwardly directed and have a capacity for possessing a perspective of their own. The essential-thinker, says Kierkegaard, knows "what she is, what she wills; from first to last she is attentive to understanding herself in her life-view."[20] The latter thinkers—premise-thinkers—are tentative and lack their own perspective. So Kierkegaard and Wittgenstein join us to help us think clearly and in an essential manner, to notice the interrelations between things, to see connections in what otherwise may seem a disconnected and fragmented life, and to help us gain a self-perspective that will see us through the tangles of our "modern" times. The authors in this book challenge the premise thinking in us all when it comes to how we reflect on culture and the moral and religious practices that are still a part of our culture.

In 1930, Wittgenstein remarked that his was "an age without culture"—fragmented and full of friction. Individual women and men had lost the means to express their values and to work in "the spirit of the whole."[21] Over fifty years later, the fragmentation in the European and American societies seem only to have gotten worse and the friction greater. It might be said that we, too, are an age without culture. This, of course, is why a new revolutionary mood is upon us. Restoring a means by which human values can be expressed and a "spirit-filled" common life can be renewed may enable us to develop an age *with* a culture. The contributions in this book, shaped in part by how Kierkegaard or Wittgenstein (or both) stand to each essay, have in a modest way this end in view.

THE GRAMMAR OF THE HEART

Why is this collection called *The Grammar of the Heart*? Although a full answer to this question will become apparent to readers of the book, a few words are in order here on the use of the concepts "grammar" and "heart" and how they are related to some specific essays. The terms "logic" and "grammar" have a resemblance in the writing of Kierkegaard and Wittgenstein. It has already been noted that Kierkegaard associated various patterns of language and human existence as having a logic to them—a logic stemming from our emotions (the human subject) and finding concrete shape in their communication in ordinary activities of life. This connected feature of emotion and language in Kierkegaard is discussed by John Whittaker, Don Saliers, Timothy Polk, and Sylvia Walsh in their essays, and Whittaker discusses the same connection in Wittgenstein. Paul Holmer in the lead essay, "The Grammar of Faith," explores the extended significance of thinking about theology, in Wittgenstein's phrase, "as grammar."[22]

Just as having a grammar in our language helps us make sense with our words, so, too, having a grammar of our emotions, or our will, or our moral action helps us make sense of our lives. In "Making Sense Morally," Holmer writes: "To know the grammar of life is like knowing the grammar of a living language; it enables and empowers one to make sense." Although the concept of "grammar" conjures up declining verbs and keeping parts of speech straight, Wittgenstein associated it with the "activity of speaking" and how such activity is woven deeply into historical and social "forms of life." Among the many things that thinking of grammar in this way can help us understand is our moral language and the manner in which we shape our religious life. Both Mason and Roberts discuss the grammar of moral language, its complexity and context dependence. Beyond what the term grammar may ordinarily imply for our moral life, it also affects the whole of human life itself. It is here that Holmer sees its importance for theology. Holmer notes: "theology does not parse verbs, arrange thoughts, and conjugate sentences. . . . Insofar as it is a grammar, it is more like the teaching that leads to a truly successful, deeply satisfactory, even blessed and happy life." "The whole business of using theology as grammar," he continues, "requires also that we refer our nation, our world, our selves, our future to God."

As these new essays address the passions of the human heart, so, too, they address the central issues of our common life. In fact, a concern in most of these essays, if only indirectly, is to show how understanding the very concept of the "heart" is to see it woven into the activities of our common life. "Heart" is not viewed as a hidden something, characterizing a separate metaphysical or emotional subject. In the midst of our individualistic preoccupations, reciprocity and partnership in common human endeavors become lost and it becomes easy to privatize the "self" as such a metaphysical subject. This is a condition spawned by what MacIntyre called our "enlightenment mentality" with its division of "objective" and "subjective," "cognitive" and "emotive," "science" and "subjectivity."

Rowan Williams meets this condition head-on in his essay, "The Suspicion of Suspicion," and notes, "If we lack a properly common language, a properly public life, we shall be increasingly unsure of what (in both the simplest colloquial sense and the more philosophical sense) other people *mean*: we shall mistrust the other until and unless we have a key to unlock the secret chamber of their 'essential' selfhood, a technique of decoding. . . ." Thus suspicion arises that all is not as it seems. We take "flight from the risks of discourse" and a greater control must be exercised on all aspects of our life. Here Williams selects insights from Wittgenstein and Dietrich Bonhoeffer, both of whom he says were "aware of living in a culture saturated with fundamental untruthfulness. It is precisely because our culture is fragmented in so many ways (by economic injustice, by nationalistic violence and threatened violence) that we are unable to speak truthfully with each other, and public language becomes a mountainous refuse heap of self-protective clichés. . . ."

Williams then shows us how Wittgenstein and Bonhoeffer provide us with clues toward greater truthfulness by sketching for us a manner of living in our world that is connected and compassionate. Williams suggests that lessons from these two thinkers "invite us to take time" and that such taking of time extends to all quarters of human life and culture—it can enable me to recall myself to myself and myself to others and others to me. Williams notes: "My obscurity to myself, yours to me, and mine to you are not *puzzles*, waiting for fruitful suspicion to uncover the real script, Marxian, Freudian, sociobiological. . . . They are to do with the inescapability of taking time. 'I do not really know myself' must be heard as 'I don't yet know what to say; how to speak so that others listen and answer and build up in their words a way for me to go on speaking so that others may answer; how to become a partner in the world.' The sense of a choked or imprisoned or elusive interiority is, on this account, a sense of skills not yet learned, and nourishment not given, or not knowing what it might be to be heard and so set free. . . ." Putting things right with greater "risk-filled discourse" in the context of our common life is an end to which Williams and others point us. Williams echoes Wittgenstein's theme that we find our self when we can locate our self within "forms of life."[23]

Jonathan Edwards once remarked, "He that trusts his own heart is a fool." For Edwards, during the Great Awakening of the 1740s in America, this remark focused on the many possibilities of both self-deception and suspicion regarding our interior feelings and the fact that they are not trustworthy and, furthermore, that such feelings must be somehow rendered public or observable. This notion of a private and inner life is precisely the picture that must be resisted today. Our own hearts can be trusted only if they are rendered accessible and public. As long as the suspicion remains that the heart is hidden and inaccessible then "mis"trust will continue, but if we can reconstrue the heart in a grammar that is consistent with a public life—our moral actions, religious practices, formed emotions in gesture, liturgy, and language—then trust can be restored and human communion as communicative understanding and mutual respect on an interpersonal and inter-communal basis can lead us toward a new sense of spirit and perhaps the recovery of a culture.

"GRAMMARIANS" AND "GUARDIANS"

D. Z. Phillips points to a feature of Holmer's work that may well characterize the spirit of these essays as a whole. Holmer, he says, moves beyond being a "grammarian" (one who seeks to understand the shape of moral and theological concepts) to being a "guardian" of the moral and religious life (one who knows how to embody those concepts in practice and thus sustain their empowering qualities). Similarly, most of the essays here explore lines along which we can restore a moral and religious order as well as clarify such a possible order in the midst of chaos.

The essays in part I of this book tend to reflect more of the "grammarian's" task. They are more philosophical in nature and offer an analysis of the grammar of our modern culture and of religious practices in general (for example, Williams, Phillips, Whittaker, Nielsen, Hustwit, and Glebe-Møller). The essays in part II tend to focus on the grammar of moral life (Holmer, Mason, and Roberts) and specifically Christian concepts and practices (for example, Roberts, Sherry, Saliers, Polk, and Walsh). By the careful look at concepts like "inspiration," "sin," "hope," "sorrow," "gratitude," and "love," and the uses of prayer and Scripture reading by the communities of faith, the role of "guardian" gets clarified and exemplified in these latter essays.

To draw out the "morphology of the life of Christian belief," Holmer, for example, says would require first that we review our moral life as preparatory to the life of Christian belief. With and through the thought of C. S. Lewis, Holmer has argued that being moral, practicing the virtues, is "the very ground of being rational."[24] Holmer and others urge upon us a rethinking of a morality of the virtues. They show us that the moral life provides an order, a coherence, and a rationale to our becoming persons, and "cardinal" virtues become foundational to the Christian practices of faith, hope, and love. While making sense morally is foundational to being rational, Holmer goes a step further to argue that "making sense morally is a minimum natural requirement" to making sense "Christianly." Here our attention is turned not only to the life of Christian belief but also to what theology is as guardian of the faith.

Learning morals often revolves around the cultivation of particular virtues like "patience," "courage," "fairness," or "truthfulness." Virtues, too, have a certain grammar. Each virtue has its patterns of action, emotion, and motivation and is embedded in what Robert Roberts calls a "virtues-system." "No virtue," Roberts says, "is an island. Each virtue gets its character from the surrounding geography of concepts and practice—what I have called the virtues-system to which it belongs." He sketches three type systems—a stoic system, contemporary psychotherapeutic systems, and a biblically Christian system—to show how virtues are appropriated differently in each and why the system makes a substantial difference in the practice of the virtues. By showing that the various psychotherapies widely practiced today do in fact constitute alternative virtues-systems, they can be seen in direct competition with other systems. To note such differences enables us to see the importance of our choices in affirming and practicing one system over another.

There is a final point to make about most of the essays in part II of this book—it has to do with the "how" of reintroducing Christianity into a person's life within the context of our culture. This was one of Kierkegaard's major tasks. For him the culture and everyone in it thought they knew what Christianity was and this made the task especially complex for Kierkegaard. Offering his own interpretation of the *Philosophical Fragments,* Kierkegaard wrote: "Because everyone knows the Christian truth, it has gradually become such a triviality that a primitive impression of it is acquired only with difficulty. When this is the case, the art of being able to *communicate* eventually becomes the art of being able to *take away* or to trick something away from someone."[25] We could say further that the suspicion lurks that the "real interpretation" lies "inside" or "hidden"—not, in fact, in how we express and live one with another in a "primitive" or first-order fashion struggling to be honest and expose our limits. Today, however, most of our culture ignores Christianity and gives only a nod to some form of "civil religion." Religion has become largely instrumental and its claims on us continually shift ground. When there is no clear religious claim on a person, then moral claims may pass easily, too. With both of these gone, the culture wanes.

Patrick Sherry, in "Inspiration and the Heart," cites this remark of Coleridge: "[I]n the Bible there is more that *finds* me than I have experienced in all other books put together. . . ." The inspiration of the biblical canon does not simply excite a response but gives shape to a whole human response—a response that not only reaches me (the reader) but has the capability of enabling me to find myself. It is the sense of biblical inspiration that Kierkegaard lifts up (what Kierkegaard would call "primitive reading") to us in his reading of the Epistle of James, as Timothy Polk's essay develops. Polk shows us the remarkable difference that one reading can make over another—it is like the difference of one placing an external interpretation on the Bible on the one hand and allowing the Bible to do its own inspirational or formative work on the reader's own heart and life on the other.

Polk's essay is a careful textual analysis of Kierkegaard's understanding of James. It is both Kierkegaard's and the apostle's intent to show that God's word shapes our Christian life by forcing an awareness on the reader of our doubts and self-deceit and by restoring a confidence whereby our faith is formed in Christian practice by the very dispositions of the human heart. Gratitude develops a heart while carelessness, sorrow, and defiance diminishes it. "To make Christian sense of Scripture," says Polk, "one must live as well as read in the expectation of (a discomforting) comfort, in courage, and in gratitude." In addition to gratitude, a Christian life is both formed and confirmed in the practice of prayer and in works of love; this is argued by Don Saliers and Sylvia Walsh, respectively.

Walsh, starting with Kierkegaard's remark that "love forms the heart," traces the logic or grammar of the concept of love in Kierkegaard, a grammar that points to the internal (heart's) connection of God's love with human love, the very relational character of God through love, and the language used in "the communication of love in 'heart to heart' talk between lovers"—language that is both ordinary and poetic, "speak[ing] out of the abundance of the heart."

Saliers' analysis of the grammar of prayer and the relationship of emotion and belief moves close to Williams' discussion of how we can use the traditional concepts of Christian interiority without reverting to "inner" and "outer" language. If the reader were to take, for example, Holmer's first essay along with Williams and Saliers (even perhaps Sherry and Polk), they could be read as providing a coherent theological perspective.

The essays here that serve a "guardian" role for Christian theology, do not go unchallenged. D. Z. Phillips raises the haunting spectre of "whether the grammar of theology allows for its own demise," that is, if the cracks in a language of faith and our very way of life become so severe, so fragmented (as many would argue) perhaps the cure of restoration through older remedies (all our attempts to "put it right") simply will not work or will no longer make any sense. There is a real risk here for the whole religious enterprise. Or even for one that seeks to resurrect a virtue ethics approach to restore some moral order as Alasdair MacIntyre's program attempts to do. Jens Glebe-Møller, like Phillips, calls into question whether there remain substantial grounds for a significant religious language in "post-modern" culture—whether the "common ground" for communication can still be said to be rooted in a religious mythology (a Christian grammar) or whether what remains common to us for purposes of communication has only the possibilities available to it arising from a secular background. There is a strong lobby supporting this latter view, and it presents a substantial challenge for the very future of theology.

CONCLUDING REMARKS

In *Either/Or*, Kierkegaard wrote:

Our age reminds one vividly of the dissolution of the Greek city-state: everything goes on as usual, and yet there is no longer anyone who believes in it. The invisible spiritual bond which gives it validity no longer exists, and so the whole age is at once comic and tragic—tragic because it is perishing, comic because it goes on.[26]

These "new essays" in one sense point toward how we may restore a "spiritual bond" in our age. But they seek not to make the spiritual bond "invisible," rather to show that our human life must be understood as a public life and that our hearts to be trustworthy must be open to view and actively involved in shaping a common life.

In his recent book *Themes Out Of School*, Stanley Cavell pursues

"his lifelong quarrel with the profession of philosophy."[27] He
believes philosophy has lost touch with its Socratic roots; it has
suppressed its "human voice" and become highly professional-
ized—a kind of meta-discipline. Philosophy has a legacy of instruction and edification in addition to clarification—it is there to help
one find one's feet and move on. Cavell asks: "And what if the
fundamental fact of philosophy lies in its recognition of a certain
social role, as in Plato's image of the philosopher as gadfly. . . ."
And then he says, alluding to Wittgenstein's remark in the *Investigations,* "perhaps 'gadfly' is the name in philosophy of what in it
forever resists professionalization. (Who but a gadfly would undertake to show the fly the way out of the fly bottle?)"[28] The essays
in this collection, too, resist professionalization in a similar manner—with a spirit of instruction and edification—and several of
their authors (especially Holmer, Nielsen, and Phillips) are known
"gadflies" among philosophers. There is a very strong effort
through this entire collection to restore a *human voice* within the
profession. When a person speaks of God or of matters of moral
worth, that person is not preoccupied with the nature of proposi-
tional claims, rather he or she speaks as an ordinary person trying
to find words to witness to what may be understood of a human
self. This is no easy task when the very idea of a self is isolated from
mutual concern, shared practices and a common life. Finding
"heart enough to be confident" in our time is often a lonely task.
Being morally responsible, as H. E. Mason insists, must be understood within the frame of common concern and a common language. If both are lost then understanding what we must do
becomes increasingly difficult.

We are a culture in transition, some would say decline. Our
retrospective view on the past three centuries has called them an
"enlightenment," but our current state often seems anything but
"enlightened"! Before we can accurately judge this period, a
clearer vantage point is required; we need a cultural perspective
that is a truly human one, one that enables us to speak in a human
voice. This remark of Wittgenstein's is hauntingly prophetic: "Perhaps one day this civilization will produce a culture. When that
happens there will be a real history of the discoveries of the 18th,
19th and 20th Centuries, which will be deeply interesting."[29] If we
could reclaim a morality of the virtues integrated with a vision of

renewed human community or a new grammar of the heart, we might "produce a culture" worth preserving as we enter the twenty-first century. Only then will the possibility arise of a "deeply interesting" history of the times we are muddling through.

What is striking about the suggestions in these essays is that the language sought to express moral and Christian values in our culture is the ordinary language of the human heart—a language that comes closer to the vernacular of human life. "Any fool," noted C.S. Lewis, "can write 'learned' language. The vernacular is the real test. If you can't turn your faith into it, then either you don't understand it or you don't believe it."[30]

Wittgenstein wrote the following, which summarizes the spirit of Kierkegaard, and Holmer's spirit, and the spirit of the writers of this book regarding how to think about religious belief and a genuine grammar of the human heart:

It strikes me that a religious belief could only be something like a passionate commitment to a system of reference. Hence, although it's *belief,* it's really a way of living, or a way of assessing life. It's passionately seizing hold of *this* interpretation. Instruction in a religious faith, therefore, would have to take the form of a portrayal, a description, of that system of reference, while at the same time being an appeal to conscience. And this combination would have to result in the pupil himself, of his own accord, passionately taking hold of the system of reference. It would be as though someone were first to let me see the hopelessness of my situation and then show me the means of rescue until, of my own accord, or not at any rate led to it by my *instructor,* I ran to it and grasped it.[31]

NOTES

1. See D. F. Pears and G. Ryle, eds., *The Revolution in Philosophy* (London: Macmillan, 1955); Antony Flew, ed., *Logic and Language* (Oxford: Basil Blackwell: first series 1951 and second series 1953) and *Essays in Conceptual Analysis* (London: Macmillan, 1956). Symbolic of the most positivistic aspect of this revolutionary mood was the publication in 1936 of A. J. Ayer's *Language, Truth, and Logic* (London: Gollancz).
2. See Richard Rorty, *Philosophy and the Mirror of Nature* (Oxford: Basil Blackwell, 1980). Rorty's book shows the inherent limitations in the epistemological outlook of the empirical and analytic tradition. He argues that we are led to a false scientism and must finally give up our attempts to gain certainty. His

alternative to this is a pragmatic and aesthetic approach to human and social interaction through more active dialogue.

3. See Alasdair MacIntyre, *After Virtue* (Notre Dame: Notre Dame University Press, 1981). MacIntyre argues that our moral bankrupty is a result of our moral language having lost all its content. What inherited moral language we do have is either placed in the service of one ideology or another or it serves highly personal and individualistic ends.

4. See Jean-Francois Lyotard, *The Post-Modern Condition* (Minneapolis: University of Minnesota Press, 1984); Michel Foucault, *Power/Knowledge: Selected Interviews and Other Writings, 1972–1977* (New York: Pantheon, 1981); and Jurgen Habermas, *The Theory of Communicative Action,* vol. 1, trans. Thomas McCarthy (Boston: Beacon Press, 1985) and *Der philosophische Diskurs der Moderne* (Frankfurt: Suhrkamp, 1985).

5. See especially MacIntyre, *After Virtue;* MacIntyre and S. Hauerwas, eds., *Revisions: Changing Perspectives in Moral Philosophy* (Notre Dame: University of Notre Dame Press, 1983); and Robert Bellah et al., *Habits of the Heart* (New York: Harper & Row, 1985).

6. Much of this discussion revolves around the work of Richard Swinburne [see his *Faith and Reason* (Oxford: Clarendon Press, 1981) and *The Existence of God* (Oxford: Clarendon Press, 1979)] and those of the so-called "reformed epistemologists" (Alvin Plantinga et al.). These are illustrative of how one can become tied to the issues of the earlier "revolution." Ronald E. Hustwit's and D. Z. Phillips's essays in this volume discuss some of the difficulties in the "reformed epistemologists." Hustwit, for example, concludes his discussion of Plantinga's account of the rationality of belief in God with this remark: "His [Plantinga's] claim that belief in God is rational, I find partly confused and partly wrong. Whichever it is, I think it works to suppress the essential features of faith that include risk, passion, paradox and duties—grammar appropriate to affairs of the heart rather than to rationality."

For a general discussion of some of the important issues found between these two revolutions see Terence Penelhum, *God and Skepticism* (Dordrecht, Holland: D. Reidel Publishing Co., 1983), especially chapters 7 and 8.

7. Holmer was a young Kierkegaard scholar on the philosophy faculty of the University of Minnesota, then a center of logical empiricism—Kierkegaard once more in the midst of the established intellectual culture was naturally volatile. In 1960, Holmer moved to Yale University where he taught philosophy and theology until his retirement in May 1987. It was at Yale where the Wittgenstein link with Kierkegaard matured.

8. There were a few notable exceptions to this—especially the Welsh philosopher, D. Z. Phillips, a former student of Rush Rhees, who, in the 1960s, actively wedded Kierkegaard with Wittgenstein in his reflections on religious language. See his *The Concept of Prayer* (Oxford: Basil Blackwell, 1981), and articles in his edited *Religion and Understanding* (Oxford: Basil Blackwell, 1967), especially the articles of Phillips, Norman Malcolm, and Peter Winch.

9. One need only conjure the names of Heidegger, Bultmann, Tillich, and the early writings of Barth.

10. It should be said that during this same postwar period another American philosopher, O. K. Bouwsma (1898–1978) was also quietly drawing together strands in the thought of Kierkegaard and Wittgenstein and educating a generation of teachers and scholars. Bouwsma had been a friend of Wittgenstein. Two of Bouwsma's works should be noted: *Without Proof or Evidence: Essays of*

O.K. Bouwsma, ed. J. L. Craft and Ronald E. Hustwit (Lincoln: University of Nebraska Press, 1984) and *Wittgenstein Conversations, 1949–1951*, ed. Craft and Hustwit (Indianapolis: Hackett Publishing Co., 1986).

Two philosophy symposia, sponsored by the philosophy department of The College of Wooster, Wooster, Ohio, brought together scholars from Great Britain and North America and had Kierkegaard and Wittgenstein as their focus. Papers from the first symposium (October 1976) were published by The College of Wooster, entitled *Essays on Kierkegaard and Wittgenstein: On Understanding the Self,* edited by Richard H. Bell and Ronald E. Hustwit (1978) and dedicated to O. K. Bouwsma. A selection of the papers from the second symposium, "The Grammar of the Heart: Thinking with Kierkegaard & Wittgenstein" (March 1987), are here published and dedicated to Paul Holmer and his wife Phyllis Holmer.

11. Paul L. Holmer, *The Grammar of Faith,* (San Francisco: Harper & Row, 1978), p. xi. Stanley Cavell, too, saw similar connections between Wittgenstein and Kierkegaard. This was articulated in his essay "Existentialism and Analytic Philosophy," *Daedalus* (Summer 1964) and reprinted in his *Themes Out of School,* see especially pages 217–34 of *Themes.* See note 23 below. Cavell remarks there: "Wittgenstein says that his *Philosophical Investigations* is a work of 'grammar,' and Kierkegaard calls his *Postscript* a 'Mimic-Pathetic-Dialectic Composition,' and he first thought of entitling it simply, 'Logical Problems.' To understand these descriptions would be to understand the works in question" (p. 225).

12. Fergus Kerr, *Theology After Wittgenstein,* (Oxford: Basil Blackwell, 1986), p. 75.

13. Ibid., p. 32f.

14. Ibid., p. 25.

15. Ibid., p. 76.

16. Ibid., p. 27.

17. See Kai Nielsen, "Wittgensteinian Fideism," *Philosophy* 42 (1967).

18. Wittgenstein, *Culture and Value,* ed. G. H. Von Wright and trans. Peter Winch (Chicago: University of Chicago Press, 1980), p. 18. This was first published in 1977 as *Vermischte Bemerkungen* (Frankfort am Main: Suhrkamp Verlag).

19. This is a phrase used by Judith N. Shklar in her *Ordinary Vices* (Cambridge, Mass.: Harvard University Press, 1984), p. 228, to illustrate the sense in which Michel de Montaigne was a background figure in her reflections on our current preoccupation with ordinary vices.

20. Søren Kierkegaard, *On Authority and Revelation* (New York: Harper & Row, Torchbook, 1966), pp. 6–9.

21. Wittgenstein, *Culture and Value,* p. 6.

22. A good bit has been written about Wittgenstein's remark in *Philosophical Investigations* #373, including my "Theology As Grammar: Is God An Object of Understanding?" *Religious Studies* 11 (1975).

23. This theme is perhaps most articulately developed by Stanley Cavell in his *Themes Out of School: Effects and Causes,* (San Francisco: North Point Press, 1984), pp. 223–24, and earlier in his book *The Claim of Reason: Wittgenstein, Skepticism, Morality and Tragedy* (Oxford: Clarendon Press, 1979), throughout.

24. Paul L. Holmer, *C. S. Lewis: The Shape of His Faith and Thought,* (San Francisco: Harper & Row, 1976), p. 54. This is a point now being vigorously pursued by Alasdair MacIntyre and others following MacIntyre's book *After Virtue.* MacIntyre has subsequently argued that "the virtues . . . always must stand in some determinate relationship to the passions, and any cogent account of the virtues

requires at its foundation a cogent account of the passions and their relationship to reason." MacIntyre and Hauerwas, *Revisions,* p. 9.

25. Kierkegaard, *Philosophical Fragments,* (Princeton: Princeton University Press, 1985), p. xxi.

26. Søren Kierkegaard, *Either/Or,* vol. 2, (New York: Doubleday, Anchor Books, 1959), p. 19.

27. Cavell, *Themes Out of School,* p. 31.

28. Ibid., p. 199.

29. Wittgenstein, *Culture and Value,* p. 64e.

30. Holmer, *C. S. Lewis,* p. 94.

31. Wittgenstein, *Culture and Value,* p. 64e.

I. CULTURE, THEOLOGY, AND CHRISTIAN FAITH

1. The Grammar of Faith

PAUL L. HOLMER

There is merit to the notion projected by Ludwig Wittgenstein that theology is the grammar of faith.[1] Calling it a grammar may seem strange and even rather forbidding. But a consideration of the role of the grammar of one's language might help a bit.

Learning grammar in the ordinary sense, that is, English, French, or German grammar, may be done in one obvious way. We learn the rules and learn them typically "by heart." But as we go along, acquiring a mastery of the language, we do not speak the grammar itself, but we say everything else in accord with the rules we have already learned. The more skilled we become in writing and speaking, the more does our knowledge of grammar inform everything we say and write. After a while we simply speak grammatically without ostentatiously remembering the grammar at all. Our practice becomes intrinsically and naturally grammatical.

Something like this also obtains with the teaching of logic. When we first teach logic, we isolate logical forms and rules and teach them in an abstract way; for this is the only procedure we can follow. But our expectation is that those who learn the logic will not actually spend their lives remembering it; instead, they will, we hope, become logical respecting everything they think and say thereafter. What starts out being a subject matter that we teach, say grammar or logic, becomes eventually no longer a separate subject matter at all, but instead a practice, a "how," by which one does his or her talking and writing and thinking. This transformation cannot be effected on paper and cannot be done for anyone else. It must be, in a modest sense of the expression, a personal achievement.

More than this, it does in fact happen. Most people speak fairly grammatically, long after they have forgotten the grammatical rules. For it is as if the rules have become embedded in the speech textures themselves; and they are undoubtedly supported there by the fact that if you want to be understood, you had better speak grammatically. So the daily concourse of speech and practice tends to support the exercise of grammatical rules, if for no other reason than verbs better follow subjects, plurals go with plurals, or we will not understand one another. But the fact that people must do it according to rules and patterns, if they are going to reason at all or to speak at all, means that the rules can also be learned from the practices. Certainly, some capacities of speaking clearly and thinking with precision are developed because we are exposed to group practices in which those rules already obtain.

We can learn grammar and logic as a separate set of rules, or we can sometimes learn to speak logically and grammatically simply by conforming to the practice of those who know how. In either case, the closer we come to successful practice ourselves, the less overt our knowledge of the rules and the more tacit and informing those rules actually become. We finally become grammatical and logical in all that we say, even if we are hard put to state any longer the rules themselves.

If theology is like a grammar, and certainly it is, then it follows that learning theology is not an end in itself. I am not denying here that theology can be learned just as grammar and logic can; most particularly, it is perfectly proper to do so. But there is the additional difference about theology that, though it is like grammar in some respects, namely, in not being the aim and intent of belief and the substance in and of itself (that is, in not being the end but the means) still it is the declaration of the essence of Christianity. Insofar as Christianity can be "said" at all, theology and Scripture say it. But what is therein said, be it the words of eternal life, be it creeds, or be it the words of Jesus himself, we must note that like grammar and logic, their aim is not that we repeat the words. Theology also must be absorbed, and when it is, the hearer is supposed to become godly.

The better and the clearer the theology, then, the more quickly the human heart will sing unbidden. For theology tells us what faith is; and the faith, when articulated with appropriateness and precision, is exceedingly good news. But appreciation and approval of the news are not the sufficient response, any more than hearty endorsement of grammatical rules and swearing allegiance to logical requisites are quite enough. No, we must become grammatical in speaking about everything else, not the grammar, before those rules have been really understood. So, too, it is of little use to be logical about logic when the point is that we are supposed to have learned to become logical about whatever we think. This is how it is, then, with theology—namely, that we are to become godly in all things, referring everything, our woes and weal, fears and joys, past and future, completely to God's love and care.

This kind of transition involves each person's spirit. There is a kind of singular and corelike Christianity, surprisingly plain yet infinitely supple, and so inclusive that it can make godly and Christlike, vulgar fishermen of the first century, sophisticates of the twentieth, Roman citizens and landless refugees, towering intellectuals and illiterate peasants. Just as grammatical rules can govern the enormous range of things there are to be said, so the theological stuff of the Church and Scripture can also be instantiated in godliness and a new life in the innumerable human host. In a peculiar way, the closer the theology gets to that necessary core, the more inclusive its grasp and the clearer its thrust in the direction of godliness.

Theology is grammar in still another way. For just as grammar of a language is not quite an invention, nor do we simply make up our logical rules, so we do not design theology just to suit ourselves, nor do we invent it as we would a pleasant saying. The grammar of a language is that set of rules that describes how people speak who are doing it well and with efficacy. A logical schematism is also that set of criteria and lawlike remarks that describe how people think when they make sense. For those of us who are just learning to speak and to think, these rules are like prescriptions and even onerous requirements. But with the practices once mastered, the rules are no longer alien and become a part of the "how," the way, we behave. Theology is also dependent upon a consensus of belief and practice, that of Jesus and the apostles, of the Scripture's teachings and the lives limned by its pages. Theology answers the question, What is Christianity? But it tells us the answer by giving us the order and priorities, the structure and morphology, of the Christian faith. It does this by placing big words, like *man, God, Jesus, world,* in such a sequence

and context that their use becomes ruled for us. And if we begin
to use those words like that, with the appropriate zest and pathos,
then we, too, become godly as those earlier believers were.

I might enlarge my thesis of what theology is by saying two more
things about it. We learn theology not by seeking God through the
cracks in the universe, as if we were spies ferreting out God's
secrets or specialists with better instruments for catching God,
either by improved perceptual capacities or by a finer conceptual
net. Neither of these ways will work. We learn about God in the
way a grammarian of language discovers the rules. A grammarian
masters the language and assesses carefully what we all have access
to already, our common working speech. So the theologian gets no
new revelation and has no special organ for knowledge. The theologian is debtor to what we, in one sense, have already—the Scriptures and the lives and thoughts of the faithful. Putting one's mind
to that, getting it straight, so that one knows what belongs, what
does not, what precedes what, what the concept of God includes
and what it excludes—these and more make up our knowledge of
God. God shows God's own self and is revealed in Jesus and the
books about him.

This, then, is one of the two important things that enlarge theology for us. For this puts theology within the grasp of conscientious
tentmakers, tinkers like Bunyan, lay people like Brother Lawrence,
and maybe someone you know on the street who shames you with
his or her grasp. Likewise it might explain why we who study so
much, who read several languages, who argue so well, are often,
as Augustine complained, chagrined to discover that others like
Anthony take heaven by storm while we wallow in indecision and
self-righteous knowledgeability. Theology is often done by the
unlikely; in fact, if it could be coolly engineered and produced for
a mass market, the world would long since have capitulated. But
the world is still alien; and to a strange degree, God's ways are still
discovered by his friends and not in virtue of techniques and
agencies of power.

But consider one more aspect of theology as grammar. We have
noted that the material is already there, the Scripture, the summa-
rized teachings like creeds, and the host of practices, stories, and
traditions that make up a Christianized historical content. For
most, these are more than enough. The advantages of theology are

like those of rules as over against the practice. Or they are like the advantage of hearing the rules of the game in explicit fashion rather than having to read them off the game itself. Surely the latter can be done—indeed must be done; for in the game itself we have both the criteria and the actual play, and we cannot get anything more than that. No one has seen God at any time, the Gospel writer warns us; so plainly enough, we are left with the game!

Those rules are like an abridgment and a more immediate access. They are rereadings that can stir us with their directness just as a grammatical rule can often frighten us into a practice sooner than leisurely exposure would do. And this is also the way Paul's admonitions corrected the early churchgoers and the way Luther's reflections on the Bible shocked Christians into a sharper definition of their lives. However, what Luther proposed finally was there already in the Scriptures, but it has been overlaid by neglectful practices and obliterated for its inattentive readers.

This theology of which I speak is infinitely more glorious, though, than the term *grammar* might suggest. For theology does not parse verbs, arrange thoughts, and conjugate sentences. Its matter is finally the whole of human life itself. Insofar as it is a grammar, it is more like the teaching that leads to a truly successful, deeply satisfactory, even blessed and happy life. This is why its promise is that thereby we make sense of our days. And there is nothing small or piddling about it at all. On the contrary, it is histrionic and magnificently dramatic, so much so that the rise and fall of empires, the tides of war and peace, the absence or presence of culture, learning, and material plenty—all of these are dwarfed in God's morphology and shaping of human destiny. Besides, one learns something from this divine grammar. We get a notion of what the world is, of what we are, and who God is. The fact that we are truly immortals, bound for an eternal destiny, and playing the whole game of God's presence—this is what the grammar of the Bible makes manifest. No wonder that it is no small thing!

Of course, we have already said that theology is an interpretation; but that does not mean that it is an arbitrary and casual refashioning of a subject matter to suit a whimsical and passing enthusiasm. Continuous redoing of the Scripture to fit the age is only a sophisticated and probably invisible bondage to the age rather than the desire to win the age for God. But if theology is grammar, then there is the task, always pertinent, of learning to extend the rules, the order, the morphology, of godliness over the ever-changing circumstances. Just as a logician is hard put to discern the rules and extend those that we already know over new things people learn and say, so, too, the grammar of a living language must always be open to the linguistic novelties and the sheer increment of vocabulary that is the fate of every living language. This, too, is a requisite of the theologian. His or her task is very modest and ought never to be overly praised or be used to justify indecision and the failure to be conclusive. There is, nonetheless, the responsibility to be continually showing that God's grammar is sufficiently flexible to take in the novelties of our changing life. And while it changes, some things also remain. Sameness in differences, likenesses in change, God's will in differing circumstances and lives—this is the Gospel's perduring theme.

But theology is still more. It is altogether too easy to assume that theology's form, its very style and shape, must be barbarously academic and formal. There are unfortunately large number of precedents for this in the history of theology. So we have Protestants of the seventeenth and eighteenth centuries who wrote lengthy encyclopedias or, if not these, then in styles that are today as fascinating as geometry books. By way of parenthesis, perhaps, we might say that Thomas Aquinas's question-and-answer style, Melanchthon's dull and pedantic outlining, and Chemnitz's clear but deadly charting in prose might have been directed to special audiences that profited greatly thereby. But one has, I believe, ample reason for still thinking that it could have been better done otherwise. And Thomas's readers surely must include few who now find God there. More likely, having found God elsewhere, they find other things in the *Summa Theologica*.

Theology is interpretation, it needs to be couched in the vernacular, and it is still a kind of grammar that passes into the "how" of a human life. But theology is also a complex and many-sided subject matter. Thus far, I have been speaking of a kind of writing that is also about God, the world, Jesus, and the manifold of human life. It is not "about" these things, however, as if theology were totally a story written by eyewitnesses. Surely Luke tells us that he writes what he saw; but he saw Jesus and the apostles. From that "seeing" and in virtue of other things, too, he goes on to write about God, salvation, and a host of other matters. It is as if in the manifold that he saw, he could also plot, like a grammarian, God's ordering of human affairs. He learned, in congress with Jesus, what *God* meant, what *love* required, what *hope* was justified, where *peace* was given. Insofar as we have knowledge of God, that is, truly theology, we get it in the use and practices suggested by Luke (and other apostles) around these and other words and teachings. Though we can learn about God from the Bible, we are also expected to become learners, to learn as we go, from living in accord with Jesus and with apostolic faithfulness in mind. Our walking by faith is also an ongoing learning about God.

This being so, theology must be more than a sum of truths. It is more than a compendium, and it is surely not just an encyclopedia. Insofar as it is put this way sometimes, its form is accidental. Theology must always move towards a present-tense, first-person mood. It must be lively and in such a form, at some occasion in its career, as first-person talk is in daily life. Theology, then, starts for us in this "about" mood—it is grammarlike and something like an account that we can get from others who have been there long before us. But we cannot absorb theology as simply the true account, nor do we really have a use for it in that form. For one thing, there is too much of it to believe or to assent to in an immediate and direct way. We cannot even begin to remember all of it, let alone savor it as it is.

So we must think of it in another way altogether. Indeed, theology is taught to us in an "about" mood, as a kind of third-person thought and language of apostles, prophets, and our Lord himself. But to use it supposes that we translate from the third-person mood of being their knowledge and language "about" God to becoming my language "of" faith. This move from *about* to *of* is again not done simply on paper, nor is it done for another, *ein, zwei, drei.* It is all the more reason for saying that theology is not done best in scholarly forms and artifices of the learned. At best, the theological research that goes on does not quite issue in real theology—instead it prepares people a bit, at the most, for appreciating the real thing. It is like logic in respect to thinking and grammar in respect to writing prose.

Theology, to the extent that it becomes knowledge of God, has to have the form of personal appropriation built in. Otherwise, it is not about God at all but is only a history of someone's thoughts. For to have knowledge of God, you must fear God and you must also love God. There is no knowledge of God otherwise. Without fearing God and loving God, one is not apprehending God but something else—maybe a concept only, an interesting story, a point of view, or something of the sort. Just as in learning grammar we must speak grammatically as the sign of understanding the grammar, so in theology, a great mistake and a fault in understanding obtains if we do not love and fear God. The grammar that is theology requires, objectively and necessarily, love and fear as the content of a person's godliness. And the very knowledge that began in the "about" mood now becomes transformed into a "how," another mood altogether. One knows God in fearing and loving God.

There is room for our saying that the love of God and certainly the fear of God also have a language. When one reads the Bible, one discovers that every page is replete with the language "of" faithfulness itself. That is the true fate of theology—not to be repeated in the form in which it was taught, but to become transmuted into another mood altogether.

The requirement, then, for those who handle theology, whether in pulpits or at podiums, is to project it with this in mind. That requires imagination, not just reiteration and a pedantic accurateness. Being sure of what was said and why is important, but only transitorily. The citing of a theological teaching also has to carry a projective thrust in the direction of suggesting the uses to which it must, not just can, be put. For without that, theology gets to be dull and misleading. It must be made clear negatively that theology is not to be believed as though it were ineluctable truths whose values were to be discovered by repeating them word for word and that often. Believing theology is different than that. I am not here denying that the acts of God stir the heart unbidden! And I am not asserting that orthodoxies have to be replaced by liberal teachings. Neither is this to deny that theology is cognitive nor is it to deny objectivity in place of subjectivity.

But I say again that theology has to be projected. The literary means have always been metaphors, parables, stories, informal conversation, everyday speech, allegories, and a rich use of vivifying materials. This is not to argue for chalk talks, buzz sessions, or tea groups; but one of the reasons these, too, arise is that theology is never perfectly done in syllogisms, arguments, and processes of verified reporting. The whole business of using theology as grammar requires also that we refer our nation, our world, our selves, our future to God. These very terms are dramatic and sweeping. It takes imagination to use them. It is as if the whole of life were God's theatre—we are all actors and God is the only spectator. Within that kind of projection, that imaginative construct, we begin to get the hang of ourselves and the world. We move, then, from saying with Paul that he lives no longer "I," that Christ lives in him, to start to live that way ourselves. This is where the positive projection of real preaching becomes theology in action. It works as it envelopes the hearer in the divine correction of disposition, of love, of orientation that is lifelong.

This imaginative projection is the proper kind of popularization. It is popularization by vivification, not by vulgarization. Think of the ways it can be done. What if human life is an examination in which nobody can cheat? What if God has humans in derision so that God laughs? What if the whole thing is like a divine comedy, with an exceedingly happy ending but certain conditions laid down for that everlasting laugh? Is the kingdom of heaven like a mustard seed? an unheard of place with no crying? a place where lions will cavort peacefully with lambs? And what about that weight of glory? Are there any mere mortals about?

The imagination I refer to is not only an optional function that some will do if they have a stroke of genius or an ear for poetry. Instead it is the outworking of the language *about* faith when it becomes the language *of* faith. It moves from being like a grammar to becoming solicitous, personal, and persuasive. One cannot be solicitous without being imaginative, for solicitude demands that we have sympathy—pathos with and for others. We cannot do that unless we project others unto ourselves as God's children, as real and as worthy as we are and maybe more. When we lack sympathy, it is usually because we cannot imagine what it is like to be poor, ignorant, dirty, and hated. God's word forces us to disregard these attributes and see everybody as God's children. But it takes imagination. That is why the commandment to love the neighbor becomes possible when we know that that most unlikely specimen is a child of the Heavenly Father. Those parables and metaphors are not decoration and little literary graces added to the hard facts. Rather, those strange imaginative projections are the very means by which love will well up in us and the grace of God grip us with heartiness.

The entire range of Christian commandments also demands imaginative deployment. We need imagination to make God's existence as our Maker, as our Father, as our Lord, and as our Judge or King at all pertinent. For only a generous dose of "supposing" will supply the detail that will make motives calling us to the new action. We have to consider ourselves as pilgrims, as wayfarers, as warriors, as runners, as lambs, as subjects, as children, in order to make those moves in God's direction. The whole thrust of theology has to be in the direction not of finding something out—for that is only at the beginning—but rather of becoming something more worthy and justified. Surely we start with having learned something about what is, but we move in the direction of becoming something that God has planned for us. Imagination is the broker between what is learned and what is, in consequence, possible.

It is often said that theology states the meaning of the gospel story or of the creeds and confessional pieces. But that is a misleading way to speak. For theology is not a more meaningful kind of prose than is, say, everyday speech or the words of the Bible. It is a mistake to say that we can have the Bible, on the one side, and then its meaning stated in another tissue of prose altogether. The entire picture is wrong; and every pastor and theologian must resist that plain and insistent request for a statement of the meaning. Just as the meaning of a piece of logic is not another piece of prose about logic but the achievement of logical acuity and accuracy of thought and inference, so the meaning of Jesus' life and death is not a theory of the atonement or an elaborate Christology. We are fooled into this, perhaps lulled into it, by the demand for meaning.

All the more is it the case that in Christian matters the formidable and somewhat angular character of Christian teachings, especially in catechisms and creeds, doctrinal summaries and position papers, be thought about most patiently. We cannot everlastingly repair to one more piece to state the meaning of the last one, one more book to give the meaning of the previous, one more commentary upon a commentary upon a text. This kind of picture is all too easy to draw for oneself; and distressingly enough, it can be drawn to include most of what is already being done in many research centers, seminaries, and pastors' studies. This process should be cut off at the beginning.

The meaning of religious sayings like those in the Bible is not something that can be gleaned from those pages and restated in a simple way—except in rare circumstances. Once more, the continuous task of theology is both to say and to resay what are the rudiments of the Bible and of the faith; and this is its simplest and never-ending responsibility. Right here, there is usually no great difficulty. When people say, "I have heard that before and I think I know what you are going to say, but I don't know what it means," then we have a model instance of not knowing the meaning. Is it the task here to state matters in the language of the day? Yes and no. We have said that the diction of the day has its claims upon all of us. But there is another matter that puts the issue in a different light.

When we do not know the meaning of Christian teaching, it is also the case that we do not have any way to put on the saying, to make it work for us. The expressions lose their life, and they become dead in our mouths. The task is not always to revivify the teachings; instead it is to place the listener in another context, so that the words will spring to life for him. The church member needs to imagine himself or herself as a lamb needing a shepherd; then the Twenty-third Psalm can become a personal affirmation, and the meaning takes care of itself. If we can conceive of having citizenship in heaven, all kinds of rights and confidences will easily accrue. The point is that the metaphors and figures of the Bible are not sufficient to have exhausted the list. Any teacher of these matters will find a thousand ways to reconceive the role of his or her hearers so that they will discover their place, opportunities, and possibilities anew. This is how theology finally realizes itself in its correct form. The teachings do not have to change at all, for they are a kind of constant stretching through the ages. But the active pedagogy in which they are exercised must insinuate the listener into a new role; the listener's self-evaluation, subjectivity, aims, wishes, hopes, desires must be altered so that the grammar of faith becomes relevant. When the right supposal envelopes her, when she understands herself to be a prisoner, a victim, a sinner, a changeling, then the teachings will come to life.

This is how theology finally becomes something besides an ideology. For an ideology is a rallying point and a strident demand allowing no other allegiances. Sometimes theology looks that way, as if it were a rationale for a cause that is relentless and unremitting. But an ideology must increase its demands and live only by further exaggeration and ever more vivid statement. Theology, on the contrary, seeks a richer role, but one that passes totally into the life history of the individual, the community, the Church, and humankind. It becomes invisible but all the more enlivening; it becomes so transparent that, like light itself, we never see it but see everything else by it.

Theology must be done by people who, scientifically trained and technically skilled though they be, must always be students of both Scripture and Church teachings, on the one side, and the passions of the human heart, on the other side. Those passions—the deep and long-standing enthusiasm for justice, for health, for everlasting life, for peace, for love, for understanding, for safety—these also permeate our common life. They are the subject matter to which all the great panaceas and all the shibboleths of politics, of science, of bright futures finally must appeal. Unless we can continually conjugate the human scene, variegated and diverse though it be, so that that aching human heart with its duplicities and deceits, vaguenesses and lies, will hear God speak to it, we will always have great tasks still to do. Theologians must always remember that unless a human heart can be addressed, the long-term aim is being thwarted.

I have noted that theology is an interpretation, that it is like a grammar of faith, that it includes metaphor, figures, stories by way of a necessary projection of imagination. All of this is so also because it must be couched in the vernacular in order to be available and assimilable. Perhaps now we can fight a few of the ghosts that hover around and espoil the rightful dominion of the knowledge of God. That, after all, is what theology proposes for its hearers. We can become God's friends by knowing about God.

Somehow this is confused for a large number of would-be Christians. Theology looks like an option, one of the subjects that bear on important things but not with particular distinction. People think they have no use for theology because it is esoteric, for specialists, and way over their heads. Although this is certainly a mistaken notion, one must admit that much of what passes as theology is fanciful and technical and does not deserve a wide audience at all. It is divorced from the plain elements and words that fashion the Christian's faith. Certainly it is time to get theology hooked up once more with the clean breeze of God's grace that blows through the centuries. Then the outlook of this age or that is swept aside, as room for the gospel is once more established. Theology states those simple "credenda," those rudimentary themes that make every age a part of God's great symphony.

There is no reason to excuse the pastor on the grounds that because he or she likes people so much, he or she must, thereby, dislike theology the more. To those who say they are practical people and have no use for theoretical matters, hence have no theology, one must say that theology, indeed, like a theory, tells you what is so; but it does it in the interest of providing a person their missing health of the spirit. Theology in the senses we have noted is not an option at all; it is the minimum and the necessary awareness of God by which counseling, Near Eastern archaeology, soul care, geriatric services, and parish life get their correct evaluation and even their point. Theology is not one field among many; nor is it quite the same as what the department of theologians offers in contrast to other departments. Theology is certainly taught and often under that very name. But the knowledge of God is also given to the pure in heart, to the fools for Christ's sake, and even to professors in theological seminaries and pastors and laity in unlikely churches.

If we are not always sure of theology's source, we certainly can be clear about our need for knowing God. And God is not without witness. The knowledge of God grows as we soak ourselves in testaments; the awareness of God is augmented as we let our moral consciousness grow; the cognizance of the Almighty is stimulated as we let godly traditions form our dispositions and capacities. This is why theology has to be taught variously. The knowledge of God does not get moved from one mind to another in a direct and immediate way. What we can mediate from one mind to another is Luther's thoughts, the words of Saint Augustine and the church fathers, the words of the apostles, and the mediations of a systematic theologian. By themselves, these are not the matters called "knowing God"; but they are like a grammar and like a means with which you, the reader, comes to know God. "Knowing God" is not done on paper. One must think about this by way of getting to know a person. Knowing a person is accomplished by knowing all sorts of other things—what she did, why she does what she does, her likes, wishes, hopes, what makes her cry or laugh. After a while one can say, "I really know her"—though that "knowing" is not a simple act or certainly not a discernible occasion or happening.

Putting it this way, then, means that it is risky not to know others who knew God. We must always begin with the saints and the prophets, the apostles and Jesus' immediate contemporaries. The Bible is our point of departure; and the tradition of theological writing, including less formal pieces in that tradition, is a kind of essential. Here is where acquaintanceship turns into knowledge, tentativeness into certainty, and obscurity into clarity. For the reader has to come to know God by knowing all kinds of other things first.

Nothing said here has disparaged the sheer "newsiness," the plain content, of the Good News. Certainly theology is important because it transmits, not the knowledge of God, but rather all the thought and action within which knowing God becomes a possibility. But what a pastor must do at length in order to meet the exigencies of the entire range of persons who make up that pastor's flock, each member of that flock can do with a single sermon, with one's own reading of the Bible and the raw material that is one's own life. Certainly this is why responsible preaching is always directed toward giving others the access to God. God can be known and even enjoyed!

One of the hard sides of addressing others in God's interest is that most of us want Christianity itself to fit our secular and everyday aims and proclivities. Religious enthusiasm begins to look useful, if not as political drug to pacify, then as stimulant and tonic.

Because the world so often suffers from a paucity of moral effort and from plain moral aimlessness, it is altogether plausible to urge Christianity upon people as a way of extracting that further degree of zest that will make for moral accomplishment. Of course, there are always thinking people around who will provide a rather thin rationale for God in Christ being the author and finisher of such grandiose attempts. This kind of thing is often called theology but is instead a kind of religious ideology.

The moral tension created by this use of quasi-theology and quasi-religion is obviously dangerous psychologically if the sources of spiritual vitality to stick with such strenuousness are not increased simultaneously. Even more acute, though, are the gross misunderstandings of Christianity this creates. Part of the confusion we always seem to manufacture for ourselves, we do in the name of theology when we tend to rationalize causes and build up impossible and utopian schemes. Much of this generates that bad odor by which theology is so often discerned. The cure for that is more theology—a responsible theology—feeding upon those who have known God and not just those who spin a web of possibilities and behave as cosmic judges on God's behalf.

All that I have said points us to the fact that theology must always be one of the ways that Christians learn to be on guard. For example, in days when Christianity is thought well of, everything claiming our attention is said to be a Christian movement. Theology is that knowledge that tells us, also, all kinds of polemical things. If only because one knows God and who God is, one knows a lot, too, that is not of God. Therefore, theology is always polemically poised; and it, too, like God, has to wound before it heals.

When we are prone to identify the Christian life and devotion with the sentiment that catches us in the throat as *Abide with Me* is sung, when we are most susceptible to a surge of emotion when taps breaks the silence, when we are likely to feel deeply as bombs burst in air and stars and stripes wave free, then, and especially then, we have to remember that these moments can all be caught up and used by cruel totalitarianism, by gross and vulgar loyalties, by impostors and frauds, too. Then it is that the religion that tells us of redemption by God's own Son, that puts a crucifixion in the center, that fixes us upon a God who sacrificed himself and whose worship must include the remembrance of all of that, must be the center of attention. Only then can we say that such faith and such worship are the declared enemy of all who put the state, themselves, moral aims, institutions, or anything else first.

Think, then, about the emotions that are called for—lovely peace, lively hopes, inclusive love, a life no longer damned by anxiety and fear. God has overcome the world, and with God we can, too. And the virtues that are called for? They are deep and pervasive, everything from a dauntless courage to a confident temperance, a fight for justice to the everyday works of love.

Theology like that tells us what is wrong and what is right; it becomes the way by which knowing God converts to serving God. Blessed we all are if in knowing such truth, we do it. Theology is directed to the essential spiritual core, our center of vitality and energy. Without such vitality we flounder in a spiritual morass, and we die. The New Testament and the theological tradition, when seen from the outside, have an extraordinary unanimity about them, for they concern the same things in a myriad of situations and times. They suppose that we have no health of the spirit save through Jesus Christ, the physician of souls. Besides, the theological tradition shows us that human beings can be certain of these things, and, certainly, that confidence is also remarkable.

Theology, again scriptural and traditional, will warn us of the frightful peril in which we all live, where the world has become deeply infected by sin. We are threatened by that contagion, the sickness unto death of our spirit, and it all happens so easily. The cumulative effect of sin is to make us captives by pleasantries and victims by easy conformity. Those striking teachings that make up the knowledge of God are also ways of training and disciplining ourselves so that we will not be taken in and will not conform to those standards.

The God we then learn about is no vague and general spirit of benevolence. That God is pure and awesome, almost a terrifying holiness, whose presence promises the destruction of everything evil. That God is a blazing light of purity in a universe darkened by sin and foolishness. No wonder that there is a story to tell to all nations; for that God causes us to see that most of the roads we tread are leading us in diverting ways. There is slight tolerance of human divergence by God, for the stakes are too high; but there is a magnificent avenue provided by God with the most costly of means: the *via dolorosa* for Jesus Christ becomes the way to eternal life for all who will take it.

Surely this puts our common life in radically different perspective, too. It becomes more like an incident rather than the main act. For its chief responsibility, weighted by theology becoming the knowledge of God, is to live this life as a preface to sharing the extravagant and timeless life of God's own self. Here, then, our emphasis upon this life is shifted into a new key, and Christianity is, again, not to be treasured for its social implication as much as for its morally transcendent content.

If anyone begins to think that theology is academic and dry, it must be that the knowledge of God has been missed. What could be more exciting and more stimulating? It is as if there has been an invasion by the Almighty and a whole new quality of life can now ensue. This is no mere ethics, nor a new code, nor a more severe law. This is not new ritual or a more impressive religion. There is a sense in which theology itself, both the Scripture and the theological thinkers who are true to Scripture, tells us about an experience of life that is a strain upon the structures of the world. Finally, none of those structures will even survive; they will all prove to be mortal and will pass away, and only people and God will be immortal.

There is high drama here. Theology has a right to create fervor, to elicit a hymnody, to cause rejoicing. Because the world is like an alien background, there is also a way in which the knowledge of God needs imaginative devices to get human attention. The story, though old, must always be readdressed to all who pass by. When Christians talk about the many difficulties of our day as if they must wait for better days before Christianity can take hold, they will have to remember that the New Testament times were far worse. The New Testament leads us to the knowledge of God, and it seeded the faith in a time when there were no churches, no books about Jesus, and virtually no inhibitions upon slavery, poverty, suffering, disease, or the rapacity of rulers. Surely if there were no vitality in the seed, it would have perished in those hard days.

Nothing whatsoever is wrong with that old knowledge of God. We do not have to make it new. It is the recipient who has to be revivified and converted. And it must be that understandings are darkened and hearts are ever hardening in the mad traffic of worldliness. Sometimes the churches are no help, for they make theology look like a constitutional document for a clerical-ridden institution. The knowledge of God is directed against that. It is instead, the declaration that we are as partakers in Jesus' life, death, and Resurrection. We are also the pioneers of a new humanity, children of light not darkness, and cofounders of a new reign of righteousness.

No imagination is too rich for such a story, no talent too strong. There is no historical tradition that has exhausted it and no Gospel writer who can make it wearisome. Thus it behooves us to use what gifts we have, not to change the story, but rather to say it with freshness and with its plenteous attractiveness. And if we are weary of it, it must be that our understanding has waned. When that waxes, the words take wing again, and theology becomes once more the Gospel according to God.

NOTES

1. For readers unfamiliar with Ludwig Wittgenstein (1889–1951), it might be well to note here that he is a major figure in British and American philosophy of the past forty years. His thought is so different from most because he called a halt to the making of ideologies in the name of philosophy. He did not write a new philosophy—if one means by that a new metaphysics or a new morals or a new philosophy of religion. Instead, he tried to get clear all kinds of elementary things, such as differences between names and concepts, and activities and capacities such as "intending," "thinking," and "believing"—matters that have produced ideologies in the past but that he thought we had not gotten clear enough about. So his writings are full of brief but very powerful investigations of this and that—often matters that are almost commonplace. But he treats them with a difference.

2. Grammarians and Guardians

D. Z. PHILLIPS

Theologians in the twentieth century have been conscious of developments in philosophy. Over and over again they have wanted to earn respectability in the academic locality and have thought that, in order to do so, they have to earn the approval of their philosophical neighbors. Expulsion from the neighborhood might result from philosophical complaints about the amount of conceptual rubbish accumulating outside theological residences.

It is much rarer today to find philosophers addressing themselves to theologians directly. Yet, that is what Paul Holmer does in his book *The Grammar of Faith.* [1] But he does not berate theologians for not paying attention to philosophical demands. On the contrary, he berates them for paying too much attention to them. As a result of this theological subservience to philosophy, widespread confusion has been wrought. Holmer considers four examples of this confusion.

PHILOSOPHY AND THEOLOGY

First, there are those theologians who think that implicit in the living faith is the philosophical foundation of it. The foundation is called theism. Many believe that rejecting theism is tantamount to rejecting religion. As Holmer says, "There is something absurd about this. Crucifying Jesus, living faithlessly, and loving the world with all one's heart, soul, mind and strength tend then to become trivialities compared with denying theism. It is almost as if the academics have made crucial what was not so initially" (p. 152). Theism is thought to be a conceptual, foundational scheme that Christianity, Judaism, and Islam are supposed to have in common. But while this is being said, the philosophical inadequacies of theism are being elucidated annually in countless philosophy classes. The traditional proofs of the existence of God, which were always flawed attempts from within the faith to elucidate its content, are turned into the even shakier foundations on which the faith is supposed to depend.

The second group of theologians has been impressed by philosophical claims that for something to be true is for it to be answerable to the facts. Faith, they argue, must be made secure through historical investigation. Holmer does not denigrate historical investigation. On the contrary, he praises its achievements with respect to the history of religions and elsewhere. Historical questions arise naturally in textual studies. But historical knowledge can never become a substitute for theology. Gathering such knowledge is not the same as coming to grips with religious truths. As far as the New Testament is concerned, Holmer suspects

it is far more important than most historical material to learn to hunger and thirst for righteousness, to learn to love a neighbor, and to achieve a high degree of self-concern, in order to understand the religious themes of the New Testament. There are, in short, personality qualifications that are also required. Perhaps it is even essential to have learned guilt because one has not done as he ought to have done. In any case, these forms of human consciousness are closer to the prerequisites for a Christian understanding than is most knowledge supplied by other scholars. (P.9)

The third group of theologians reacts to difficulties involved in basing religious truths on secular historical investigations by saying that there are special facts, religious facts, on which the faith depends. These facts are found in a religious conception of history. Liberal theologians who argue in this way create a technical vocabulary to accommodate this new conception of factuality. But the living faith is not dependent on these new categories. What it proclaims is the need to understand that God has reconciled the world to God's own self in Christ. Conservative theologians, anxious to retain what they take to be an ordinary conception of factuality, proclaim this fact of reconciliation as if it were prior to the gospel; something on which the gospel depends. But, Holmer insists, it is only with the gospel that one can find the sense of saying that such reconciliation has taken place. Appropriating that sense, finding out about it, is not something one can do impersonally *before* becoming religious. On the contrary, the appropriation called for is a personal matter, itself a stage in religious growth.

In thinking otherwise; in thinking that the facts can be appropriated "all at once," the conservative theologian becomes an example of what Kierkegaard calls "impatience"; such a theologian attempts to take eternity by storm.

The fourth group of theologians, if they can be called that, despairing at the array of theologies on offer and the various confusions associated with them, emphasizes the importance of a religious experience independent of all theologies. Although Holmer has some sympathy with this reaction, he sees that theology cannot be jettisoned in the way suggested, since there are internal relations between it and religious experience. When theological concepts are not intellectualized out of all recognition by theologians, Holmer argues, we can see that to appropriate a theological concept is to develop a capacity:

The Christian concept of *agape*, or love, is a typically familiar one. But there are more—God, hope, grace, repentance, sin, guilt, sanctification, holiness, faith, creation, Savior, Lord, crucifixion, gospel, forgiveness, and many others. Many of these words are otherwise familiar; but it does seem that in specifically Jewish and Christian contexts, one does something distinctive with them. This distinctive power is tied up very concretely with the expectations and dualities of being a Jew and/or a Christian with attendant forms of life, of concern, and of emotion. (P. 142)

So to appropriate theological concepts is to learn the authorization for

all kinds of dispositions, feelings, passions, virtues, and deeds that make one's daily living something distinctive. They even produce another view of the world and human life. . . . So we have to remember that theological teachings have also the power to commission their hearers. To be commissioned is to be given something to do. Religious teaching challenges people out of their complacency into a radical kind of behavior. It makes disciples of the hearers. Therefore, to understand theology and to evince a command of its concepts is to be spurred, to be humiliated, to be stirred to contrition, to be prepared for joy. There is even a way to understand all human beings as if they were profoundly sick. This is also a Christian way. The Christian mode of talking is supposed to completely alter the way of sick lives, and the task is to cure one person at a time. (Pp. 145–46)

In the light of these remarks, we see how confused it would be to desire a divorce between theology and religious experience. Without theology, religious experience degenerates, for example, into various forms of romanticism.

The four kinds of theological confusion Holmer cites have one common characteristic: instead of being *of* the faith, they are *about* the faith. They stand in external relation to a living faith. As a result, Holmer asks, Is it any wonder to see the discredit in which, so often, theology stands today? From the point of view of the religious laity, "theology is painfully abstract . . . a specialist's domain . . . impractical . . . of no use to the laity . . . about matters that do not and cannot concern those who are non-academic" (p. 1). Within universities, theology may become a self-perpetuating game.

In such places, the sheer opulence of points of view and the thick harvest of historical antecedents gives a revivification of scholarship and cause dim overviews to develop about the development of doctrine and the necessity that one succeed another. After a while, it becomes a lot easier to believe this vague metaview that makes one skeptical about any particular theology of an individual or of a church than it is to be a lively believer and hearty participant in any one theology and its related practices. The point that seems so disturbing here is that these chaotic developmental views are so easy to teach and that they are no longer linked to anything save the most obvious accommodation to the "Zeitgeist." They serve also to divorce most people from the practice of religion itself, and instead create a sophisticated clientele that is interested in theology as one more artifact cast up in the course of time. (P. 3)

But if, in fact, this use of theology has uprooted it from its natural context; if, to use Wittgenstein's phrases, its language is idling or has gone on holiday; then its intellectual aspirations will come to nothing. "And then theology is (just as unfortunately) lumped with speculative concerns, with metaphysics, with subjectivity and special interests, and, by its detractors, finally, with astrology, prescientific thought, mythology, and make-believe" (p. 1).

The exposure of theological confusion by Holmer is radical in character. What is the reaction to it likely to be? Apart from the well-known academic strategy of silence, Holmer predicted it. Once a metaphysical view on which, a theologian believes, religion depends comes under attack, that theologian's tendency will be to look for an alternative metaphysical view. It will hardly occur to him or her to locate the confusions in the tendencies of thought which led to the metaphysical view in the first place. There is something comic in the way in which theologians have hopped from one metaphysical view to another. The theologian, along with his or her philosophical counterpart, will not admit that an overthrown metaphysical view need not be replaced by another one. What, then, will he or she do with a book like *The Grammar of Faith*, which is an attempt to rescue theology from its metaphysical view of itself, to bring the practice of theology back from its metaphysical to its ordinary use? As Holmer foresaw, the radical attack of his book can be blunted, if not ignored, by suggesting that it, too, offers an alternative metaphysical view. An excellent example of such a suggestion is found in a review of *The Grammar of Faith* by Cornel West, Holmer's former colleague at Yale Divinity School. West locates four paradigms in contemporary North American theology: *the historicized Kantian paradigm* derived from the influence of H. Richard Niebuhr; *the process paradigm* stemming from the work of Alfred North Whitehead and Charles Hartshorne; *the hermeneutical paradigm* informed by the work of Husserl and Heidegger; *the liberation paradigm* initiated by James Cone. West outlines the drawback in each paradigm, but then characterizes Holmer as offering a fifth paradigm to better the four that have proved unsatisfactory. In this way, a continuity of enterprise is suggested where none exists. We are told: "Holmer has performed an invaluable service by presenting and promoting a new and exciting viewpoint—the Wittgensteinian-Kierkegaardian paradigm—on the North American theological scene."[2] The academic practitioners can breathe a sigh of relief, a new label has been provided, and now *it* can be discussed. This would have undoubtedly been the fate of the Wittgensteinian-Kierkegaardian paradigm had not another label, Wittgensteinian fideism, beaten it in consumer appeal. The preference for discussing theological labels, rather than matters of substance,[3] reminds one of Kierkegaard's humorous story to illustrate the point. One day, a man went to get his suit pressed. He saw a shop with a sign in its window, "Suits Pressed Here." He went inside, but found that only the sign was for sale. In West's exposition, Holmer's attack on metaphysics is presented as though it were a metaphysical thesis: "Holmer's metaphysical thesis is that theology ought to be a *part of* the language of the faithful, not *about* this language."[4] In this way, the metaphysical game perpetuates itself.

If we turn from the confusions Holmer exposes, we discover theology's proper task. It is to be the grammar of faith. It presents the parameters within which believers can come to know God. It may appear in codified form, but it cannot be appropriated by rote. As we have seen, in this context, appropriation is always personal appropriation. Once we appreciate theology's grammatical role, two important consequences follow. First, we see that "the theologian gets us no new revelation and has no special organ for knowledge. He is debtor to what we, in one sense, have already in the Scriptures and the lives and the thoughts of the faithful" (p. 21). Second, "this puts theology within the grasp of conscientious tentmakers, tinkers like Bunyan, lay people like Brother Lawrence, and maybe someone you know down the street who shames you with his or her grasp" (p. 21).

It may seem that compared with the rejected conceptions of theology, the theologian's remaining task is a relatively modest one. Nothing could be further from the truth. Many theologians feel that the only informative theology is a systematic theology. Starting from the true apprehension that religious faith informs the whole of life, they conclude, wrongly, that one thing can only bear on another as parts of a system. But conversations bear on one another, too, but not in a systematic way. Similarly, as Holmer says,

the language of faith is not an artificial or contrived tongue. People speak in this way and in conjunction with Apostles, saints and the proposers of law and gospel. *Faith, hope, grace,* and other words become internal to one's life and its vicissitudes. Fairly soon, that language of faith is extended to all of one's planning, judging, wishing, and even remembrance of things past. Judgments are formed and ideas are formulated as to what life is all about. (Pp. 198–99)

All this could never take the form of a system, since it constitutes what Brother Lawrence called "the practice of the presence of God." In this practice, humans become aware of their own pride and are humbled. Holmer concludes, "Surely the one who is then humbled is also the one to whom the Lord God gives His Grace and His Spirit (I Peter 5:5). But this is also how one becomes a true theologian, one who actually knows God" (p. 212).

THEOLOGY AS GRAMMAR

So far, I have been concerned to identify Holmer's audience, those he takes himself to be addressing. As we have seen, he identifies forms of theological confusion and attempts to recall theology to, and remind it of, its proper role as the grammar of faith. There are two questions of general interest that can be asked of what Holmer has said about theology's grammatical role.

The first question is whether, in stressing the internal relations between theology and the primary language of faith, Holmer fails to do justice to the heterogeneity that exists at the primary level, and to the equally heterogeneous relations that exist between religious beliefs and secular movements in the culture.

Holmer admits that "Orthodoxy in theology is never capable of much more refined definition than that supposed by the somewhat loose consensus of the faithful" (p. 198). But are there not deep differences between more than one loose consensus? Cornel West is correct in saying that Holmer's analysis reflects "those situations in which there has been close personal contact, or when a group is culturally homogeneous or held together by bonds of trust—in short . . . those situations in which an organic, cohesive tradition exists."[5] But there are also deep religious differences that, at the extremes, result in the response, "Your God is my devil." It is simply not feasible to account for these differences as theological misunderstandings of an agreed primary language of faith. Religion is a mixed bag, the scene of accusation and counteraccusation. If, in a philosophical analysis, Wittgenstein is right in saying that what is ragged should be left ragged, we would expect Holmer to pay more attention than he does to this phenomenon. After all, he says himself that an essential part of his task is not to settle all theological issues or internecine controversies, but "to give them a better setting" (p. xi).

Similar considerations arise in considering the relation between theology and secular movements. Although misunderstandings of the character of religious belief are common enough among secular critics, secular perspectives cannot be explained away as varieties of conceptual confusion. The post-Enlightenment attempt to characterize religious belief as the product of confusion was itself a muddled enterprise.[6] It is equally muddled, however, to suggest, as some contemporary reformed epistemologists have done, that atheism is a product of self-deception.[7] Such totalitarian claims in epistemology cannot be sustained, and Holmer does not make them. On the contrary, he has this to say of powerful secular opponents of Christianity:

> Nietzsche's aversion to Christianity was so profound and so detailed that his pages outline a faith in Jesus that is worthy of offense. For this reason, his work helps us to see how blessed someone is who is not offended by Jesus. Nietzsche understood but was antipathetic. Voltaire's conception that Pascal's account of Christianity is misanthropic suggests that both Voltaire and Pascal had seen the logic of faith correctly. In one sense, both had the grammar straight—one so that he could accept it, the other so that he could at least reject the right thing. (P. 194)

Holmer has depicted genuine clashes, counterclaims of truth and falsity. How is the grammar of these claims and clashes to be understood? In a world in which, as Flannery O'Connor kept insisting, theology cannot take its audience for granted, these are important questions. In elucidating what is meant by calling theology a grammar, Holmer sometimes speaks like this: "It is more like the teaching that leads to a truly successful, deeply satisfactory, even blessed and happy life. . . . We get a notion of what the world is, of what we are, and who God is" (p. 22). Does Holmer think that these notions of success, satisfaction, blessedness, personal identity, and the character of the world, which he invokes, are external checks by reference to which religion can be shown to be superior to its secular rivals? It is difficult to believe this since, for most of the time, he is emphasizing the need to understand religious concepts in their natural contexts and the foolishness of thinking that they can always be cashed in terms of some common conceptual coin of the realm. These tensions indicate the need for further enquiry into the character of perspectival clashes. Such enquiry would lead us to the issues raised by Newman in his discussion of clashes between what he called "antecedent presumptions."[8] It would also lead us to ask, with Wittgenstein, whether believers and unbelievers are contradicting each other in their basic claims. Central to such a discussion would be an investigation of what Wittgenstein meant, in *On Certainty,* by that persuasion to which one comes when all reasons have come to an end.[9] It is hard to overestimate the importance of such issues for the epistemology of religion on the one hand and for theological apologetics on the other.

The second question I have to ask is whether Holmer believes that part of the grammar of theology involves the denial of the possibility of its demise. Holmer speaks of theological truths as abiding truths:

> There is a deep and abiding truth that theology proposes, which, like a "de profundis" is a criterion and standard for all of human life. Amid the mad whirl of our common life, this theological stuff, this news about God and man, helps to redefine the human boundaries, to tame its vagrants, stimulate the indifferent, energize the slothful, and give scope and promise to all those who feel hedged in and even utterly defeated. Amid the highs and lows, where ethico-political aims engulf us, where empires organize and disorganize human passions so that we stumble in confusion, there is still a great and level *via,* a narrow way, across these frightening chasms. (P. 12)

Holmer is rightly opposed to those thinkers who, emeshed in some intellectual fashion of the day, accuse the language of faith of being outmoded and suggest their own linguistic revisions:

> The diagnoses are rather vague and several; and the prognoses are equally disquieting. The themes that are struck are rather familiar in the long historical scene. Popular religion is vague, more chauvinistic than Christian, not well-conceived, and not quite responsible socially and intellectually. The churches with their avid members are pictured as grand but ill-founded. In fact, there are cracks everywhere. . . . Who are the specialists for God's creaking house? Are there any at all? Quite a few hands are up. (P. 85)

These enterprises distort and seek to displace the primary language of faith. Holmer concludes, "it only sustains a confusion to ask for a revision of language, as if this were the seat of the difficulties" (p. 117). But the difficulties Holmer concentrates on are difficulties in coming to terms with the language of faith, a language he contrasts with the dead metaphysical language that obscures it.

For it is a question of which part of religious language is really so dead today. Is it the discourse of the metaphysical theologians? Is it the language of the hymn writer? Is it the language of the psalmist and other Biblical authors? If we are talking about certain kinds of elaborate metaphysical theology, I believe it is quite clear that much of this is very dead indeed. (P. 128)

But *could* the language of the psalmist and other Biblical authors die? Cornel West thinks that Holmer is not being Wittgensteinian enough and that he fails to recognize that it is the very religious responses he thinks are central "which are being called into question by the realities facing our churches, our seminaries, our communities, our society, our world."[10] Let us assume that the challenges West has in mind are religious revisions of which Holmer would disapprove. West is quite right in saying that if these responses became pervasive, then Wittgenstein would say that this is what religion had become. West is wrong, however, in thinking that it follows that it would be incumbent on Holmer, or on anyone else who opposed these religious revisions, to accept them simply because they are pervasive. West has forgotten that Wittgenstein said that language games can pass away and be forgotten.

But the question is whether Holmer, too, has forgotten this aspect of Wittgenstein's discussion of language games. There are times when he seems to suggest that the primary language of faith cannot be in jeopardy. I am not now referring to the confused view that it *has* to be in jeopardy because of its alleged magical or prescientific character. I am referring to the possibility of the language becoming increasingly unavailable because the well is poisoned at its source. Holmer asks, "Do beliefs crack, sag and sink?" T. S. Eliot certainly thought it made sense to say so of the words we speak:

> . . . . Words strain,
> Crack and sometimes break, under the burden,
> Under the tension, slip, slide, perish,
> Decay with imprecision, will not stay in place,
> Will not stay still. . . .
>
> *Burnt Norton*

Holmer is well aware that religious concepts, like any others, have their meanings in the life that surround them. As a result, he is able to say, "If the concepts no longer have any life in them; if they mean nothing, then it must be that all the rest that goes into giving people confidence and faith that there is a God has also disappeared" (p. 131). But it is not clear that Holmer is always prepared to allow this possibility, a reluctance that leads him to separate words from usage in a way that, usually, he would not allow: "It is not the words that are at fault, as much as the persons speaking them. Therefore, the religious words are vain when nothing follows their usage, where the individual does not seem to know anything about the matters to which they refer and the way of life in which they were born. Then we can say, sadly, that people do not know what they are saying. To teach them is one of the theologian's tasks" (pp. 134–35). The circumstances we are envisaging, however, is one where the theologian would be as much part of the predicament as anyone else. It was the perception of such pervasive shabbiness that concerned Kafka in *The Trial* and that led him to conclude in the fourth of his Prometheus legends: "Everyone grew weary of the meaningless affair. The gods grew weary, the eagles grew weary, the wound closed wearily."[11] This is the world that Eliot described as ending, not with a bang, but with a whimper.

The point at issue is one of some philosophical importance. Holmer and I could argue about loss of meaning, loss of concepts, in specific contexts. We could discuss, for example, Ian Robinson's claim that the language of the *New English Bible* cannot express certain notions of divine authority.[12] But that would not be a philosophical issue between us. The philosophical issue is whether the grammar of theology allows for its own demise. Someone may predict, truly or falsely, that there will always be a Christian witness while humankind survives. Such a prediction poses no problem. But what if someone said that there *must* be such a witness? What sort of necessity would that person have in mind? Part of the confusion may come from thinking that an abiding truth in religion, in the sense of an eternal truth, is one that abides forever in a temporal sense. There is no contradiction, however in the supposition that all people could turn their backs on an eternal truth. A religious truth is not less eternal, for those who believe it, if it can be said to disappear from the face of the earth. To think otherwise is to think that religious faith is dependent on the kind of external conceptions of necessity that Holmer has condemned elsewhere in his work. To say that God will see to it that a religious epistemic practice persists, is to abstract talk of God's activity from its natural sense without that epistemic context.

THE THEOLOGIAN AS GUARDIAN

Having located the audience Holmer takes himself to be addressing and having asked some critical questions of what he has to say, a final question of a different kind awaits us. We know who Holmer is speaking *to*, but where is he speaking *from*? Is Holmer simply a philosopher pointing out important conceptual confusions? There is reason to think that his is a task that goes beyond purely philosophical concerns. He not only reminds us, conceptually, of the grammar of faith, but calls us back to an embracing of that faith with something approaching an evangelical challenge. He is more than a philosophical gadfly.

The analytical philosopher is concerned with clarity. Certainly, Holmer does not disparage close philosophical analysis. "On the contrary, it can be asserted that the most detailed and seemingly disinterested analysis is very frequently also the most useful. Great detail and great skill are essential to becoming clear. Furthermore, religions, not least Christianity, do live in part by concepts, and these, in turn, become muddied by dubious associations and are frequently misconstrued by virtue of their resemblances to concepts found in the sciences, in aesthetics, and surely in morals" (p. 167). The struggle for clarity is obscured if we think of philosophy as the provider of meanings. Those who think of philosophy as such a provider, will fail to realize that "the recent shift in philosophical emphasis is not the better way, analytic instead of speculative, to do the same thing. In fact, Wittgenstein's reflections on these matters are more in the direction of liquidating philosophy as the science of meanings than of inventing one more permutation of methods to provide them" (p. 132). Wittgenstein teaches us differences by waiting on differences and unraveling those tendencies of mind that lead us to ignore them. Holmer, too, wants to emphasize that there can be no generic theory of meaning by which we can say that scientific language is more meaningful than religious language. . . . In fact, the whole notion of meaning is itself confused and it might be better simply to say that we can learn the differences between ways of speaking and ways of understanding. . . . One way to express this fully is to declare that the logic of the discourse of science is not the same as the logic of religion. Another way is to note all the different ways that we explain things to ourselves. For again, there are many kinds of explanations. Each kind has its context, its occasion, its own province, and its own function, relative to a specific need. We are gradually learning that kinds of explanations are not necessarily incompatible. They are, in fact, incommensurable with one another, and hence, there is no logical incompatibility of the radical sort. (Pp. 68–69)

When philosophy achieves clarity concerning such matters, having revealed the routes by which we are so easily led astray, its task is over. Philosophy leaves everything where it is; a far more difficult undertaking than is generally supposed. Holmer emphasizes that this philosophical search for clarity deserves to be carried on in freedom, free from "alien and extraneous demands, be they political, religious, ethical, or even institutional" (p. 62). Thus, despite the current institutional success it enjoys in America, there is no such thing, no such subject, as Christian philosophy. There can be an epistemology of religion, but the concept of a religious epistemology is a confused one. Thus, when contemporary reformed epistemology seeks to replace the logos of the Greeks, or the post-Enlightenment concept of sovereign reason, with the sovereign God of Christianity, it does so because it is still within the grip of the conception of philosophy as the provider of meanings, presuppositions, and perspectives. All this shows how little actual appropriation there has been of Wittgenstein's philosophical methods in the philosophy of religion. In his own philosophical practice, Holmer would stress the importance of philosophy's independence of religion, even if the philosophical enquiries are carried on within theological or religious institutions.

But, having come to these conclusions, Holmer wants to go beyond them. He asks, "All of these things remembered, is there not still another way of speaking that is theology proper? Is there not a way of speaking that is a more intimate expression of the religious life, a greater clue to its province, a greater help to learning to be religious, than all the learning *about* religion?" (p. 62). Holmer says that the meaning of religious and theological utterances "has to be earned and achieved in its original forms." To earn the understanding *he* seeks, the philosopher must pay attention to the grammar of religious concepts in their natural contexts. But if the philosopher *earned* and *achieved* these meanings *in their original form,* the philosopher would be a *hearer* of the Word, too, in its primitive form, namely, a believer. Is to understand the Word to hear the Word? Not if by "understanding" we mean the conceptual clarity the philosopher achieves. The philosopher need not personally embrace what he or she becomes clear about.

The philosopher leaves the unconfused theologian alone. It is right that the philosopher should do so. But the theologian, of the kind Holmer wants to show us, does not leave the philosopher alone, nor does the theologian think that it is right to do so. This is because Holmer tells us "the true judgments that theology proffers, like the judgments of the morally enflamed man, are made to incite, not merely to inform" (p. 67). Of course, the philosopher can, in turn, inform himself or herself of *this* feature of theology's task; the philosopher can become clear about it without being religiously incited and without wanting to incite anyone else.

When we read *The Grammar of Faith,* it is clear that Holmer is doing far more than informing himself and his audience of theology's proper task. He is also engaged *in* the task himself. Holmer not only informs, he also incites. Holmer says that when he does his work properly, the Christian teacher, the theologian, dares to become the guardian of the language of the faith. So does Paul Holmer.[13]

NOTES

1. Paul L. Holmer, *The Grammar of Faith,* (San Francisco: Harper & Row, 1978). All quotations from this volume will be cited in the text.
2. Cornel West, review of *The Grammar of Faith, Union Seminary Quarterly Review* 40, nos. 3 and 4 (Spring/Summer 1980): p. 284.
3. For an illustration of such a tendency, see my review of Don Cupitt's *Life Lines, Times Literary Supplement,* 26 December 1986.
4. West, review of *Grammar of Faith,* p. 281.
5. Ibid., p. 284.

6. I have discussed some of these muddles in *Religion Without Explanation* (Oxford: Basil Blackwell, 1976).

7. See Nicholas Wolterstorff, "Is Reason Enough?" *The Reformed Journal* 34, no. 4 (April 1981).

8. See James R. Cameron's stimulating essays on Newman in *The Night Battle* (Baltimore: Helicon Press, 1962).

9. Again, this is one of my main concerns in *Faith After Foundationalism* (London: Croom Helm and Methuen, 1988).

10. West, review of *Grammar of Faith*, p. 284.

11. I explore these issues at greater length in "Meaning, Memory and Longing" in *Through A Darkening Glass* (Notre Dame: University of Notre Dame Press, 1982) and in a forthcoming volume on religion and voices from twentieth-century literature.

12. See Ian Robinson, "Religious English," in *The Survival of English* (Cambridge: Cambridge University Press, 1973).

13. An earlier version of this essay was delivered at Yale Divinity School in the fall semester 1985. I am grateful to Paul Holmer for his comments on that occasion and for later discussions with David Gibson.

3. The Suspicion of Suspicion: Wittgenstein and Bonhoeffer

ROWAN WILLIAMS

Fergus Kerr's fine book, *Theology After Wittgenstein,* [1] devotes a good deal of space to expounding Wittgenstein's therapeutic dismantling of the myth of the solitary subject living "inside" the visible body and goes on to suggest some of the possible consequences for religious thought of this demythologizing. We shall need to rethink much of what we habitually say about "authentic" or "interior" prayer, about acts and intentions, about mortality and eternal life; theology must rediscover itself as a language that assists us in *being mortal,* living in the constraints of a finite and material world without resentment. We are not, in fact, "in" the world as selves contained inside some other sort of thing—the shell or husk of flesh: what we are *are* our limits, that we are here not there, now not then, took this decision, not that, to bring us here and now. And if this is true, understanding a person is understanding their limits, their materiality. Kerr quotes Nietzsche on the Greeks, who knew how "to stop courageously at the surface, the fold, the skin, to adore appearance. . . . Those Greeks were superficial—out of profundity!" [2] And he continues after this quotation: "the depth of the world is on the surface, so to speak: but also, what is most secret about the self is public knowledge." [3]

We are frequently told that we live in a time of "suspicion" in our thinking and interpreting. Paul Ricoeur [4] famously identified Marx, Nietzsche, and Freud as "masters of suspicion," those who pressed the Cartesian doubt to its most extreme point, the doubting of consciousness as well as the doubting of things. All three assume that consciousness is in need of decoding: "For Marx, Nietzsche, and Freud, the fundamental category of consciousness is the relation hidden-shown or, if you prefer, simulated-manifested."[5] How are we to reconcile the imperative of decoding with a recognition of the profundity of surfaces? Is Ricoeur wrong, still trapped in the Cartesian framework at whose outer edges the three "masters" stand? Or is Wittgenstein absurdly overreacting to the Cartesian problem and asserting that all language, all "presentation," must be taken at face value, so that we are left only with an essentially uncritical behaviorism?[6] Ricoeur is apparently endorsing a diagnosis of the post-Cartesian malaise in terms of insufficient skepticism; the remedy is an ascesis of thought by way of the suspicions of one or other of the masters, so that language ceases to function as a delusive protection against the unfathomable and uncontrollable world.[7] Wittgenstein refuses the terms of such a discussion, it seems, denying that we can usefully analyze consciousness (whatever that is) into simulation and truth: consciousness is not another object-to-be-known, it *is* what language shows (as the statue *is* what the stone shows, *is* the stone seen or recognized like *this*);[8] and what is shown is what we all know and all we know.

In what follows, I intend to explore this tension further, in an attempt to see whether it adds up to a contradiction. I shall briefly examine Wittgenstein's critique of Freud and his general attitude to the idea of interpretation as "decoding." And I shall try to elucidate what conception of "interiority" remains after the demythologizing of the imprisoned self, with the help of another of the century's major critics of certain notions of the inner life, Dietrich Bonhoeffer (in the letters written from prison in his last years). The comparisons and contrasts with Ricoeur's project of Christianized post-Freudian suspicion can then be assessed with greater clarity, and the sense in which Wittgenstein and Bonhoeffer may justly be counted as *critical* thinkers will emerge. Perhaps we need not, as philosophers or theologians, be left with the bald alternatives of false naivete about ideological or pathological distortions of speech, and manipulative reductionism.

WITTGENSTEIN AND FREUD

Wittgenstein's positive appreciation of Freud is in no doubt; both Rush Rhees[9] and Maurice Drury[10] record his conviction that Freud had "something to say," particularly in *The Interpretation of Dreams,* and the conversations with Rhees and others testify to the degree to which he took Freud seriously. However, after a passing enthusiasm for the idea of practicing as a psychiatrist (1934; though he had apparently begun to read Freud shortly after the First World War),[11] he both described himself[12] as a "follower" or "disciple" of Freud and insisted that the father of psychoanalysis had misunderstood his own project[13]. By 1946, he believed that the "way of thinking" represented by *The Interpretation of Dreams* was positively dangerous and needed the sharpest criticism.[14] A phrase in one of the 1943 conversations with Rhees indicates one reason for this hostility: Freud "wanted to find the essence of dreaming."[15] Dreaming is seen by Freud as a kind of language or, more accurately, a set of determinate symbols, "a way of saying something" (I'd be inclined to underline *way* in this phrase). Given the correct tools, the dream can be decoded into "ordinary speech." Yet, as Wittgenstein points out, there is no means for reversing the procedure, for *encoding* "ordinary speech" in dream symbolism: we cannot suppose that there is a content that can be indifferently expressed in ordinary and in oneiric language as two "ways of saying." This means, then, there may be no "correct" interpretation of a dream: its detail resists assimilation to a single pattern, a controlling latent meaning that orders the symbolism of the dream. Does this mean that dreaming is a matter of chance, that we refuse to face the questions of scientific causality?[16] But why should we oppose chance and determination in this simple way? Of course, there may be *reasons* for oneiric symbolism of various sorts, and Freud's readings may have a good deal to offer; but why assume a single pattern? What if dreaming is simply something we do, like a children's game, like art, like ritual, like story telling—like speech itself?[17]

The attraction of systematic Freudian interpretation is precisely in its concentrated simplicity. Our lives, thoughts, acts, imaginings are not, after all, contingent, but have the nature of a dramatic script being enacted: "it may then be an immense relief if it can be shown that one's life has the pattern rather of a tragedy—the tragic working out and repetition of a pattern which was determined by the primal scene."[18] The same point is already made with some force in the earlier lectures on aesthetics: reductive explanation has "charm."[19] This attraction is at least twofold. The *hidden* is attractive to us, says Wittgenstein—the idea of things buried and uncanny, (Why do we do this sort of thing? This is the sort of thing we do do.)"[20] and also we are sufficiently afraid of self-deceit, sufficiently mistrustful of our speech and images, to be ready to embrace the "ugly" or disedifying interpretation of what we do ("It is charming to destroy prejudice").[21] A Freudian interpretation of a dream is therefore essentially a rhetorical technique: it is about *persuasion,* not discovery, it is a practice intelligible only in the context of a performance by analyst and analysand.[22] The interpretation, as Wittgenstein says elsewhere,[23] is a "solution" because it is agreed to be such. "Someone seeing the unfolded picture might exclaim 'Yes, that's the solution, that's what I dreamed, minus the gaps and distortions.' This would then be the solution precisely by virtue of his acknowledging it as such. It's like searching for a word when you are writing and then saying: *'That's* it, *that* expresses what I intended!' Your acceptance certifies the word . . . as being the one you were looking for."

"Successful" analysis is in fact, so it seems for Wittgenstein, itself a game of sorts; its rules have to do with ritually offered and accepted transformations of selected narrative material. Like other kinds of systematic interpretation, it trains one in *ignoring* certain features of what is concretely present;[24] which is why it does not in itself necessarily contradict or exclude other readings.[25] The claims to exclusive truth ("x is *really* y" or "x is *only* y") cannot be sustained because the ideas of abstract convertible content in two kinds of utterance cannot be sustained (translation works only one way; we cannot establish reciprocally equivalent expressions for "the same thing" in ordinary and oneiric language). This again recalls the more general point about aesthetics: a putative account of how a particular aesthetic sensation might be neurologically analyzed and reproduced would not be capable of delivering the aesthetic stimulus, the artwork itself, in all its detail.[26] If analytic reduction of dreams or behavior patterns is seen (correctly) as the playing out of a particular option among several interpretative strategies, it may open possibilities to us; if presented as the uncovering of a deeper and determinative truth, it deprives us of possibility.[27] And it does so by taking us away from the constraint of here and now and persuading us to ignore and discount the complexity of what determines that here and now. It is a claim to know independently of agreement (that is, of community and conversation)—to have a knowledge that is nobody's in particular.[28] What Wittgenstein seeks to combat in Freudianism is the flight from particularity and the endlessness of difference (concrete detail) and the inexhaustibility of social converse,[29] the flight that for him represents the bondage of European thought to an epistemological problematic that remains obstinately dualist and so obstinately discontented with finitude. Specific interpretations are always exercises in ignoring difference and uncontrollable converse;[30] their danger lies in their potential for ignoring the fact of their ignoring.

In principle, the critique is applicable to any totalizing interpretation, Marxist, sociobiological, religious schemes of some kinds; and it is important to remember that Wittgenstein is not rejecting interpretation as such in favor of a passive reception of what presents itself but is rather defending the pluriform vitality of interpretation. The same notes of 1948 that contain his remark about the sort of Freudian exegesis of dreams that deprives us of possibilities also have a long and suggestive discussion about "understanding and explaining a musical phrase,"[31] very reminiscent of certain passages in the lectures on aesthetics. You explain to someone that the phrase is like *this* (how? by gesture, by movement, by comparison). They say, "Yes, I see" (but they don't have to). If they go on to perform the phrase in a way responding to what has been said, there has been an agreement in understanding—though what "understanding music" means is only establishable in relation to how an entire life is lived, how hearing and performing music relates to what else is seen and done. Understanding, explaining, interpreting are not efforts of an individual to penetrate a surface: they are *social* proposals for common reading and common, or at least continuous, activity (a gesture or performance that in some sense goes on with or takes up from mine). They do not, therefore, see what is to be interpreted as setting a problem to be solved: interpretation is not designed to put an end to puzzlement for good and all, though it may remove specific puzzles ("When a dream is interpreted we might say that it is fitted into a context in which it ceases to be puzzling;"[32] but, as the 1948 notes make plain, a final end to puzzlement—" 'Oh, *that's* how it was?' "—is an end to potential stimulus).[33] The interpretative proposal is precisely one that is made at a point in time and space; it acknowledges the finite and so acknowledges other possible voices; it is, in fact, suspicious of a suspicion that looks for a determinate hidden content to consciousness or phenomena.

BONHOEFFER'S SUSPICION OF THE PRIVATE SELF

The same polemic is at work—with a more immediately recognizable Christian motivation—in Bonhoeffer's prison letters. In June and July 1944, Bonhoeffer wrote two letters to Eberhard Bethge in which he developed a critique of "unaristocratic" apologetic.[34] With the withdrawal of God from the public sphere of human language, it had become necessary to look for religious meanings in the private, the interior; and a Christian apologetic faced with what seems to be a contented and self-sufficient human world struggles to persuade this world that it has a diseased *inner* life, a secret and hidden misery. "Existentialist philosophy and psychotherapy have worked out some quite ingenious methods in this direction."[35] This works on the assumption that the private sphere is of final, central significance. Just as the gutter press wants "revelations" of the secret life of public figures and is suspicious of anything that looks like a guarded privacy, so the apologist hunts for the "intimate" level—"as if you couldn't adequately appreciate a good play till you had seen how the actors behave off-stage." "Anything clothed, veiled, pure, and chaste is presumed to be deceitful, disguised, and impure."[36]

With a social confidence that rather takes aback the liberal reader, Bonhoeffer dismisses all this as "the revolt of inferiority," the pervasive and pathological mistrust felt by the socially disadvantaged or isolated (echoes of Nietzsche's *resentment,* perhaps). The Word of God cannot be allied with this vulgarity, this urgency to know what is discreditably secret. Setting aside the unmistakable tones of the cultivated upper bourgeoisie of pre-Hitler Germany, there are at least two very serious points being made here. One is that the assumption of an equivalence between the "inner" and the "essential" is controversial and historically conditioned;[37] the other is that a large part of what conditions it, is the development of cultures in which isolation has become an increasingly widespread experience. If we lack a properly common language, a properly public life, we shall be increasingly unsure of what (in both the simplest colloquial sense and the more philosophical sense) other people *mean:* we shall mistrust the other until and unless we have a key to unlock the secret chamber of their "essential" selfhood, a technique of decoding. Before we can effectively say what we have to say to another person, we must be able to establish that it will be rightly and safely received, by setting in advance certain criteria of truthfulness that must be accepted by the other. If you won't listen, it's because of your hidden guilt or sinfulness; if you won't listen, we shall have to deal with your resistance; if you won't listen, it is because of ideologically induced false consciousness (any or all of these may be *true,* of course, but that is not the point: the "audibility" of their truth can only emerge as a common, agreed world is actually shaped in the discourse between us). Bonhoeffer is alerting us to the fact, familiar enough now, rather less so in 1944, that the notion of an essential private self is a sociohistorical construct, and that hermeneutical suspicion arises from the universal "modern" (post-Enlightenment or post-Renaissance) experience of cultural fragmentation and consequent mistrust. We constantly feel we need to know more of the other because some directness, some presence or certainty eludes us, and that lack menaces us. As Stanley Cavell puts it in the brilliant concluding section of *The Claim of Reason,* "we are rather disappointed in our occasions for knowing, as though we have, or have lost, some picture of what knowing another, or being known by another, would really come to—a harmony, a concord, a union, a transparence, a governance, a power—against which our actual successes at knowing, and being known, are poor things";[38] we are tempted always to "the conversion of metaphysical finitude into intellectual lack."[39]

The second of these two summer letters to Bethge is followed by Bonhoeffer's poem, "Who am I?"[40]—at first reading a slightly banal presentation of the outer and the inner person, concluded by an abrupt transition into piety. It is, in fact, a subtle commentary on the letter's argument. The calm and cheerful exterior that Bonhoeffer was aware of presenting to his jailers and fellow prisoners ("They often tell me / I would step from my cell's confinement / calmly, cheerfully, firmly, / like a squire from his country-house") is contrasted with the anger and impotence within, so that the question "Which is the real me?" is raised; but it is raised to be itself exposed to suspicion. Why should the analysis be in terms of a false exterior persona cloaking a "real" weakness; what if the truth is that the interior self is in flight from the "victory already achieved" of the visible person? And all these are in any case "lonely questions," the indulgence of a certain kind of solitude; whatever or whoever is there, he belongs to God. In other words, the question "Who am I?" is not about an "intellectual lack," to be filled by an account of the real (hidden) self: the private sense of self, in this case, humiliating and wretched, may represent another kind of fiction or evasion, a construct out of the chaos of passing emotions. But Bonhoeffer's flesh and blood were in the prison at Tegel, offering sanity and comfort to other prisoners: how if at all that indubitable victory (both the imprisonment and his manifest response to it) should be harmonized with his inner fears is essentially an abstract problem posed in an unnatural isolation. The "answer" is the simple self-commitment to God: the wholeness of Bonhoeffer's selfhood lies in its belonging to God, a wholeness achieved in trust or hope rather than analysis. The pinning of knowledge, especially self-knowledge, to "metaphysical finitude" is secured by putting the entire situation in the context of God. My own identity's "ungraspable" quality thus becomes not an elusive level of interiority, but the unknowable presence of the creator's absolute affirmation, the mysteriousness of grace, past, present, and future, not of the "true self" as a hidden thing. My unity as a person is always out of my field of vision (I can't see my own fact), just as the divine condition for there being fields of vision at all, for there being a world or worlds, is out of my field of vision (I can't see my own origin).

This is further elucidated by some of Bonhoeffer's throwaway remarks on perfection. There are the cryptic notes of June 1944[41] on humanity, animality, and perfection, in which he implies that the human is irreducibly animal, resistant to the pathos of nostalgia, "the delight in death" (yearning for the unmediated absolute: somehow the "animal," though clearly not the whole of human identity, is our guard against *hubris;* which is why it is "the perfect human form" that is the focus of what? thought in general? theology in particular? "The divine, not in absolutes, but in the natural form of man." "To meet again, then, is a God": Bonhoeffer cites this remarkable line from Euripides' *Helen* apparently to illustrate the manifestation of the gods *within* human converse, the encounter of speech-using animals. It is this encounter that decisively relativizes the inner *Sehnsucht* of the isolated soul. Perfection does not lie in this inner world; in July he writes, "I should seek the 'perfect' in the human, the living, and the earthly, and therefore not in the Apolline, the Dionysian, or the Faustian"[42]—not, presumably, in the static determination of a psychological type, but in the world of temporal engagement and growth.

A year earlier, he had written to Bethge of a friend's horror at the spectacle of "a film that showed the growth of a plant speeded up; she said that she and her husband could not stand it, as they felt it to be an impermissible prying into the mystery of life."[43] This occurs—strangely, at first sight—in the context of a discussion of honesty and reserve and the nature of truthfulness. As in the reflections of 1944, there is a distinctive blend of simple old-fashioned *pudeur* and philosophical and theological acumen. Since the Fall, concealment is necessary and good in the sense that there is plenty in human thought, feeling, and experience that *should not* be part of shared discourse. We are alienated, divided, and corrupted; but to bring this into speech (and to assume we thereby tell a better or fuller truth) is to collude with sin. This is less than perfectly clear in the 1943 remarks; but what Bonhoeffer wrote in 1944 suggests that it is precisely the self-isolation that regards the complexities of the "inner life" as the primary reality that is the source of at least certain kinds of sin. The interior struggle should be hidden because, once brought into the light of speech, it is caught in the trap of mistrust, the fragmenting of discourse: "I tell you that I am not what I seem; and so I know that you are not what *you* seem, and I shall not be able to hear you until you, like me, renounce semblance for truth (here, let me help you . . .)." Bonhoeffer finely sums up in 1943 with a surprising allusion: "Kant says quite rightly in his *Anthropologie* that anyone who misunderstands or questions the significance of outward appearance is a traitor to humanity."[44] And the last few words should be taken quite seriously in the light of the writings of 1944: we are capable of betraying the reality of what we in fact are, where we in fact stand, of body and speech, of the bonds of sociality that constitute us as human, discounting the tangible, utterable contingency of what is there for the senses, in claiming to strip (oneself and others) to what is held to be true and essential and which is, in fact, the product of certain alienating or fragmenting forces in the social and linguistic world.

The same principle, incidentally, is applied to history as a whole. Bonhoeffer declares his suspicion of an Hegelian philosophy of history on the grounds that any notion (Hegelian or otherwise) of history as a continuum is bound to be a distortion.[45] The "essential" story of humanity is a scheme that always leads to the ignoring or misreading of the concrete phenomena of the past by forcing them into a pattern of *development*. We either absolutize or dismiss classical antiquity by categorizing it as "primordial": perhaps "classical values" are more accessible to us in other (medieval or modern) forms. Why should we suppose there is a single story to tell of humankind? "Until we can see further into it, it will be as well to base our attitude to the past, and to classical antiquity in particular, not on a general concept of history, but solely on *facts* and *achievements.*" Thus there can be no facile reduction of the complexity of the past to a single "inner" structure. Both relativism and systematic traditionalism are ruled out: we cannot distance the whole of the past as "foreign" (any more than we can distance the contemporary foreign by calling it archaic),[46] nor can we say that the ways we differ from a "classical" past are the measure of our decline and unseriousness, so that truth is discovered by stripping away the extraneous forms of contemporary life to return to fundamentals. Conversing with the human past is (in Wittgenstein's phrase) simply something we do, and, like other conversations, it has its unexpected convergences and its unexpected gulfs in understanding. The search for the single story of humanity reflects, once more, an age of alienation and mistrust, the flight from the risks of discourse.

There is, of course, much more that could be said about Bonhoeffer's analysis of faith and of Christian language from this point of view, the celebrated and much misunderstood "nonreligious" interpretation of the gospel.[47] But enough has been said to indicate that Bonhoeffer as a theologian shares much of Wittgenstein's project of "suspecting suspicion." But it should also be clear that their commitment to the profundity of surfaces cannot be written off as a *faux naif* rejection of interpretation itself. Wittgenstein believed most emphatically in the possibility of deception and self-deception,[48] and he, no less than Bonhoeffer, was aware of living in a culture saturated with fundamental untruthfulness. It is precisely because our culture is fragmented in so many ways (by economic injustice, by nationalistic violence and threatened violence) that we are unable to speak truthfully with each other, and public language becomes a mountainous refuse heap of self-protective clichés. Starting from such a context, how can we not be suspicious? And how can we not have a certain longing for "uncovering," for a language that will show us what is *really* happening? Yet that longing for a *unifying* discourse, to the extent that it urges us away from the particularities before us, colludes with our fragmentation, persuading us to ignore what is awkwardly or meaninglessly *there*. Because our speech and, therefore, our common life are so fragmented, we must be suspicious equally of the untruthfulness of what is offered us and of the untruthfulness of our own refusal of it (for we have no language or consciousness that has not been given us, and the great seduction is to think we can arrive at "our" truth by isolation). In Kierkegaardian terms, irony reaches into the very heart of consciousness; it does not stop at the frontier of my liberated or autonomous selfhood.[49]

RICOEUR AND THE TASK OF INTERPRETATION

If we now turn back to Ricoeur on Freud, it is something very like this pervasive irony that Ricoeur finally sees emerging from a sustained thinking through of the task of interpretation. Ricoeur begins, as we have noted, with the statement that modern critical hermeneutics assumes that the dialectic of concealment and manifestation is "fundamental" to consciousness. However, his discussion of Freud leads him to the conclusion that Freudian interpretation carries within it a severe tension. Symbolization, for the later Freud, is both a "making friends with necessity," a dealing with the imminence of death, and some kind of liberation, some affirmation of desire to which the imminence of death is immaterial.[50] Although Freud is sharply critical of the way in which the latter too easily and quickly offers resolutions that are, in fact, only possible by way of the former, he is not, Ricoeur claims,[51] entirely without sympathy for the lyrical, the aesthetic, and (in the widest sense) erotic claiming and transfiguring of reality in symbolic vision: the conclusion to the great "Leonardo" essay seems to point in this direction.[52] But if this is so, symbolization is not in fact capable of the reductive reading Freud insists upon; in the terms Ricoeur uses, it is not simply a matter of the "economics" of the psyche, the release of tensions, outlets for repressed forces. Symbolism is "over-determined," not simply to be read as a single and "real" language of the subconscious as opposed to the conscious, but a discourse in which both our origins and our final meaning (the goal of irreducible human desire) speak and are spoken of.[53] So the primary "dispossession" or displacement or decentering of ordinary consciousness to show what it conceals does not finally yield another closed explanatory structure (the subconscious simply doing the job of pre-critically conceived rationality). The hidden voices are many and complex in their relations. They can only be heard in their fullness by listening again to the pluriformity of what is shown or articulated—back to the surface, in fact, to what Ricoeur calls "the second naivete," a phrase peculiarly his own.

Ricoeur's proposal is carefully paradoxical: to think with or through symbols, they must first be unraveled or decoded, so that their overdetermined, even chaotic complexity appears. They must be reduced to show their irreducibility, then "reappropriated" in "concrete reflection" and "living speech," in the particularities of hermeneutics; and it is in the constant dialectic of the loss and the recovery of the symbolic particular that the symbol opens out on to the endless horizons of desire refining itself into the love of creation and creator.[54] In its return to the spoken word, reflection continues to be reflection, that is, the understanding of meaning; reflection becomes hermenuetic; this is the only way in which it can become concrete and still remain reflection.[55]

This comes close to saying (but doesn't quite say) that, at the end of the day, interpretation is simply responsive action: the creation in communicative behavior of a new moment in the historical configuration, generated by a fruitful and irresoluble puzzlement at what this "historical configuration" addresses us with. Wittgenstein can say that the most significant interpretation can be a gesture; Bonhoeffer looks forward to an unimaginable future religious language that (like Jesus' parabolic speech) will not offer a "reading of the world, but will liberate and renew it." Not interpretation, but change—a Marxist resonance that has not gone unnoticed by some readers of Wittgenstein[56] who have declined the facile and popular misinterpretation of Wittgenstein's dictum that "philosophy leaves everything as it is"[57] (*philosophy* is not itself interpretation but the questioning about the conditions for intelligible, unmythological interpretation: it is not itself passion or action, faith, hope, or charity, and shouldn't try to be).[58] If there remains (as I think there does) a tension between Ricoeur and the two exponents of the profundity of surfaces, it is in the way in which his language can still be read as presupposing a privileged status for consciousness and for theory—though this is in some respects modified in later essays. Wittgenstein and Bonhoeffer more clearly presuppose that to interpret the symbolic, linguistic, and behavioral complex that "addresses" us in the human world is to have one's own pattern of speech and action conditioned (not determined) by it, to be provoked (called forward) by the ways in which it touches, confirms, resonates, or questions what we have done and said. To interpret means interweaving a text (words or actions, words *and* actions) with our own human project, acquiring a partner, a pole of difference that refuses to allow our "project" to return endlessly on itself, as if it were indeed generated from a well of unsullied interiority, "self-consciousness."

INTERIORITY AND TAKING TIME

Are we then (if Wittgenstein and Bonhoeffer are right) simply to stop talking about the "inner" life of persons? This would be an odd conclusion. Both are writers whose lives and words show the sort of patterns we associate with interiority: solitude, chosen or enforced, meditation or prayer, acute and painful awareness of injury or falsity in relationships (penitence), passionate and reflective reading, a struggle for openness or honesty of a kind (granted Bonhoeffer's hostility to the idea of honesty as merely unexamined candor, irrespective of what you might call the moral grammar of a society or a situation). If we gather up such patterns of behavior under the term "interiority," and if we want to avoid the idea that they are patterns stemming from a "true" life beneath the surface of fleshly being in time, what is it that we are speaking of?

It may be that an analogy from visual art will help. Sometimes you will hear people talking about the "life," even the "inner life," of a picture: the sense that the viewer has of not exhausting the object when all its details have been taken in, a quality that can sometimes be called enigmatic, sometimes warm, spacious, or deep. A self-portrait by Rembrandt or a landscape by Turner or Corot or Nash or one of Klee's elusive linear statements would have this kind of "interiority." Now in this case, there is manifestly nothing there except the work itself: there is no *region* behind or beyond what is seen and sensed that would explain the "inner life" of the work, nothing that is private or secret. Everything is "on the surface," *is* the material surface, in fact. But, if we speak of its inner life as what teases and eludes us or what invites us simply to look and absorb, without "results," without decoding, we mean, I think, that the picture strikes us as sufficiently solid, sufficiently realized in itself or worked through, that it resists being mastered and made to serve some function in our mental program. It invites us to take time. Our relation to it isn't just spatial (eye to object, stimulation of the optic nerve in a sort of chronological vacuum, the speed of light) nor just a matter of a clearly determinate period (until I've found out what use this is, until I've solved/decoded this problem): we do not know what time is demanded of us, nor what it will issue in. We respond to the work as to a claim on our attention, of indeterminate scope; a presentation of multiple possibilities for assimilation and action.

Is interiority as a moral or "spiritual" concept comparable to this? We show our "inner life" not by the desperate effort to say everything, to externalize the stream of unspoken fantasy or dialogue that accompanies our material and public speech, but by so speaking and acting as to invite the taking of time. The person struggling with the former enterprise "has become a virtuoso of confession, an entertainer with his suffering," *assuming* that the basic fact is the unwillingness of others to know him or her and so constructing an ideal identity that cannot and, in fact, is not really meant to reveal what is hidden: "the very capacity for intimacy measures the fact of isolation; measures the depth of privacy unshared, i.e., refused."[59] The confessional style can, at the end of the day, produce simply a spectacle, not an invitation, because it takes for granted the inadequacy of conversation, the fact of *learn-*

ing the nature of another human being. Cavell draws our attention to the tragic possibilities of taking for granted the inadequacy or falsity of such learning: there is the risk of ultimate terror and madness, the image of the other as lie, as contradiction, as threat, even while we know at the same time our bondedness with the other, our dependence and partiality.[60] At the end of *Othello*, "the two bodies lying together form an emblem of this fact, the truth of skepticism. What this man lacked was not certainty. He knew everything, but he could not yield to what he knew, be commanded by it. He found out too much for his mind, not too little."[61] Othello, in other terms, wants to know and to *have done with knowing;* but that enterprise is the death of the specifically human mind, a dream of final orgastic possession that entails the voiding of one's own identity (limit, flesh, words, time).

My obscurity to myself, yours to me, and mine to you, are not *puzzles,* waiting for fruitful suspicion to uncover the real script, Marxian, Freudian, sociobiological (though all these stories may be true, need finding out). They are to do with the inescapability of taking time. "I do not really know myself" must be heard as "I don't yet know what to say; how to speak so that others listen and answer and build up in their words a way for me to go on speaking so that others may answer; how to become a partner in the world." The sense of a choked or imprisoned or elusive interiority is, on this account, a sense of skills not yet learned and nourishment not given, of not knowing what it might be to be *heard* and so set free—which is why the resolution suggested by a religious believer like Bonhoeffer has such powerful pertinence: I have been "heard" by God, and I have been given words—of praise and penitence and thanks—that direct me away from the question of how I shall "know myself."[62] I have been given time to learn what to say, with the help of the language of praise; because this is a language in which my finitude and limit are affirmed at the same time as my freedom and value, I may better learn from this how to speak to others without assuming their refusal, giving time to them and inviting them to give it to me.

Religious interiority, then, means the learning of patterns of behavior that reinforce the awareness of my finite and provisional status, my being in time. It is neither a flight from relation, not the quest for an impossible transparency or immediacy in relation but that which equips us for knowing and being known *humanly,* taking time with the human world and not aiming to have done with knowing (and desiring). Religious language can be the ally of projects of "suspicion" to the extent that they question the easy, restrictive social practice that discourages taking time (puzzlement, invitation, dialogue)—the kind of practice or discourse we label "superficial"; the "false consciousness" of the Marxist. The point at which suspicion itself is under criticism is when it comes itself to the point of discouraging the taking of time. The religious critique, as formulated by the writers we have been looking at (I have no qualms about seeing Wittgenstein's polemic as "religious" in this context),[63] directs itself against the potentially tragic and inevitable self-and-other-diminishing fantasy of abstracting knowledge from attention and response, from a material history of action—from the world, in fact. But what sets it apart from pure humane pragmatism is that it proposes to us a self-description enabling us to set aside once and for all the illusion that our value or "reality" depends on the success with which we can activate a suprahistorical knowing subject in penetrating to the hidden structures beneath the world of time and flesh. As Augustine memorably put it, we are driven at last to fling ourselves down upon the human mortality, the skin and bone, in which the Wisdom of God speaks to us so that "in its resurrection we too shall rise."[64]

NOTES

1. Fergus Kerr, *Theology After Wittgenstein* (Oxford: Basil Blackwell, 1986).
2. Ibid., p. 188.
3. For further discussion of this, see the four articles by Fergus Kerr in *New Blackfriars* 1983 and the third part of his "Rahner Retrospective," "Transcendence or Finitude," *New Blackfriars* 1981, pp. 370–79, especially the quotation on p. 378 from Valery, "Le plus porfond, c'est la peau."
4. Paul Ricoeur, *Freud and Philosophy: An Essay on Interpretation* (New Haven and London: Yale University Press, 1970), pp. 32ff.
5. Ibid., pp. 33–34.
6. The use of Wittgenstein in theoretical discussion of psychoanalysis by Roy Schafer (for example, *A New Language for Psychoanalysis* [New Haven and London: Yale University Press, 1976], *Language and Insight* [New Haven and London: Yale University Press, 1978]) has provoked accusations of this kind. See,

for example, Roy C. Calogeras and Toni M. Alston, "On 'Action Language' in Psychoanalysis," *Psychoanalytical Quarterly* 49 (1980): pp. 663–96, especially pp. 680–82 for the remarkable assertion that Wittgenstein believed language to be unfalsifiable.

7. Ricoeur, *Freud and Philosophy*, pp. 550–51.

8. Compare Stanley Cavell, *The Claim of Reason: Wittgenstein, Skepticism, Morality and Tragedy* (Oxford: Clarendon Press, 1979), p. 398.

9. Introducing "Conversations on Freud," in Wittgenstein's *Lectures and Conversations on Aesthetics, Psychology and Religious Belief* (Oxford: Basil Blackwell, 1966), p. 41.

10. Maurice Drury, "Conversations with Wittgenstein," in *Recollections of Wittgenstein*, ed. Rush Rhees (Oxford: Oxford University Press, 1984), p. 136.

11. Ibid.

12. Wittgenstein, *Lectures and Conversations*, p. 41.

13. Ibid., pp. 44, 49, 51–52.

14. Ibid., pp. 41, 44, 50ff., Drury, "Conversations with Wittgenstein," p. 137.

15. Wittgenstein, *Lectures and Conversations*, p. 48.

16. Ibid., pp. 42, 49; compare Wittgenstein, *Culture and Value* (Oxford: Basil Blackwell, 1980), p. 68.

17. Wittgenstein, *Lectures and Conversations*, pp. 49–50.

18. Ibid., p. 51.

19. Ibid., p. 24.

20. Ibid., p. 25.

21. Ibid., pp. 23–24.

22. Ibid., p. 27.

23. Wittgenstein, *Culture and Value*, p. 68.

24. Wittgenstein, *Lectures and Conversations*, p. 27 ("There are certain differences which you have been persuaded to neglect").

25. Ibid., p. 23.

26. Ibid., pp. 28ff., 37–40.

27. Wittgenstein, *Culture and Value*, p. 69 ("it is really as though I have been deprived of something").

28. A major theme of Cavell, *The Claim of Reason*, especially chapter 8, pp. 204–21.

29. Compare Wittgenstein, *Lectures and Conversations*, p. 27.

30. This is an area in which—as my phraseology in the text may hint—I would agree with those who see *some* convergence between Wittgenstein and Derrida; but the shadow of idealism hangs far more heavily over Derrida insofar as the *physicality* and temporality of discourse is so imperfectly dealt with.

31. Wittgenstein, *Culture and Value*, pp. 69–70.

32. Wittgenstein, *Lectures and Conversations*, p. 45.

33. Wittgenstein, *Culture and Value*, p. 69.

34. Dietrich Bonhoeffer, *Letters and Papers from Prison*, enlarged edition (London: SCM Press, 1971), pp. 339–42, 343–47.

35. Ibid., p. 341.

36. Ibid., p. 345.

37. Ibid., p. 346 ("The discovery of the so-called inner life dates from the Renaissance, probably from Petrarch"—a typically sweeping summary; one would need to look further at the difference between the medieval Augustinian tradition of entry into the depths of the self and the Renaissance idea. The former might be said to be the movement to awareness of the *fact*, not the experiential contents, of reflective activity, presence to oneself).

38. Cavell, *The Claim of Reason,* p. 440.
39. Ibid., p. 493.
40. Bonhoeffer, *Letters and Papers from Prison,* pp. 347–48.
41. Ibid., pp. 331–32.
42. Ibid., p. 376.
43. Ibid., p. 158.
44. Ibid.
45. Ibid., p. 230.
46. The point is made by J. Fabian in his excellent and provocative study, *Time and the Other: How Anthropology Makes Its Object* (New York: Columbia University Press, 1983), which argues that "scientific" anthropology achieves control over the cultures it studies by denying that they and the observer share the same time: the object culture belongs to the past (as "primitive") and so cannot be an interlocutor.
47. This is worth comparing with some of Wittgenstein's remarks to Drury in *Recollections of Wittgenstein* (above, n.10), p. 114.
48. Ibid., pp. 174–75, on the dangers of self-deceit; compare Wittgenstein, *Culture and Value,* p. 34.
49. Compare R. Williams, " 'Religious Realism': On Not Quite Agreeing with Don Cupitt," *Modern Theology* 1 (1984): p. 21, on "ironic" detachment as itself a cultural construct in need of being seen ironically.
50. Ricoeur, *Freud and Philosophy,* pp. 331–32.
51. Ibid., pp. 333–35.
52. Ibid., pp. 336–37.
53. Ibid., pp. 494–95.
54. Ibid., pp. 529–31, 536ff.
55. Ibid., p. 496.
56. Kerr, *Theology After Wittgenstein,* pp. 66–68; compare A. R. Manser, *The End of Philosophy: Marx and Wittgenstein,* an inaugural lecture, University of Southampton, 1973.
57. Compare Wittgenstein, *Philosophical Investigations* (Oxford: Basil Blackwell, 1953), I #126, 128, 496; and also take careful note of the remarks on "progress" in philosophy, *Culture and Value,* pp. 15, 86–87.
58. Wittgenstein, *Culture and Value,* pp. 53, 56, on "wisdom" as distinct from faith.
59. Cavell, *The Claim of Reason,* pp. 464–65.
60. Ibid., pp. 492–93.
61. Ibid., p. 496.
62. See Bonhoeffer's poems of summer 1944, *Letters and Papers,* pp. 347–56; and compare pp. 370–71, 391–94.
63. How else should we read *Culture and Value?* The impetus of philosophical critique here is manifestly a commitment to the world *against* the fantasies of the will and the egotistic imagination—which I take to be one mark of what might count as religious. And—in the light of this last section—see *Culture and Value,* p. 80: "This is how philosophers should salute each other: 'Take your time!' (or perhaps, 'give yourself time'—'*Lass Dir Zeit!*')."
64. Augustine, *Confessions* VII. 18.

4. Christianity Is Not a Doctrine

JOHN H. WHITTAKER

If there is an excerpt that summarizes Kierkegaard's *Concluding Unscientific Postcript,* it is the enigmatic saying that Christianity is not a doctrine.[1] This remark startles us because it is counter-intuitive; surely in the normal sense of the word, Christianity *is* a doctrine, or perhaps a set of doctrines. But Kierkegaard had a special sense of the word "doctrine" in mind, and he wanted to bring out a feature of Christian teachings that is overlooked when they are indiscriminately classified as "beliefs." Yet the special sense he had in mind can be more confusing than the remark itself, for the explanation of this remark usually turns out to be more puzzling than the original saying.

Let me explain what I mean. The *Postscript* contains observations, ironic comments, and hypothetical analogies designed to clarify the "logic" of Christian assertions. Kierkegaard, writing as Johannes Climacus, draws numerous distinctions to bring out the peculiar features of religious claims, and saying that Christianity is not a doctrine is designed to further one of these.

Christianity is not a doctrine but an existential communication expressing an existential contradiction. If Christianity were a doctrine it would *eo ipso* not be an opposite to speculative thought, but rather to a phase within it.[2]

He wants to contrast the nature of Christian claims with the nature of *speculative* claims, a point to which he returns again and again in the *Postscript.* Speculative doctrines are "not relevant to existing," whereas Christian claims are beliefs to be inhabited or filled out with our lives. We are to pour ourselves into the molds of such teachings so that the form of our lives matches the shape of Christian existence. To acknowledge this special connection between believing and reforming one's life, he called the claims whose affirmation brings about such changes "existence communications." Existence communications are the opposite of speculative hypotheses; for unlike speculative claims, they are essentially the means of life transformation. If they are not so understood, then they are misunderstood.

However, it is far from clear why speculative doctrines could not also play the role of life-transforming beliefs. What is it about them that prevents this? One must dig deeper here for Kierkegaard's answer, which has to do with the way in which the two types of claims are judged. Existence communications are to be "realized in existence,"[3] or evaluated from the standpoint of one who has undergone the life changes that they imply. This amounts to saying that the connection between believing a teaching and conforming one's life to it cannot be broken, so that there is no time when one considers the evidence for an existence communication in abstraction from the way in which it promises to refashion one's life. The only way to judge such a belief true is to gather the cares of an unhappy life together and pour them into the new form that it provides, hoping that the new life available through them brings the peace of mind that one seeks. The only way to defend such beliefs, moreover, is to make one's life a testimony on their behalf, so that the peace that one finds in these teachings might move others to faith.[4]

Yet it is just the opposite with speculative beliefs. In weighing them, one abstracts the weight of one's personal concerns from judgment, since one's personal cares have nothing to do with the truth or falsity of the issues. The truth or falsity of speculative doctrines depends solely on the way the world is, not on the private concerns of individuals; so one needs to gather evidence of the way the world is without allowing subjective desires to spoil one's deliberations.

Kierkegaard tries to draw out the same contrast between Christian claims and speculative hypotheses in the *Postscript* by saying that "truth is subjectivity."[5]

When the question of truth is raised subjectively, reflection is directed subjectively to the nature of the individual's relationship; if only the mode of this relationship is in the truth, the individual is in the truth even if he should happen to be thus related to what is not true.[6]

This remark is not as extreme as it sounds, for we are not to imagine a person believing in a known speculative or a scientific error yet having some kind of personal relationship with it that renders it true. I don't even know what such a suggestion could mean, but it is not Kierkegaard's point. His comment is restricted to "essential truths" (which are the same as "subjective truths" or "existence communications").[7] When such truths are at stake, ordinary means of objective judgment (weighing evidence, testing consistency, etc.) no longer apply; so these beliefs cannot be *known* to be false without mistakenly construing them as hypotheses. An entirely different manner of evaluation applies to them—the appropriate question is whether or not one can *live* by them. If belief reorders the priorities in which the passions of one's life are invested, changing his concern for happiness from frustration to hope, then even if the belief *appears* to be false as speculative doctrine, it might nevertheless be a subjective truth.

Of course, one's concern with lasting happiness must be aroused before his or her passion for it can be reinvested according to the guidelines of an "essential truth." Since Kierkegaard thought that such truths appeared to have little credibility as speculative hypotheses, he thought that their affirmation required an enormous amount of passion in order to be affirmed at all. In fact, he thought that the amount of passion required to affirm an essential truth is inversely proportional to the claim's susceptibility to objective judgment. The less amenable a belief is to being confirmed by factual evidence or abstract criteria, the more passion it requires for its affirmation. Christianity requires an infinite amount of passion because the belief on which it rests (the belief that God was in Christ reconciling the world to himself) *absolutely* resists objective confirmation. Yet the passion required to affirm basic Christianity is not *spent* in the act of belief; it is sustained by a new way of life governed by a new order of concepts. This new life makes one's hopes less dependent on worldly events and less subject to worldly disappointments. It is made for those whose spirit can only be restored by the improbable, impractical, and unprovable hopes that Christianity fosters. In such dispirited souls, suffering has evoked the passion that faith requires.[8]

These are some of the distinctions that Kierkegaard draws to explain his fundamental contention that Christianity is not a speculative doctrine. They can be expanded, of course; "passion" might be better explained, "objectivity" might be further elaborated, and "subjectivity" might be rescued from the confusion that surrounds it. But even when that is done and one is satisfied with the contention that religious claims are existential communications, a modern philosopher cannot help but ask if this means that Christian claims are really *beliefs*—beliefs that the world truly is as it is described. If Kierkegaard means that "existential communications" consist of *truth claims,* then it is hard to see how he can deny the relevance of evidence and the logical propriety of considering consistency and coherence in their judgment. But if he means to deny that faith claims are either true or false, then his view seems totally at odds with believers and their understanding of faith.

In any case, Kierkegaard is largely ignored by hardheaded philosophers of religion, who tend to think of him either as an irrationalist or as an early noncognitivist. For these philosophers, it may come as a surprise to realize that his intense preoccupation with the nature of Christian faith was shared by Ludwig Wittgenstein. Actually, it has been known for some time that Wittgenstein was familiar with Kierkegaard, apparently reading him with great respect.[9] But only since the publication of some of Wittgenstein's disconnected notes, issued under the English title *Culture and Value* in 1980, has there been much evidence that Wittgenstein's thought moved within the orbit of Kierkegaard's ideas. On what subject?—that Christianity is not a doctrine.

Several closely related Kierkegaardian themes, in fact, come to the surface in Wittgenstein's notes. He struggles with the relationship between historical scholarship and Christian faith, for example—the very topic that moved Kierkegaard to write the *Postscript* in the first place.[10] His comments sound uncannily like those of Kierkegaard.

Christianity is not based on a historical truth; rather, it offers us a (historical) narrative and says: now believe! But not, believe this narrative with the belief appropriate to a historical narrative, rather, believe, through thick and thin, which you can do only as the result of a life.[11]

Elsewhere, he recalls a Kierkegaardian theme in distinguishing Christian beliefs, which involve *passion,* from the passionless wisdom of philosophers.

> The point is that a sound doctrine need not *take hold* of you; you can follow it as you would a doctor's prescription. But here you need something to move you and turn you in a new direction. . . .
> Wisdom is passionless. But faith by contrast is what Kierkegaard calls a passion.[12]

No point, however, is as typical of Kierkegaard as his effort to distinguish Christianity from speculative hypotheses.

> Christianity is not a doctrine, not, I mean, a theory of what has happened and will happen to the human soul, but a description of something that actually takes place in human life.[13]

When Wittgenstein says that Christian teachings are not to be read as a theory about what happens to the soul, his meaning is clear enough. The *point* of such assertions is not the point of speculative hypotheses, which is simply to describe the nature of reality. Christian teachings are *religious* beliefs, and their purpose is not to disclose facts about supersensible realities. They are to do more than this. But what is this *more?* Exactly what kind of claims are they?

In the last passage quoted, Wittgenstein goes on to say that " 'consciousness of sin' is a real event and so are despair and salvation through faith." "Those who speak of such things," he continues, "are simply describing what has happened to them . . . ."[14] This suggests that Christian claims about supernatural occurrences actually refer to changes within the believer's experience. One who thanks God for the gift of salvation articulates the changed state of his or her own disposition toward himself or herself, but one does so in the form of a narrative about receiving something from a transcendent being. Here the form of the believer's description is metaphorical; the true content of the belief concerns inward facts about the believer. Yet if this is what Wittgenstein means, then his account ought to be suspect. Believers who think that they have been saved believe that something has happened *to them* and that their inward state is the result of their relation to something outside of themselves. Any analysis that changes this cannot be acceptable as an explanation of *their* meaning. For they relax their inward relationship to themselves *in consequence* of a gift from on high, and their belief expresses this supposition.

Still, it is by no means clear that Wittgenstein intended anything like what I have described. His lectures on religious belief come from the same period of his life as this note from *Culture and Value,* but they suggest another view entirely.[15] In these lectures he describes religious claims as "pictures" that play a regulative role in believers' lives.[16] He implies that the meaning of a religious belief might be understood in terms of its role, since the point of such a belief depends on the place that believers customarily afford it in their thinking and living. A belief's regulatory role, as we might say, belongs to its *essence.* One does not first understand the belief, then gather reasons for believing in it, and finally decide to attend to its practical implications. Rather, one believes in it by adhering to it, so that there is no middle step in which the belief is considered in abstraction from its regulatory role and assessed in the light of evidence.

The difficulty with the account from the *Lectures,* though, is still the problem of cognitive significance: how does the claim to truth fit in here? Do religious people simply affirm rules that are dressed up as beliefs about the world, or do they affirm truths with practical applications? If it is the latter, what is wrong with attending to a belief's regulatory role to gain a better understanding of its meaning and then looking in a detached way for evidence that supports it?

In a later passage from *Culture and Value,* Wittgenstein provides a comment that dispels some of the haziness of his ideas. He does not answer this question directly or even face the issue as I have posed it; and yet the perspective that he offers opens up the vista we need to answer this last question for ourselves.

It strikes me that a religious belief could only be something like a passionate commitment to a system of reference. Hence, although it's a *belief,* it's really a way of living, or a way of assessing life. It's passionately seizing hold of *this* interpretation. Instruction in a religious faith, therefore, would have to take the form of a portrayal, a description, of that system of reference, while at the same time being an appeal to conscience. And this combination would have to result in the pupil himself, of his own accord, passionately taking hold of the system of reference.[17]

Here the idea that religious beliefs serve a regulative function is presented as the natural consequence of these beliefs framing systems for the *assessment* or the *interpretation* of life. A believer adheres to a certain way of life because she sees life in a certain way, a way given by the picture that her beliefs present—and the regulation of her behavior goes hand in glove with that. Everything, including the practical implications of belief, depends on the pattern outlined in one's system of reference. Yet this system of reference must be *believed* to be adopted. One must take hold of it *as true*.

Here, too, Wittgenstein notes the passion that moves a believer and that arises out of hopelessness—both Kierkegaardian themes. But the thing that I would like to emphasize is Wittgenstein's reference to *belief* in a *system of reference*. Though he does not say so explicitly, he implies the necessity of committing oneself to truth claims if one is to have faith. But the claims in question are the definitive elements of a system of interpretation for the assessment of life, and believing in them means entering into the system that they outline. It means adopting such claims as principles and regulating one's thoughts accordingly. But does it mean accepting *speculative doctrines?* Does the believer first have to decide the truth or falsity of his or her beliefs *metaphysically* if he or she is to abide by them practically?

I do not think that a religious believer needs to assess his or her beliefs as metaphysical speculations about transcendental realities in order to believe that they are true. There is no level on which religious beliefs might be treated as philosophical hypotheses. Rather, "the belief in God" is the doorway to a new pattern of judgment about oneself, one's neighbors, and the surrounding world. The commitment that one makes in entering that domain is a commitment to thinking that this pattern is called for or that the judgments one makes in accordance with such a principle brings understanding. It is not a commitment to an alien realm of speculative endeavor in which judgments are made with little regard for the role of these beliefs in working systems of judgment, and there is no need to detach these beliefs from the role they play nor to judge them dispassionately.

But I am getting ahead of myself. These last remarks need considerable explanation, but they take us to the limit of Wittgenstein's remarks on religious belief. Wittgenstein, after all, never claimed to have answered all questions about the logical features of religious belief. He wrote only *notes,* and he expected those who understood him to think for themselves. To explain the idea that Christianity is not a doctrine—and to save the idea that religious claims are truth claims—we will have to venture some thoughts of our own.

To see how it is that Christianity neither is nor depends on a speculative doctrine—yet *is* a truth claim—let us compare it to a simpler case. Imagine a person who is ill with a poorly understood disease, let us say a painful rash of some kind. This person believes that this rash, like bodily ailments in general, is the result of being exposed to too many "negative energy waves." To combat such negative waves, the body sends out positive "relaxation waves," which counteract the harmful effects of the incoming energies. These "relaxation waves" are generated from states of deep relaxation, which a wise person tries to cultivate in periods of daily meditation.

What are we to say about these beliefs? Are they farfetched scientific hypotheses? I don't think so. Just as Kierkegaard and Wittgenstein denied that Christianity was a speculative doctrine, one might deny that this belief in "relaxation waves" is a scientific doctrine. It *looks* like a scientific doctrine, just as Christianity *looks* like a set of metaphysical hypotheses about supernatural reality; but one wonders if it is what it appears to be. Unlike an empirical hypothesis, this one resists objective testing. Most waves have a physical origin; they can be classified (sound waves, light waves, etc.), they can be measured, and their effects on other phenomena can be observed. But not "relaxation waves." Other than being somehow produced by the body, their origin is unspecified; their size cannot be measured; and other than effecting cures (supposedly), they have no observable effects on physical things. Let's say that the believer admits all this, saying that "relaxation waves" are mental phenomena, not detectable in the physical world—yet still produce cures. Maybe they do; but if so, these cures are not correlated with measurable states of relaxation. If the person meditates and his or her ailment continues, then this meditation is said to be too shallow. If the person does not meditate, and the condition improves, he or she is said to enjoy the effects of relaxation subconsciously in his or her daily affairs. No explanation is given for the fact that some people die after being in comas, where their relaxation would appear to be complete—none, that is, except the ever-available supposition that they somehow had not relaxed enough. This makes the relaxation diagnosis foolproof, since there are no circumstances in which it cannot be invoked. But it also makes it *empty* as a scientific claim.

Is the belief simply foolishness, then? Maybe. But there is also the possibility that it plays a quite different role in the thinking of believers, not the role of a scientific hypothesis but the role of a practical guide, a key to *coping* with illness.

To follow out this possibility, let us redescribe the belief in "relaxation waves" as a means of *construing* illness. In common language, construals show the way the believer "looks at" his or her disease; but it does more than this. It evokes a certain *disposition* toward the disease. And, indeed, one might say that the evocation of this disposition is the purpose of the belief. For construing a disease as the result of destructive energies impinging on the body entails adopting a set of attitudes toward oneself and the world: it is unhealthy to be too busy, to be uptight, and it is healthy to stop worrying over everyday affairs, banishing all anxiety and dissolving into utter relaxation. Feeling this way about the relation of disease to one's larger life gives one a therapeutic strategy. Instead of feeling victimized by a disease, one who thinks of disease as a relaxation disorder feels responsible for his or her illnesses; and instead of relying passively on medical aids, he or she takes an active role in trying to rid his or her life of anxieties.

Since there are behavioral consequences riding on this belief, one could also describe it as a regulative belief. It regulates the way that people think about diseases, the way that they feel about them, and, to that extent, the activities that grow out of this underlying disposition. The belief in destructive energy waves and their counterbalancing relaxation waves also presents a "picture" of disease.

"Yes," some will say, "this construal of diseases contains a *metaphorical* picture that people use to express their attitudes toward disease." Similarly, I can imagine people saying the same thing about religious beliefs. They, too, contain "pictures" of various supernatural realities, and these pictures help them to adjust themselves to the transcendent realm. There is nothing wrong with this idea, yet it hides an important ambiguity—and I think that we should go back to the case of the rash to bring it out.

The ambiguity can be spotted if we ask how the *metaphorical* nature of the relaxation-construal is to be recognized. The usual answer is that metaphorical descriptions are identified by means of a *contrast* between them and a *literal* description. That is to say, one who has an accurate knowledge of something can recognize the figurative nature of an alternative description simply because the alternative is only partially true or true only by way of extension. He or she can see this contrast, furthermore, because he or she knows what the object of the metaphorical description is like. But in the case at hand, no one has a true and accurate knowledge of the disease, since its cause—its etiology—is unknown. We know the disease only by way of its symptoms. Thus, we lack the literally true description of the illness to contrast with the way in which the disease is pictured, and we are in no position to compare our *exact* knowledge with the *inexact* account we're given. Indeed, it may seem as if we are in no position to say that the construal is figurative at all; for all that we *know,* it might be completely true. Yet we do describe it as a metaphor and with good reason. The recognition of its metaphorical nature, therefore, must come from somewhere else.

It comes from the knowledge that some of the things that we say in connection with an expression are not appropriate in the context in which this expression is used metaphorically. For instance, we might ordinarily speak of waves as having a particular origin, but in the case of "relaxation waves" we do not. Their origin is the "spirit" or the body in general, not any particular point. Or we might suppose that energy is used in the production of waves, but in the case of "relaxation waves" this is not the case; they are emitted in inverse proportion to the consumption of energy. So the ordinary grammar of the concept of a wave is only *partially* invoked in speaking of "relaxation waves." That is how we know that the word is being used metaphorically. Its grammar is abridged, and we *know* this simply by understanding the concepts involved. We do not have to compare our figurative descriptions to literal knowledge.

Consequently, we do not need to assume some kind of literal knowledge of the divine realm in order to say of our religious beliefs that they are metaphorical—and this is important. Just as construals of a disease may be metaphorical pictures designed to engender certain attitudes toward it, religious construals may serve the same purpose. They engender attitudes toward our life, but the "pictures" that they present of it may be known to be figurative without presuming accurate knowledge of the divine.

In describing religious claims as construals, then, I would like us to remember this point. Yet another ambiguity needs to be cleared up, and the use of the word "construal" should help to avoid misunderstanding on this issue as well. That ambiguity is this: if we describe religious claims as "regulative beliefs," one might suppose that they might be followed simply by imitating the outward forms of behavior associated with them. Thus, one might attempt to *live* in a Christian manner while holding none of the beliefs of Christian faith to be true. The behavior, as it were, might be valued but not the beliefs, which are discarded in the mind of such "believers." On the other hand, regulative beliefs might be regarded as genuine truth claims, so that their regulative influence would only affect those who were convinced of their truth. Those who attempted to imitate the behavioral consequences of a religious belief could never quite do so without actually *believing* in them. For the attitude that accompanies them *as beliefs* requires commitment. Pretended belief, on this account, could never do as a substitute.

If we think of religious beliefs as construals, the former view of religious claims clearly won't work. For if true Christian behavior is an outgrowth of a Christian disposition, then a believer will need to share this disposition to share Christian faith—and this disposition is a product of a *construal.* What a person needs to share, in other words, is not the outward form of behavior, which might be valued from an alien perspective, but the manner of valuing that belongs to the construals themselves. A person needs to see the world after the fashion of a believer, construing it as believers do. This sharing of a construal is believing.[18]

How, then, does one come to believe that a religious construal is true? What are the reasons underlying good judgment on such questions, and what does it mean to describe a religious construal, usually a figurative expression, as true? These are the most difficult issues in this whole analysis; and to be truthful, the questions are too complex to be dealt with in a general way. I have only two points to contribute: one observation about a factor that might be described as a "reason" for belief and one observation about the meaning of affirming a religious belief as *true*.

The truth of a construal such as the one I've presented might be judged, following Wittgenstein, in terms of the whole "system of reference" of which it is a part. If the manner of thinking, which reflects the dispositions and the feelings behind a construal, proves helpful in illuminating experience, in drawing disconnected fragments of it together, or in settling the believer into a more honest relation to his or her life, then one might affirm those beliefs that provide these advantages. This, I realize, is not the only factor to be considered in the evaluation of empirically untestable construals, but it is one of the most important. And it is problematic enough to occupy all our attention.

In general, the view that the "adequacy" of a belief forms one basis for judging its truth sounds like pragmatism, and there are well known objections to pragmatic theories of justification. Even so, I would like to make some distinctions that distinguish the account that I am suggesting from the usual variety of pragmatism. Wittgenstein himself ran into this same problem, so maybe I should start with some of his remarks. In discussing the obvious truisms that we ordinarily take for granted, Wittgenstein suggested that such certainties were not items of knowledge, since items of knowledge rest on evidence. When one knows something, one can always say *how* he or she knows by citing the evidence from which the belief follows.[19] But not so for certainties, for they are as certain as any of the evidence that one would like to use to defend them. Thus, Wittgenstein emphasizes the "groundlessness of our believing" when it comes to fundamental certainties.[20] At the same time he tries to acknowledge the role that the world plays in limiting the conventional agreements that people can incorporate into their lives. "Doesn't it seem obvious that the possibility of a language-game is conditioned by certain facts?"[21] Our ungrounded agreement in treating certain beliefs as certainties is *borne out* in our lives;[22] we do not have to "get out of the saddle" because facts about life keep bucking.[23] Rather, our ungrounded agreements have a kind of practical sustenance inasmuch as they are suited to our lives in this world. But here Wittgenstein says that he is thwarted by pragmatism, which is obviously not what he intends.[24] So what can he mean?

He means, I suggest, that there is no way to turn the practical utility of a certainty into an *argument* for its truth. The pragmatic value of a certainty is not *evidence* for its truth; for if it were, certainties would not be groundless but would rest on *pragmatic* grounds. Yet neither are practical considerations irrelevant to the question "Why is a groundless certainty held?" This issue plagued Wittgenstein, who struggled with it repeatedly, speculating that the experiential success of our linguistic conventions might be the *cause* of their being held, but not their *ground*.[25] Now I don't think that this explanation does justice to the significance the world has in supporting our linguistic agreements. Somehow it is logically appropriate that *suitable* beliefs are held, even though one cannot present their suitability as evidence of their truth.

I would like to defend a qualified version of pragmatism, then, and apply it to religious construals. The pragmatic utility of a belief never counts as direct evidence for its truth, but it does more than to explain causally why a belief is held. It has a role to play in informing good judgment, but that role cannot be so specified as to become a standard of good judgment.

Let's go back to the case of the rash to see why. Since the things that one does to relax—resting, remaining comfortable, putting anxieties out of mind, etc.—are generally conducive to health, it is obvious that "relaxation therapy" will cure a lot of diseases. But there are two ways to judge its success here. *Success* can be understood independently of the way that diseases are construed as "relaxation ailments," as, for example, when success is understood to be simply a matter of eradicating the symptoms of disease. From that point of view, the success of a therapeutic regimen will count for the truth of the beliefs the regimen is based on, as long as one assumes that cures could not be produced in any other way—which is an assumption that we have reason to doubt. Thus, the pragmatic value of construing a rash as a "relaxation ailment" *might* count as evidence for its truth *if* this additional assumption could be made. But it cannot be made, and so the practical utility of the belief in "relaxation waves," etc., amounts to very little in the way of evidence.

On the other hand, the success of "relaxation therapy" might be understood in a way that *presumes* the truth of the general perspective on which it rests. Thus, if the symptoms of a rash are made to disappear by the administration of drugs, this will not necessarily be considered a successful therapy. Rather, such drug therapy will be thought to mask a serious condition under the guise of a healthy appearance; for in the minds of those who construe diseases as relaxation disorders, people who lose the symptoms of a rash may still have the anxiety conditions that caused the ailment in the first place. Consequently, they may still be *vulnerable* to the outbreak of other unhealthy symptoms. To be *really* cured, a person must not only lack the symptoms of an ailment but must also show a marked increase in relaxation. For without this increase, there are no truly successful cures—none, at least, for a person who judges the success and failure of these therapeutic techniques in terms of relaxation.

According to this way of understanding success, to argue that the success of one's therapeutic techniques proves the truth of the underlying beliefs is simply to argue in a circle. Applied to religious beliefs, such an argument is tantamount to arguing that the goal of human life is to become Christ-like, and since the beliefs of Christianity underlie the most resolute attempts to acquire a Christ-like character, these beliefs must be true—which proves nothing since Christian beliefs are involved in the original definition of the goal of life. Thus, however one interprets "success" (independently of the construal whose truth is at stake or in a way that presumes it), pragmatic arguments lack evidential force. And we seem to have gained little by talking about the adequacy of those dispositions that accompany empirically empty construals.

But surely there is some value in the way in which we construe "success." One way of construing diseases and the success of their cures must be more valuable than another way of construing these things, even though one cannot mount pragmatic arguments or advance pragmatic evidence apart from an underlying agreement as to what counts as utility. That is why we would like to say that our standard medical diagnosis of diseases and the therapeutic techniques associated with these diagnoses are superior to the system in which diseases are construed as relaxation failures. Perhaps this example is not the best, since we are comparing empirically testable medical theories to an empirically empty way of interpreting them. But then again, do we not think that an empirically based way of handling disease is superior to purely psychological techniques? We do, but if we try to *argue* for our manner of interpreting illness pragmatically, we will not be able to share common standards with one who sees the value of therapy in terms of relaxation. We lack the common agreement on standards that arguments presume. But is there not an *inarticulate* sense in which we feel our system of interpretation to be superior to theirs?

I think that Wittgenstein thought so, even though he offered but few clues about what this inarticulate sense of superiority might be. In *On Certainty,* he briefly describes a situation in which people disagree in what they consider good grounds of arguments to be and in which "arguments" are no more than slogans to belittle opposing views. Having admitted this, however, he says that *persuasion* might take the place of reason giving.[26] Might not this persuasion include *showing* the value of one's system of beliefs by training a person in it? Here the only way in which the value of a system of thought can be articulated is in accordance with the principles of that system; but when another stands completely outside this system, the value of the principles and the conception of utility that they presume can only be shown. Yet it *can be shown,* or at least, one can try to show it, which is exactly what reasonable persuasion involves.

In short, I think that there is an adequacy that systems of belief might have that is *not* the kind of adequacy that can be articulated according to set standards and used to judge the truth of conflicting principles. It is the adequacy of construing *values* in certain ways—of defining the ends of inquiry or conceptualizing the purpose to which understanding is to be used. These various construals have their own utility, one that lies deep down, as it were, beneath conceptualization. This inarticulate utility makes *training* possible and *persuasion,* too. One can be taught to believe, and the one who teaches can hope that the learner will see for himself or herself the worth of those capacities that believing brings. To that extent, one can be justified in maintaining principles for which he or she lacks convincing grounds. This person might *persuade* someone else of these beliefs, and do so appropriately, though he or she might not be able to *argue* for them successfully.

The same, I suggest, applies to religious beliefs. They are construals that cannot be shown to bear truth on pragmatic grounds. The basic principles out of which these construals are formed are so fundamental that they affect not only the interpretation of evidence (making arguments for them circular) but also the conceptualization of the values that they promote (so that attempts at pragmatic justification also fail). Yet I see no reason why religious construals might not be supported and communicated through a process of rational persuasion, which is all that we can ask in the way of justification for any truly fundamental principles.

Still, though, one must ask what it means to affirm a religious construal—a mere metaphor expressing an attitude—as a *true* belief.

In the case of the disease construals, one could say that the empirically empty theory of relaxation disorders is not the same *kind* of belief as those in conventional medical theories. The conventional medical theories coordinate hypotheses with empirical findings, but not the relaxation view. Instead, the relaxation view helps people to *cope* with diseases whose specific causes are unknown, being only loosely associated with vague notions of relaxation. The *point* of the relaxation construals, therefore, seems to differ from the point of conventional medical theories. These construals provide a helpful *psychological* technique for handling illness but not a helpful *physical* therapy—even though some physical ailments disappear under the regimen of the relaxation view.

Similarly, the point of religious construals is not the same as scientific theories. Science, in general, describes whatever may be found contingently to be the case. Religion appears to offer a parallel description of supernatural facts, but it actually serves a quite distinct function. Religious construals do not state value-free facts about transcendent realities; they place known facts about life into an *evaluative* perspective. For that is what construals do—portray facts in a value-laden perspective that expresses an attitudinal disposition. They show how people *feel* about things, where "feeling" means adopting an evaluative attitude. Being metaphorical, they borrow only part of the grammar of the concepts they involve, but the part that they borrow is precisely that part that evokes the relevant attitudes.

The particular kind of evaluation that religious construals provide is *teleological*. I'm not particularly fond of the word "teleological" since it is both academic and imprecise. But I mean by it that religious beliefs provide the kind of construals in which people see the purpose of their lives. These construals enable them to count one way of life more worthwhile than another. They propose cosmic evaluations to do this, and they thereby provide a "system of reference" in which to bring one's life-evaluations into line with the values that render all of creation worthwhile. This makes the life lived in consequence of these construals a *meaningful* life.[27]

Since this evaluative dimension is part and parcel of their logic, religious assertions cannot be compared with purely descriptive claims. This means that the "facts" that they state are *not comparable to empirical facts*. In the usual sense of the word "fact," religious construals are not factual judgments *at all*. The truths that they state are not descriptions of any given states of affairs, natural or supernatural. No point here is more important than this one, and it bears repetition: religious truths are not comparable to scientific or metaphysical descriptions but are instead the cornerstones for teleological, evaluative construals.

We tend to think that religious beliefs state facts of a sort that give life a purpose, as if the question of fact was prior to the particular implications that follow from it. For example, we suppose that there is a God who *gave* life a purpose that it would not have had if God did not so create it. But the question of whether such a God exists and the question of whether life has a certain kind of purpose are not distinguishable; the belief in God *is* a belief in the godly purposes of life. So religious construals cannot be judged by separating the "question of fact" from the "question of purpose" that attaches to the facts. The two questions are really one. The facts involved are facts about purposes. The truths at issue are truths about meaning.

This view of religious assertions as teleological construals may be difficult to accept in view of our tradition of interpreting religious claims metaphysically, yet I wish to complicate it further with another suggestion. We commonly say that true beliefs "accord with reality" or "correspond with the nature of things." This form of affirmation, however, applies only to those circumstances in which we can verify our assertions: when we can verify them, we say that they correspond with the facts because we have factual evidence to support them. "Reality" and the description of it in our evidence come to the same thing so that the agreement between a proposition and reality is simply the agreement between a proposition and the evidence that supports it. But in the judgment of religious construals, there is little or no factual evidence that one can rely on for the support of religious claims since the evidence is colored by the very construals at issue. Then the judgment that there is truth in our beliefs comes from a vague sense of being capacitated by these construals or having settled into a meaningful view of life through them. Because we cannot turn this vague sense of being capacitated into an argument, I don't think that we should say that our beliefs "accord with reality." Rather, I think that we might mark the distinction here by saying that there is *some* truth in them.

Let there be no misunderstanding here; I'm not saying that believers should stop affirming their beliefs as *truths*. I'm saying that there is a difference in the way that religious beliefs are logically supported and that, whenever it is important to note this difference (in philosophical discussions, for example), it might be indicated by a corresponding difference in the *way* we claim truth for our beliefs. If one says that a religious belief is true, meaning that it corresponds with reality, this form of expression is apt to mislead. People may think that the belief's correspondence with reality can be shown in the way that other beliefs' correspondence with reality can be shown—through the presentation of favorable evidence. But if one says only that there is *some* truth in one's beliefs, we might avoid this misleading implication. Then the vagueness involved in the justification of religious construals might be matched by a vagueness in their affirmation of truth.

Again, I'm only recommending this change in usage in certain specialized contexts in which we need to be very careful with the words we use to express ourselves. In other contexts, where such precision is not expected, saying that various religious beliefs have some truth in them would be more likely to confuse rather than to clarify the nature of belief. For in many contexts, such a qualified affirmation of a belief prepares us for criticisms to follow: we say that a belief has *some* truth in it only if we want to criticize it or to formulate it more exactly. Thus, when one knows *precisely* what another knows only *approximately,* one might say that the other's statements have some truth in them. But this is certainly not the case in religious belief, since no one knows precisely what the supposed objects of religious discourse are like. Nor is this the case in the example of the rash, since no one knows exactly what the etiology of the rash is. So the claim that the relaxation account of the rash bears some truth is not advanced on the basis of an *exact* knowledge of the disease but on the basis of the loose, pragmatic, unformalizable way in which that account stands or falls. And it is no different with religion. Most religious claims also rest on an unformalizable sense of being capacitated, not on independent evidence—"facts"—that serve as their justificatory ground.

To summarize, then, we can repeat Kierkegaard and Wittgenstein's claim that Christianity is not a doctrine. It is not a doctrine because its claims are construals portraying human life in ways that make it subject to final appraisals of its value or purpose. These construals are recognizably metaphorical, not because we can compare them with literal truths about their objects, but because we can understand that the figurative terms that they utilize serve only to express certain attitudinal dispositions. Yet they are truth claims. We judge their truth or falsity in large part by their adequacy in satiating our hunger for a meaningful life; but we have no standard of adequacy that can be used to make comparative judgments of rival religions possible. Instead, we can only try to persuade nonbelievers that our pictures of life's meaning are capacitating enough to be reasonably held. Accordingly, we might affirm our religious beliefs, not by saying that they correspond exactly with reality but by saying that they bear *some* truth. That is all that religious belief requires.

There is much more that might be said about the logic of religious belief. For one thing, we might agree with Kierkegaard and

Wittgenstein that the breeding ground of faith is the individual's acquaintance with suffering, death, and despair. The more deeply that one knows these ills, the more hungry one will be for an understanding that will bring peace to his or her troubles. But perhaps I have said enough already.

I would add only this—that I am conscious of having talked in generalities, as if there were one thing that is Christianity or one kind of belief that is religious. This, of course, is not true. But I can only ask the reader's indulgence on this point. As in sorting the papers in a cluttered office, there are two things that need to be done. One is to put everything in its proper file; the other is to arrange a proper filing system to begin with. I obviously have not struggled to put the many varieties of religious claims in their proper files. Instead, I have tried to accomplish the preliminary business of creating a better filing system. But that, it seems to me, is one of the contributions that the philosophy of religion might make.

NOTES

1. Søren Kierkegaard, *Concluding Unscientific Postscript*, trans. Walter Lowrie (Princeton: Princeton University Press, 1941).
2. Ibid., p. 339.
3. Ibid., see footnote.
4. Søren Kierkegaard, *Attack Upon Christendom*, trans. Walter Lowrie (Princeton: Princeton University Press, 1972), p. 271.
5. Kierkegaard, *Postscript*, book 2, part 2, ch. 2, pp. 169–224 and throughout.
6. Ibid., p. 178.
7. Ibid., see footnote.
8. Kierkegaard uses "passion" interchangeably with "subjectivity" and "inward-ness," all of them the consequence of the desire for eternal happiness. Everyone has such passion because everyone has such a desire, but not everyone has it consciously or explicitly before him or her. Suffering can help to make one consciously aware of this need and so, too, can the promise of eternal life conveyed by an objective uncertainty. Christianity does this to an infinite degree.
9. See, for example, Norman Malcolm, *Ludwig Wittgenstein: A Memoir* (Oxford: Oxford University Press, 1958), p. 71.
10. Kierkegaard wrote the *Postscript* as a clarification of themes that he began in *Philosophical Fragments*, which dealt with the relation of an existing individual to the historically dated claims of Christianity.
11. Ludwig Wittgenstein, *Culture and Value*, ed. G. H. von Wright and trans. Peter Winch (Chicago: University of Chicago Press, 1980), p. 32.

12. Ibid., p. 53.
13. Ibid., p. 28.
14. Ibid.
15. Ludwig Wittgenstein, *Lectures and Conversations on Aesthetics, Psychology and Religious Belief,* ed. Cyril Barrett (Berkeley: University of California Press, 1967).
16. Ibid., pp. 54–56, 63–64, 66–72.
17. Wittgenstein, *Culture and Value,* p. 64.
18. Actually, construals can be seen in two ways. They can be understood as expressions of transient sentiments, in which case they need not be taken seriously as truth claims. Or, they can be understood as expressions of lasting attitudes, in which case the fact that they *last* reflects their intended status as truths.
19. Ludwig Wittgenstein, *On Certainty,* ed. G. E. M. Anscombe and G. H. von Wright, trans. Denis Paul and G. E. M. Anscombe (New York: Harper & Row, 1972), par. numbers 11–18.
20. Ibid., par. number 116.
21. Ibid., par. number 617.
22. Ibid., par. number 603.
23. Ibid., par. number 616.
24. Ibid., par. number 422.
25. Ibid., par. numbers 429 and 474.
26. Ibid., par. number 612.
27. For a fuller account of this idea, see my "Religious Beliefs as Purpose Claims," *International Journal for the Philosophy of Religion* 20 (1986): pp. 17–30. This essay argues that religious beliefs can be truth claims solely as *purpose claims.*

5. A Meeting of Minds on Water

H. A. NIELSEN

[W]ater . . . is a profound truth which becomes more interesting the more one plumbs its depths. . . .[1]

While still at school our children get taught that water *consists* of hydrogen and oxygen. . . . Anyone who doesn't understand is stupid. The most important questions are concealed.[2]

This essay reflects on what I take to be a meeting of minds between Kierkegaard and Wittgenstein. Each has something to say about the commonest stuff on earth: water. Water is a profound truth, says Kierkegaard. I don't remember getting taught that in school. The most important questions are concealed, says Wittgenstein, when Mr. Science teaches our young people about water. In what sense can we call water a *truth?* And what exactly are those "most important questions" concealed by scientific ways of speaking? Our authors do not slow down to unpack their remarks, so it is up to us.

Both Kierkegaard and Wittgenstein, I am suggesting, have something like this in mind. Nobody understands water, but our educational system outfits every generation of young people with a standard, official, thin, and impersonal understanding of water, a lame understanding most briefly expressed in the formula H_2O or definitions such as "a liquid oxide of hydrogen."

What does it mean to say nobody understands the nature of water? In science as in other school subjects, let's remember, understanding is obligatory. Over every classroom door hangs the motto, "Understand—Or Else." What the pupil can do, of course, is cough up the right sentences on demand, and the sentences are easy enough to learn, tailored in their difficulty to the various grades. "Water consists of hydrogen and oxygen" is a piece of cake for a sixth grader who might have trouble with an eighth grade version such as, "Water is a slightly compressible liquid oxide of hydrogen." In this kind of learning process the child is acquiring a habit of thought that might be expressed this way: "I must never consult *myself* to see if I understand; I must always consult the textbook and learn the right sentences." It would be bad form if a youngster asked, "But what good are the right sentences if I don't really understand?"

Now whether *I* in fact understand this or not is just enough of a personal question so that I ought to hesitate to accept my old teachers' assurances that I do indeed understand. Here I might feel the need to avail myself of a distinction such as this. "For purposes of passing biology quizzes, I guess I understand well enough. That is, I never had much trouble *repeating back on paper* what the textbook or lecture said. But whether I personally understand is another question. When I'm alone and try to *think the transition* from those gases to water, I can't do so." The textbook conceals its truth.

Dwell on this for a few minutes. If the teacher had said, "Nobody knows how it comes about, but when hydrogen combines with oxygen, guess what we get—water!" This would invite the child into the circle of those who *in their own minds* cannot imagine where the new properties come from. Instead, the child finds himself or herself in the circle of those who think it not at all surprising that the visible should emerge from the invisible, the wet from the dry, the noisy from the silent, the multiform from the uniform. In the second circle, the controlling assumption is that it is only a matter of time before we learn exactly what in the infrastructure of hydrogen and oxygen atoms makes the properties of water emerge.[3] This assumption gets across to our children, and we can hardly expect youngsters of school age to *resist* joining the second circle, even though it puts cramping restrictions on their license to wonder. Wonder asks, "How does it happen that watery phenomena, from the microscopic to the majestic, tie back to those two docile gases?" We should not assume that this expression of wonder is an instance of asking for information or even that it is a first step toward finding out the answer. An alternate expression might be, "When it comes to figure out water, cleverness gets me nowhere."

Something like a corporate mentality, that of the science textbook with its official criteria of what shall count as understanding, crowds out the individual mentality that is part of the child's original endowment. A high school science teacher writes this assignment on the board: "When you have stated what water is composed of, ask yourself if you personally understand how contrary properties come forth when the elements unite." A strange, unlikely assignment in a context cool toward personal comprehension and its shortfalls!

The scientific community imposes its understanding of water on everyone by means of its formulas and definitions, which I want to characterize as abstract. We find it possible, in other words, to speak of water in terms of a standard table of elements, and this is called the scientific concept of water. One might want to agree that water *in the abstract* consists of hydrogen and oxygen, bearing in mind, of course, that water in the abstract does not exist. In the abstract, or at the furthest remove from our senses, water is always the same thing, but in existence water is endlessly varied and on the move. The contrast between abstraction and existent becomes overwhelming if you compare the scientific account of water with the enormous variety of things we observe about an existing body of water such as the Niagara River. The actual river is individuated by the shape of its bed, its quantum of free oxygen, the types of life it supports, its levels of contaminants, and on and on.

What sort of abstraction are we speaking of? To start with, the ways of its own that water possesses do not figure very centrally in the notations in which science tells us what water consists of. Understandably, no formula or definition could begin to list its millionfold ways, even its repertory of operations in the life of a mouse or minnow. The standard account of what water consists of *abstracts,* then, from everything it does and can do. No harm in that, someone will say; if we disallowed abstraction, how could we build a surveyable science of chemistry or biology? Yet the ways of its own that water exhibits, the ways that enable it to perform, can slide out of the picture when we look at water through those stripped-down notations, even if we remember that it is indispensable for life and much besides. That is, we can learn to speak about water as if it had no more ways of its own than a Euclidean plane figure, which has only those characters implicit in the rule for constructing it and none of its own. A circle or a right triangle does not deliver performances, nor does it have any functions in the sphere of existence. Its nature is limited to what it consists of. But with water no such restriction applies; in a sense one could say that what water is composed of is quite irrelevant to everything it does and everything it had been doing for eons before anyone had a notion that H and O enter into its composition. To the extent that one thinks about water in the abstract, it can be alluring to imagine that understanding water amounts to having a firm grasp of a formula or definition, as is true of ideal Euclidean figures. Just as there is nothing more to a right triangle, no secret ways of its own that defy fathoming, one can learn to speak as if there is nothing more to water than H and O and whatever throb of energy it takes to bond them. No wonder we meet people even today who are deeply impressed by myths that predate the Genesis accounts of creation and who respond with bright eyes to the notion that *water came first,* that H and O are in some dim sense derivative rather than constitutive of the real thing!

In short, official ways of speaking can obscure the borderline between understanding and seeming to understand water or some other prime component of existence. It can be hard for young minds to resist the idea that science can help us comprehend water in the same way that cleverness can get a clear fix on Rubik's Cube, an artifact, or on Euclid's ideal circle, a nonperformer.

Here someone might say, "But don't you see, in science we try to get at *water itself?*" No, I don't see. What on earth do you mean by "water itself"? When is it *not* itself? Perhaps when a chosen way of speaking drops existence out of account? What keeps us from seeing that water in existence has as many manifestations as a symphony orchestra has sounds? On this question Wittgenstein offers help on page 46e of *Philosophical Investigations* where he cautions against predicting of a thing what is characteristic of our mode of representing it. At the bottom of the same page we find the following detached citation: "Faraday in *The Chemical History of a Candle:* 'Water is one individual thing—it never changes.' " Isn't this a classic instance of what Wittgenstein warned against? Water changes in a millionfold ways, though the formula H_2O never changes. Science can dull not only the imagination but our very eyes!

At this point I'd like to go back to the two quotations that started off this essay. What does it mean to say water is a *truth* and a profound one at that? Here is a possible answer. As a human being, I see actual water in all its symphonic performances as an actualized idea. It obviously wasn't my idea, in fact, I can't even understand it. It is as an idea, I am assuming, that water is a truth, specifically the idea of getting new and amazing properties and performances out of two gaseous components of air. What an idea! Here I don't mean to be saying that God has ideas and burns the midnight oil working the bugs out. Those mental operations do not fit smoothly with the grammar of "to create." The truth that is water is profound in the sense that no individual mentality can get to the bottom of it. Water makes so much else possible as it goes through cycles of purifying and soaking the world that our minds are simply too small to take in the range of its virtuosity.

We turn next to the quotation from Wittgenstein, alerting his reader that, where scientific ways of speaking prevail, "the most important questions are concealed." When a textbook tells me that water consists of two hushed, well-behaved components of air, according to Wittgenstein I should come storming back with important, unanswered questions such as, "But how can that be? *How* can two airy elements produce the showstoppers, the great rhythms, the tempests, and all the supporting performances we expect of water?" These I take to be examples of Wittgenstein's "most important questions." By voicing them I reveal myself in the ignominy of failing to understand. "There goes the fellow who can't understand water!"

Here is a case at least of consulting myself. I might not add anything to my understanding of water, but I restore my awareness of a certain stubbornly baffling side to water. Mr. Science might not give thanks with the cry "Bafflement regained!" but it seems to me an individual might do so, and that cry belongs to the grammar of the heart—the grammar, even, of human thought itself.

How does liquidity, for example, make its way into existence? Here a college biology text might present an account of loose hydrogen bonding, complete with diagrams. Then there is a quiz: "Explain the composition of water." Suppose a student hands in these remarks: "Water is made up of hydrogen and oxygen loosely bonded as per diagram, plus whatever it takes to give those bonded gases the properties of actual water, but I'm unable to say what the extra something is." That student might well be invited to repeat the course, but let's imagine for a moment that the science teacher is patient. The teacher calls the student in and tries to explain. "The chemical bonding *itself* confers those properties on water, just as in another example it confers sweetness on sugar. We have experiments that show we get water every time when we bond hydrogen and oxygen, and when we electrolyze water we get hydrogen and oxygen every time."

It would be hard, I think, for a young person to know what to say next. Maybe a young Socrates would know. However, I think there is an answer to the science teacher implicit in the quotations from Kierkegaard and Wittgenstein. Someone might reply in this way. "I can't quite make out your assurance to me that the bonding itself confers the properties of water. I see nothing in hydrogen or oxygen that could accomplish such a bestowal, and I don't understand how the properties of precisely *water* are laid up in the phenomenon you call 'boiling.' The fact that you can produce a drop of water by sparking a mixture of the two gases doesn't move you to say the *spark* confers the new properties, since the spark doesn't have them to give. The transition to water, which I can't get through my head, isn't explained by reminding me that hydrogen and oxygen are invariably involved. What I don't understand is how their union results in an astonishingly sovereign set of properties. I'm not even asking *exactly* how the new properties come into being. Just a clue, a crumb will satisfy me. Until you toss me that crumb, though, I'll have no choice but to go on thinking of water as a prime wonder of nature, understood by no one."

This reply wouldn't necessarily leave a science teacher speechless. He or she could go on to say, "You know, you're really asking about the nitty-gritty of the formation of compounds in inorganic chemistry. The literature on that is too vast to carry around in my head, but I can refer you to a couple of first-rate texts." If our student takes the bait, the science teacher, in Kierkegaard's words, "Instead of saying summarily, 'I do not understand this' . . . encumbers the student with a mass of detail and very fascinating, engaging knowledge, which nevertheless always ends with the fact that he cannot, after all, explain the ultimate."[4]

Kierkegaard and Wittgenstein have put us on alert. We have all been propagandized into thinking we understand a lot more than we do concerning nature's productions and performances. Water is simply a case in point, though a dramatic one. A hint that comes through from both authors suggests that recognizing the limits of one's personal understanding helps maintain a healthy level of roughage in the intellect. On the other hand, when natural science communicates an official and talkative understanding of water, springtime, the origins of life, and so forth, this puts the individual at risk of confusing his or her personal mentality with an official, corporate one.

How can an individual reduce the risk of confusion? Think of water as a truth, says Kierkegaard. Remember the most important questions, says Wittgenstein. I have tried to weave those provocative bits of advice into some lengthier remarks. After finishing the attempt, I came across a passage by George Macdonald, a nineteen-century English clergyman. Here is the passage that struck me, entitled "Water."

Is oxygen-and-hydrogen the divine idea of water? Or has God put the two together only that man might separate and find them out? He allows His child to pull his toys to pieces: but were they made that he might pull them to pieces? He were a child not to be envied for whom his inglorious father would make toys to such an end! A school examiner might see therein the best use of a toy, but not a father! Find for us what in the constitution of the two gases makes them fit and capable to be thus honored in forming the lovely thing, and you will give us a revelation about more than water, namely about the God who made oxygen and hydrogen. There is no water in oxygen, no water in hydrogen; it comes bubbling fresh from the imagination of the living God, rushing from under the great white throne of the glacier. The very thought of it makes one gasp with an elemental joy no metaphysician can analyse. The water itself, that dances and sings, and slakes the wonderful thirst—symbol and picture of that draught for which the woman of Samaria made her prayer to Jesus—this lovely thing itself, whose very wetness is a delight to every inch of the human body in its embrace—this live thing which, if I might, I would have running through my room, yea, babbling along my table—this water is its own self its own truth, and is therein a truth of God. Let him who would know the truth of the Maker, become sorely athirst, and drink of the brook by the way— then lift up his heart—not at that moment to the Maker of oxygen and hydrogen, but to the Inventor and Mediator of thirst and water, that man might foresee a little of what his soul may find in God.[5]

NOTES

1. Søren Kierkegaard, *Søren Kierkegaard's Journals and Papers*, trans. and ed. Howard and Edna Hong (Bloomington: Indiana University Press, 1975), vol. 3, "Nature" #2826.

2. Ludwig Wittgenstein, *Culture and Value*, ed. G. H. von Wright and trans. Peter Winch, (Chicago: University of Chicago Press, 1980), p. 71e.

3. A recent discussion puts the matter this way: "Knowing the properties of the atoms hydrogen (H) and oxygen (O), both of which are gases at room temperature under normal pressures, in principle we should know what water would be like. Antireductionists point to the 'emergent properties' of water—so unlike the gases which its constituent elements form when uncombined. But proreductionists reply that, present ignorance aside, in principle the properties of H_2O would be predictable given sufficient knowledge of H and O. Despite the appeal of 'emergent properties,' reductionism pervades the minds of most active scientists today. . . ." Niles Eldridge and Ian Tattersall, *The Myths of Human Evolution* (New York: Columbia University Press 1982), p. 13. Note that the expression "given sufficient knowledge" in the proreductionist's reply gives the whole reply the aspect of a tautology, since no one would deny that *sufficient* knowledge would do the trick. The tautological aspect makes the reply safe-sounding and thus masks another aspect that asserts a lot more than a tautology. It lets on that the properties of water come forth by necessity or that the bonding of H and O could issue in *nothing else but* water. Is that sort of knowledge within reach of human beings? If not, we are looking at a confusion veiled by a tautology. For a further account of reductionism, see Ernst Mayr, *The Growth of Biological Thought* (Cambridge, Mass.: Belknap Press, 1982), pp. 57–63.

4. Kierkegaard, *Journals and Papers*, vol. 3, #2807.

5. C. S. Lewis, *George Macdonald: An Anthology* (London: Geoffrey Bless, 1946), p. 61.

6. Professor Plantinga on Belief in God

RONALD E. HUSTWIT

Professor Plantinga argues, in the essay "Reason and Belief in God," that belief in God is "properly basic" and that it is "rational."[1] This is a counter to those who argue that such belief is not properly basic and is irrational. Clifford, Huxley, Russell, and Flew are cited as presenting a challenge to those who profess belief in God on the grounds that it is wrong or irrational to believe when there is not enough evidence. Plantinga calls these challengers "evidentialists" and proceeds to argue against them. He calls "foundationalists" those who are uncritically drawn into the evidentialist's objection and its assumptions—attempting to provide foundations for their belief in God. Saint Thomas, who derives belief in God from self-evident first principles and truths of the senses, is the paradigm foundationalist. Plantinga argues against this position as well, showing self-referential inconsistencies in their claim that everything believed must be self-evident or known immediately from the senses or derived from either of those. His claim that belief in God is "properly basic" and "rational" is set against both the evidentialists and foundationalists. Belief, he argues, does not necessarily require evidence nor foundation to be "properly basic," and the believer may be quite "rational" in believing without evidence or foundation. This is a very brief statement of the claims central to Professor Plantinga's essay. In my essay, I intend to examine his claim that belief in God is properly basic and rational.

In order to focus my discussion, I want to get several sentences of Plantinga in front of us. They come close to the end of his essay and form part of a set of summary remarks. He does not say directly in these sentences that belief in God is properly basic, although he does so several sentences later. They present the position of the "Reformed epistemologist," which he says is his own position. According to Calvin, Plantinga relates, everyone has a tendency to apprehend God's existence and something of God's nature. This apprehension is just as natural as our apprehension of other basic truths about perception, the past, and other minds although all such knowledge can be suppressed by the effects of sin. In this context, Plantinga provides the sentences that I find interesting and that I want to use to try to get a handle on what he is doing:

Belief in the existence of God is in the same boat as belief in other minds, the past, and perceptual objects; in each case God has so constructed us that in the right circumstances we form the belief in question. But then the belief that there is such a person as God is as much among the deliverances of reason as those of other beliefs.[2]

What struck me about these sentences was the inclusion of belief in God with these philosophical beliefs. What could Plantinga possibly have in mind? This is where I propose to begin.

The oddness of including belief in God in this set is glaring. Belief in God is something shared and acknowledged by many; there are organized religions, churches, even countries acknowledging belief in God. But no such body of testimony exists for the belief in other minds, the past, and perceptual objects. Even if one argued that everyone really does believe in these things, one would still need to go on to say that most who believed such things did not realize that they believed them. No one organizes churches or workshops in connection with them. Neither anthropologists nor historians nor political scientists study them. They are not found in the subject themes of poems or novels. Their believers do not make sacrifices to them or for them. It would seem that only philosophers are aware of these beliefs and only philosophers discuss and describe them. On the face of it, Plantinga has put an apple in the onion bin.

But let us now consider why he did put belief in God in this company. Here I need to return to the basic idea in Plantinga that I am trying to understand—the idea that belief in God is properly basic and rational. Plantinga makes this claim over against the challenge of evidentialism and the mistaken response of foundationalism. To say that belief in God is properly basic is to say that it needs neither evidence nor foundations to be believed. It is a kind of foundation in itself and is epistemologically appropriate or "proper." But what makes it proper—how is it shown to be proper? Up to this point, Plantinga's arguments have been against evidentialism and foundationalism, and not directly for his own view of properly basic beliefs. His argument against evidentialism essentially comes to showing that the evidentialist has no argument for his or her claim. The evidentialist simply claims that we need sufficient evidence for every belief that we hold. But why, Plantinga asks, why can we not believe something without any evidence? So Plantinga's argument is that there is simply no support provided for this claim. However, that argument in itself does not yet show us that, in general, there are beliefs with no evidence nor that, in particular, belief in God requires no evidence. For the latter we need to take notice of the fact that there are such beliefs that require no evidence and that belief in God is one of them. And this is what Plantinga is doing, I believe, when he groups belief in God with belief in other minds, the past, and perceptual objects. He is giving, or intending to give, examples of beliefs that do not require sufficient evidence nor foundations and placing belief in God in their good company.

It must be, as Plantinga sees it, that we have beliefs in other minds, the past, and perceptual objects and that we do not have evidence for these beliefs. I am not clear on whether he would treat all three the same way, saying that we have no evidence for any of the three, or if he would claim some evidence for one and less or none for the others. It is true, for example, that some philosophers have argued that there is some, though not conclusive, evidence for other minds (for example, Mill) but no evidence or very little for perceptual objects (for example, Berkeley). The history of philosophy would display mixed results on all three of these subjects. In any case, Plantinga does not make clear here the extent to which the three beliefs have evidence. It is safe, however, to conclude that he is claiming (1) that they are of the class of beliefs believed without sufficient evidence, (2) that they might be believed without any evidence, and (3) that one is entirely rational in adopting these beliefs, that is, they are properly basic beliefs.

It is interesting that he calls these "beliefs" in other minds, the past, and perceptual objects. I do not intend to propose a better label for them. They have been called by other philosophers "presuppositions," "apriori truths," "apriori principles," "first principles," "ungrounded assumptions," and by other names. To call them "beliefs" is supposed, I take it, to call to mind that we have a certain attitude towards them, namely that of accepting them as true without being able to know that they are true. But I should like to point out that labeling them "beliefs" might also call to mind that we might choose not to believe them, that we have thought about them, that we have considered evidence for and against them and made a decision about them. And these features of belief do not seem to be functioning as Plantinga sees it. Again, my intention in making this observation is not to propose another label for them, but to present a warning that in trying to understand Plantinga on this point one might not know how to proceed with the word "belief" in "the belief that other minds exist," etc. I find this difficulty repeatedly in Plantinga's essay: he does not make clear what sorts of beliefs he is referring to and what possible differences there are between beliefs that would make a difference to what he is saying.

I find this unanalyzed concept of belief in Plantinga the obstacle to understanding his account of belief in God as a "properly basic belief" and to understanding his paper in general. He speaks everywhere of belief as if it referred to a single state of mind or attitude. If he does think that there are important differences within the concept of belief, he does not indicate what they are. There are points in the paper where it would be very helpful to see what they are and where serious confusions result from proceeding without them. I want to try to show more of that in what follows.

As I tried to show above, there are aspects of the concept of belief that do not seem to apply to Plantinga's examples of belief in other minds, the past, and perceptual objects. Not only is there philosophical debate about whether and how much evidence there is for these beliefs respectively, but outside of philosophy there does not seem to be any such thing as people deliberating and choosing to hold such beliefs. In fact, in Plantinga's view, it must be that nonphilosophers hold them without even knowing that they do—and not even philosophers will hold them on the basis of sufficient evidence. But there are, surely, other beliefs that we hold that we *do* have evidence for and about which we *do* deliberate and *are* aware that we hold them because they are conclusions at which we have quite deliberately arrived. I believe that twelve tomato plants will produce more tomatoes in the same small area than eighteen plants will. Why? Because last year I put eighteen in that same space, and they grew together and crowded each other out. Evidence, deliberation, drawing conclusions, and forming beliefs—these are all involved in many such cases of belief. These beliefs, of course, would not be "properly basic beliefs," but they are perfectly ordinary beliefs—ones that we would most readily think of if we were giving an account of how the concept of belief worked. Now if he were clear about these differences in the concept of belief, he might choose to say that belief in God is not like my ordinary belief in garden planning. And I think that Plantinga thinks that, although he does not discuss it. But that is the problem with understanding him; he does not seem to be sensitive to these differences. Perhaps, in thinking to himself that belief in God is not like many ordinary beliefs, Plantinga is led to say that it is like these epistemological beliefs in other minds, etc., and there are similarities between them, though, as I have tried to show, there are startling differences, too: no churches whose needs and worship proclaim belief in other minds nor commitment to live a certain kind of life. These are differences that Plantinga takes no notice of. He makes only general claims: belief needs no evidence; belief in God is properly basic; belief in the existence of God is in the same boat as belief in other minds. There are glimpses of things that may be right or partially right in these claims, but I cannot get clear on them until I can see the differences in the concept of belief worked out in connection with them.

Such distinctions are precisely what Plantinga needs to discuss in order to critique evidentialism. The evidentialist is looking at belief in God on the model of many ordinary beliefs—such as my garden planning belief—on the model, that is, of forming and confirming a belief in science. There are a variety of reasons for this: there is one word "belief" and it should name one state of affairs; the success of science; and others. The evidentialist demands that belief in God measures up to scientific beliefs and the logical features of the process leading up to those beliefs: "What is the hypothesis to be believed? What evidence supports it? What counterevidence is there, and how does one explain that? Has one been judicious in forming the hypothesis and weighing the evidence? Does one have the proper tentative attitude towards the belief so that the belief might be changed or rejected at some future time?" The evidentialist wants belief in God to be treated in a way similar to this. And, as it would be unscientific or improper or even wrong to believe in something without sufficient evidence, it would be wrong to believe in God without sufficient evidence.

I would think that pointing out the distinction between this scientific model and belief in God would be precisely what Plantinga needed in showing how evidentialism came to be and in showing what was wrong with it. As it is, he only asks, in connection with evidentialism, why it is not perfectly rational to believe something without any evidence at all. If the answer is not that some beliefs do not function according to the model of science, then I would have no idea of how to answer this question. However, Plantinga seems mystified by the evidentialist, as if the latter were pulling totally unsupportable claims out of the sky. Plantinga asks: "Why does the objector think these things? Why does he think there is a *prima facie* obligation to try not to believe in God without evidence? Or why does he think that to do so is to be in a deplorable condition? Why is it not permissible and quite satisfactory to believe in God without any evidence—proof or argument—at all?"[3] I cannot tell from these questions whether Plantinga has any idea of why the evidentialist would say the things that he or she does. Developing the distinctions in the concept of belief would help him to understand and explain evidentialism and its deficiencies better.

The same kinds of difficulties surround Plantinga's discussion of foundationalism. Foundationalism, as he presents it, accepts the legitimacy of the evidentialist's challenge, but has an answer to it. There is enough evidence for belief in God, according to the foundationalist, and "enough" here means that belief in God is logically entailed from propositions that are self-evident or evident to the senses. So foundationalism has the same confusions about belief packed into it. Of course, Plantinga rejects foundationalism, but the difficulties about belief are still there, lurking in the background as confusions. The foundations for belief in God according to Aquinas's proofs are either self-evident truths, such as "The whole is greater than the part," or propositions evident to the senses, such as "There is a tree before me." The sentences "No contingent being can bring itself into existence" and "There are now contingent beings before me" are supposed to be the foundations for belief in God. But is it really belief in God that these support? Do not Aquinas's foundations support propositions such as "a necessary being must exist" and "a first cause must exist"? Are these propositions the same as belief in God? How does one know that this necessary being or first cause is the one who is called "God" in the Scriptures? And is belief in God the sort of thing that is supported by such foundations? None of this is unpacked in Plantinga's refutation of foundationalism. His refutation does not involve that there is a difference in the way these beliefs are to be treated, but rather that the principle of foundationalism is self-referentially inconsistent, that is, that the principle of foundationalism cannot be the foundation of itself. This is a resourceful and correct refutation, but it does not show a thinker how to begin to sort through the confusions of foundationalism.

Some, though not all, of the confusion that underlies Plantinga's discussion of these topics could be dispelled by an appreciation of the differences between "belief in God" and "belief that God exists." Without playing this out far, "belief in God" is manifested by the paradigms of faith: Abraham, Noah, Moses, Saint Paul. It involves risk, trust, obedience, a way of life. "Belief that God exists," by contrast, is a philosopher's expression or at least has an odd ring to it. It sounds like "belief that a thief exists" (when one is not sure) and "belief that the universe is expanding." And yet it is different from both of these also. Belief that X exists, by these models, ought to involve that there is evidence and argument. Theses about thieves and expanding universes are hypotheses about states of affairs; they can be supported to varying degrees by evidence; they can be modified and replaced. Does Plantinga know and understand this distinction? He clearly knows of it; whether he understands it or not, I cannot determine. I have doubts. He knows the distinction because he refers to it in the paper: "I have been speaking," he writes, "of 'belief in God,' but this is not entirely accurate. For the subject under discussion is not really the rational acceptability of belief in God, but the rationality of belief that God exists. . . . And belief in God is not at all the same thing as belief that there is such a person as God. . . ."[4]

But whether he has understood this distinction and what it would come to is doubtful. After discussing "belief in" as involving trusting and accepting and "belief that" as involving propositions, he goes on to write: "Having made this distinction, however, I shall ignore it for the most part, using "belief in God" as a synonym for "belief that there is such a person as God.""[5] If there is a significant distinction here, how can one ignore it? How can one take the language of trusting, accepting, risking, and obeying as a synonym for the language of hypothesis, evidence, and dispassionate objectivity? And would it not be precisely the language of "belief in God," and not the language of "belief that God exists," that would allow one to show that evidentialism and foundationalism were confused in asking for evidence? Plantinga wants to speak of the belief that God exists, but not accept the demand for evidence that would seem to go with it, as if it were like belief in God. This, I think, is a conceptual confusion that follows from not taking these distinctions seriously.

As I turn over the expression "belief that God exists," I am not sure that it is even understandable. Above I noted that it appeared to be like belief that a thief exists when one is not sure and belief that the universe is expanding. But how much like belief that God exists are these others? A closer parallel to this would be belief that Gerald or John exists where the proper name of a person replaces "God." But I cannot easily imagine having a use for such an expression. In what circumstances would I form the belief that Gerald exists? I might form the belief that a thief exists, if something is missing, or perhaps that Gerald is the thief, but I cannot imagine needing to believe that Gerald exists. This gives me nothing to go on in understanding "belief that God exists." Neither can I get "belief that God exists" to look very much like "belief that the universe expands." If the universe expands, then certain things will be true, for example, a light shift in all stars indicating that they are receding from the earth. And, certain things will be false, for example, that some stars will move towards the earth. This is collecting evidence, falsifying and supporting hypotheses, and behaving objectively. Belief in God, as I have been trying to emphasize, shares none of this. But what of belief that God exists? The comparison to the expanding universe is supposed to show us how to proceed with the latter, but how is it supposed to work? Are there propositions that will be true or false in connection with God? What could they be? How is the expression to be understood? The distinction between "belief in" and "belief that" is understandable, but the distinction between "belief in God" and "belief that God exists" has an element in it that I do not yet understand. Plantinga has gone too fast in all of this. He has not grasped, and consequently ignores, these differences in the concept of belief.

Although Plantinga's work harbors these confusions and his lack of analysis prevents the reader from understanding how he wants to be read, there is, nevertheless, something right and important in the kernel of what he is trying to get said. To call a belief a basic belief and to say of it that it needs no further evidence nor foundation is to begin to call attention to some fundamental features of certain kinds of belief. In *On Certainty*, Wittgenstein writes: "At the foundation of well-founded belief lies belief that is not well-founded."[6] Wittgenstein intends to be describing how some beliefs are founded. They do not rest upon propositions that are known finally with certainty. Cartesian doubts, for example, cannot be overcome by countering them with logically necessary propositions that in turn stand as the foundation for all other beliefs. Neither will appeals to common sense overcome such doubts, as if tone of voice and insistence that one knows such things as "here is a hand," amounted to establishing foundations with certainty. Beliefs, rather, form an interrelated system with some explained or derived from others and none being independently established certainties. The grounds of belief, basic beliefs, are not established as true or false, but establish other propositions, other beliefs, as true or false. Wittgenstein intends this, not as argument, but as description. His descriptions, by the way, are long and detailed and many faceted. They are meant to counter the very foundationalism that Plantinga is worried about and the partly wrong response of G. E. Moore to that foundationalism.

Now Plantinga's suggestions about basic beliefs, at least in the kernel, bear some resemblance to some of Wittgenstein's remarks in *On Certainty*. One of Plantinga's examples of a basic belief is "God is speaking to me." If one believes this, one might believe also that he or she is supposed to build an ark or a church or to go to Damascus or Dallas. The second belief would be founded on the first, and the first would, most likely, not be founded on anything. How could one establish that it is God's voice? How does one know when God is speaking to him or her? This is not something we can systematically question or establish. In addition, Plantinga claims that we have basic beliefs in the existence of perceptual objects, other persons, and the past. One's belief that he or she had breakfast more than an hour ago is a basic belief upon which other beliefs are built—perhaps the belief that it would be unwise to eat again in the next hour or that one's food is not yet digested. Again, the second belief rests upon the first, and the first does not have to rest upon anything else. Of this sort of relationship Wittgenstein writes: "One cannot make experiments if there are not some things that one does not doubt. . . . If I make an experiment I do not doubt the existence of the apparatus before my eyes. I have plenty of doubts, but not that. If I do a calculation I believe, without any doubts, that the figures on the paper are not switching of their own accord, and I also trust my memory the whole time, and trust it without any reservation."[7] I believe that to the extent that Plantinga has seen this aspect to belief—that basic beliefs function to found other beliefs without being well founded themselves—he is on his way towards describing an important element of belief in God. But by comparison to Wittgenstein, his remarks, like Moore's, seem right-headed but not careful enough.

Moore claims that he knows that there is a hand here while looking at his hand. Wittgenstein chips away at this and similar knowledge claims that Moore makes. Knowing involves finding out, and finding out involves relying on other propositions and beliefs. But there is no finding out in connection with seeing a hand, no reliance on other propositions, no grounding. Moore speaks as if there is no room for being mistaken in connection with knowledge, but he is forgetting such expressions as "I thought I knew." Where there is knowledge there can be doubt, but doubt makes no sense in connection with knowing there is a hand here. In these and other ways Wittgenstein chips away at Moore's claim. Plantinga's claims to belief seem to be like Moore's claims to knowledge. Instead of claiming we know these basic propositions, Plantinga claims we believe them—we believe such propositions as "I see a tree," "That person is pleased," and "I had breakfast more than an hour ago." But while "belief" is better in some ways than "know" in connection with these propositions, it still presents problems of which Plantinga seems unaware. Does "I believe I see a tree" or "He believes he sees a tree" make sense? Under some very peculiar circumstances they might, but generally not. Does belief not require similar investigation and founding as knowledge? In which case there ought to be evidence and argument for it, too. To say that these propositions are believed requires some analysis and distinctions, and Plantinga fails to provide them.

I want to turn now to the attached idea that belief in God is rational. (The full claim is that belief in God is properly basic and rational.) In the sentence that I have been working on, Plantinga writes that as "belief in the existence of God is in the same boat as belief in other minds, the past, [etc.] . . . then . . . [it] . . . is as much among the deliverances of reason as those of other beliefs." He uses this expression "among the deliverances of reason" repeatedly and in other places calls belief in God "rational." Particularly, in connection with his objections to the evidentialists, Plantinga insists that belief in God is rational: "Why is it not entirely acceptable, desirable, right, proper, and rational to accept belief in God without any argument or evidence whatever?"[8] Here "rational" and "proper"—including "properly" in "properly basic belief"—are meant to be equivalent. This is what I want to focus on then: Plantinga's claim that belief in God is rational.

Why does Plantinga make such a claim? To say that someone is rational or that one's belief in something is rational is not a claim made on a regular basis. What I mean is that there generally has to be some particular occasion on which it would be appropriate to offer such an opinion. The sort of occasion I am thinking of would be that of someone's rationality being doubted. If there were some question about your rationality or about the rationality of some belief you hold, I might say to another who has noticed this, "Sarah is still rational" or "Sarah's belief is rational; you just have to see it from her perspective." Now I think there has been just such an occasion for Plantinga to make his remark. The occasion is that of the evidentialist's denial that belief in God is rational, proper, acceptable, or even morally right. The evidentialist is not the only sort of nonbeliever that would make this kind of challenge—no doubt Plantinga has heard the others as well. So now when he and his belief in God are challenged in this manner, he makes the direct and natural reply, "But I am rational and my belief in God is rational as well."

In this frame of mind, Plantinga perhaps thinks in the following way: "There may be insufficient evidence here, but are there not other beliefs that are believed without sufficient evidence—even without any evidence at all? In fact are not some of our most basic beliefs—those that epistemologists have been uncovering and attempting to justify for a long time—are those beliefs not believed without evidence? And are not these basic beliefs—such as the belief in other minds, the past, and perceptual objects—paradigms for how reason builds from starting points, paradigms that is, for rationality? Why should belief in God not function in the same way, among these other 'deliverances of reason'? Furthermore, there are arguments that can and have been used to defend the belief in God. There are arguments against the objections to belief in God. There are arguments showing that certain philosophical views are compatible or incompatible with belief in God. What are all these arguments if not exhibitions of rationality? In fact, all of this argumentation, including the idea of basic beliefs, mirrors exactly what epistemologists have discovered about any belief system. This belief is not only rational, but is the paradigm of rationality." So might Plantinga have spoken to himself, having been told that his belief in God is not rational.

I have been trying to show the account by which Plantinga might have been tempted. I do not know that this is the way in which he came to say that belief in God is rational. It seems likely to me, however. Someone says, "You are not rational." This is not a compliment. So one spends one's time defending and explaining. It may be that Plantinga sees nonrational aspects to what he believes. This too might make him defensive. In any case he answers the charge by denying it: "Belief in God is rational!" Plantinga should have asked what it means for someone or someone's belief not to be rational. That may have slowed him down some, and he may then have been less likely to reply that it is rational. All these expressions that belief in God is rational, not rational, or irrational are puzzling. They seem to have a grammar at home in a clinical setting, and yet they exhibit some features that do fit with religious belief. This seems to me to be a mixing of categories ripe with possible confusions. Belief that quarks exist is rational. Belief that communists set fire to the Reichstag is irrational. Belief in the voice that told the Son of Sam to kill is irrational. Belief in God is . . . rational? Belief in God's telling Abraham to sacrifice Isaac is . . . ? Again, the analysis of "belief" is lacking here, but also of what it means to call someone or someone's belief "rational."[9]

In calling attention to Plantinga's claim that belief in God is rational, I have not intended to show that religious belief is irrational but rather to show that there is something confused in his claim. In fact, in all of what I have been trying to do with Plantinga's work on belief in God, I have not argued against his view of basic beliefs as if the evidentialists or foundationalists are right and his view is wrong. I have been trying rather to show that he has not been clear in his view. And I believe that showing where and how he has not been clear will help one to understand this concept properly. But understanding belief in God properly will take more than analysis of what Plantinga has said about basic belief and rationality. The reason for this is that focus on basic belief and rationality means focus on truth, inference, assumption, and evidence. But belief in God involves risk, passion, paradox, and duty, and it involves them not incidentally but in a way that is deep and central to the essence of the concept. Plantinga's focus on the former has kept the latter suppressed.

I would like to call the language of belief in God relating to risk, passion, paradox, and duty "grammar of the heart" after the title of this collection of essays. Grammar of the heart is found everywhere in the Scriptures where the stories of faith are told. I would like to recount some features of one of these stories in order to bring back into view the grammar of the heart that Plantinga's discussion of basic beliefs and rationality has kept suppressed. One of Plantinga's examples of a basic belief relating to belief in

God is the belief "God is speaking to me." The Scriptures, to be sure, are full of such accounts where people believe that God is speaking to them. The story of the shepherds outside Bethlehem receiving the news of the birth of Jesus is such a story, and, I will suggest, a typical one. According to Plantinga's view of this story, we should take notice of the fact that these shepherds were entitled, without further foundation, to believe that God was speaking to them and that they were perfectly rational in believing so. But without denying this, let us take notice of what is omitted from this account of their belief.

What is absent from Plantinga's view is, to begin with, the fear and astonishment of the shepherds. They had a vision on a dark night; an angel of the Lord appeared to them, and they were, according to one translation, "terror-struck." There was, then, a declaration of an event—the birth of the Messiah. And they were given the details of where and when he was to be born and of what he would look like. They were given these details, presumably, so that they might go and look for him, and this task they immediately took up. They went to Bethlehem to the place where Mary and Joseph had taken refuge; they found the baby lying in the manger as the angel had described, and they gave praise and glorified God.

Their belief is not one that I would immediately think to modify by the word "rational." It was, by contrast, fearful and astonishing. There was, for them, no reckoning of the likelihood of the veracity of the message nor attempting to verify the presence of the heavenly hosts—things that the idea of a rational belief might suggest. There was no conceptual investigation of the idea of the Messiah or of what it would mean to be God incarnate in a manger. The Scriptures only record that they were fearful and astonished, that they went to see the event with all speed, and that they glorified and praised God.

What the Scriptures record in this respect is what I am calling grammar of the heart. The shepherds believed what was, by reflective standards, paradoxical. They were overcome with astonishment and fear at the presence and message of the angel—passion. They acted on the belief that God had given them a sign—risky, but what could they do but pursue the sign and then praise and glorify God—duty. This is grammar of the heart appropriate to those who believe that God is speaking to them. Such grammar is not the only thing to be recalled in connection with belief in God, but it can hardly be ignored nor suppressed by attention to properly basic belief and rationality.

Where have I been in all this? I have tried to understand Plantinga's account of belief in God as "properly basic" and "rational." I have had mixed results. Much of it I have not understood or understood poorly because he has not, in my judgment, provided enough analysis of the concept of belief. Some of what he has said about basic belief as ungrounded, I think I have understood and, in part, agree with. His claim that belief in God is rational I find partly confused and partly wrong. Whichever it is, I think it works to suppress the essential features of faith that include risk, passion, paradox, and duties—grammar appropriate to affairs of the heart rather than to rationality.

NOTES

1. Alvin Plantinga, "Reason and Belief in God," in *Faith and Rationality* (Notre Dame: University of Notre Dame Press, 1983), p. 16ff. Hereafter referred to as *RBG*.
2. Plantinga, *RBG*, p. 90.
3. Plantinga, *RBG*, p. 39.
4. Plantinga, *RBG*, p. 18.
5. Ibid.
6. Ludwig Wittgenstein, *On Certainty*, ed. G. E. M. Anscombe and G. H. von Wright (New York: Harper & Row, 1969), p. 33e, s.253.
7. Wittgenstein, *On Certainty*, p. 43e, s.337.
8. Plantinga, *RBG*, p. 39.
9. O. K. Bouwsma and J. L. Craft have each written helpful papers on this subject. Bouwsma's is titled "Is Belief in God Rational?" It is in the collection of his papers at the Humanities Research Center in Austin, Texas. Craft's paper goes by the same title and was published in an issue of *The Personalist*.

7. Two Views of Religion in Wittgenstein

JENS GLEBE-MØLLER

Wittgenstein has two views of religion. *The first,* and explicit, is characterized by a first person point of view with respect to a person's relation to God; it reflects a highly subjective or personalized view of religion. *The second* could be described as a more "sociological" account of religion where religion as a "world-picture" arises from the social background and develops in a social context by virtue of the rule-governed behavior of a group of people. Let me discuss each in turn, then ask if they are compatible or complementary with one another.

The first view is exemplified by this remark of Wittgenstein's from *Zettel:*

"You can't hear God speak to someone else, you can hear him only if you are being addressed."—That is a grammatical remark. (*Zettel* 717)

Wittgenstein might be quoting himself (as he so often does), however, the quotation also has a certain Kierkegaardian ring to it. Compare, for example, Kierkegaard's discussion of "Christ's answers" in *Works of Love:*

Not the prolix discourse does he warn against futile questions which only give rise to quarreling and evasions; alas, prolix discourse against such questions is not much better than the object of its opposition. No, as he taught, so does he answer, with divine authority, for authority means precisely to set the task . . . divine authority . . . is like the single eye; it constrains the person addressed to see who is talking with him and then fastens its piercing look on him and says with this glance, "It is to you whom this is said."[1]

Whenever Christ addresses you, you are set a task, and every question you might ask is just another way of trying to evade it. Or compare again, from *Training in Christianity,* the discussion of the sermon, aimed at Martensen, where Kierkegaard writes the following:

This, you see, is the reason why Christian truth does not allow itself to be presented for reflection or expressed eloquently as a reflection; it has itself, if I may say so, ears to hear with, yea, it is as if we're all ears, it listens attentively while the speaker talks; one cannot talk about it as about an absentee or as a thing present only objectively, for since it is from God and God is in it, it is present in a very special sense while one is speaking about it, and not as an object, rather it is the speaker that is the object of its regard, in speaking he has conjured up a spirit which examines him.[2]

Obviously, these are not Wittgenstein's precise words, and yet the affinity to Kierkegaard's thought lies at hand. If you could hear God speak to someone else, then the Word of God would indeed be a fact (*Gjenstand*) among other facts, and you might take the stance of a neutral observer and try to verify or falsify the alleged fact: God speaks to someone else. But this is not possible according to Wittgenstein or Kierkegaard. Religious talk, in so far as it *is* religious, is neither verifiable nor falsifiable. It has, in a certain sense, nothing to do with the facts of the world. Like ethical or aesthetic talk it is confined to first-person utterances. As Wittgenstein said, referring to the concluding remarks of his "Lecture on Ethics":

In my "Lecture on Ethics" I have in conclusion spoken in the first person: this, I think, is something quite essential. Here nothing can be stated any longer; I can only step forward as a personality and speak in the first person.[3]

Conversely, if and when you come across a confusion of the religious and the secular, you are bound to step forward and criticize. This was what Wittgenstein did when he turned against the notion of a scapegoat. "Sin" is a religious term and a personal term. Therefore, the notion of laying your sins upon someone else, for example, a scapegoat, does not make sense. It is a false picture:

The scapegoat, on which sins are laid and which goes out into the wilderness with them, is a false picture, like all the false pictures of philosophy. Philosophy might be said to purify thought from a misleading mythology.[4]

So, what our initial quotation implies, whether it stems from Wittgenstein himself or in some derived way from Kierkegaard,[5] is that whenever God addresses you, the hearer's neutral stance is excluded. Either you are listening to God and correspondingly set a task, or you are not listening. *Tertium non datur.*

We must ask: In what sense is this "a grammatical remark"? Let us recall #373 of the *Philosophical Investigations:*

Grammar tells what kind of object anything is. (Theology as grammar.)[6]

"Theology as grammar" for Wittgenstein means that words are being used in religious discourse by a religious person. If someone said that he or she could hear God speak to someone else, this would be ruled out as a nonreligious statement because, as we have seen, religious statements are not objective but personal. Strictly speaking, they are not statements at all, but rather, value judgments. Therefore, if someone says, "I was addressed by God," this is a grammatical remark, not a factual one; it speaks of God—it is a "theo-logical" remark.

Wittgenstein speaks of two kinds of grammar, a surface grammar and a depth grammar (*Philosophical Investigations,* hereafter *PI,* #664). The surface grammar refers to the part of the use of a word that can be taken in by the ear. "God speaks" *sounds* like "Wittgenstein speaks." But, if I understand "theology as grammar," then theological expressions are not the sounds one hears spoken; they cannot be taken in by the ear. Rather, they go "deeper." In *Zettel,* Wittgenstein had remarked, "How words are understood is not told by words alone. (Theology)," (*Zettel* 144). On the level, then, of depth grammar, "to hear God speak" only makes sense if and when we understand what it means to be addressed by God and set a task. "Theology as grammar" points to that dimension in a person's life where he or she is placed in such a position that he or she either has to accept or reject the task. "Will you or will you not fulfill the demand and do the works of love?" A person addressed by God no longer occupies a detached position—can no longer "leave everything as it is (*PI* #124) but is confronted with a choice, a personal choice.[7]

This, then, is Wittgenstein's first view of religion and the one to which he adhered throughout his lifetime, from the "Tractarian" period onwards. However, there is another aspect that has to be considered.

In the *Philosophical Investigations* we find the well-known discussions of rule governed behavior or "following a rule." In #232 Wittgenstein compares the grammar of following an inspiration to that of following a rule. He then imagines being trained in a sort of arithmetic where the children are told to listen only to the voice within when calculating. Such calculating would be like composing, Wittgenstein says. He then continues in #234:

> Would it not be possible for us, however, to calculate as we actually do (all agreeing, and so on), and still, at every step to have a feeling of being guided by the rules as by a spell, feeling astonishment at the fact that we agree? (We might give thanks to the Deity for our agreement.)

What we have here is first a description of what goes on when we normally do arithmetic. We agree (compare #224: "agreement" and "rule" are cousins) upon a certain procedure; we follow common rules. Nevertheless, even if it is seemingly plain and obvious what we are doing when doing arithmetic, we might still feel that there is magic *(Zauber)* going on here. It is as if the rules are leading us. We fail to see why we agreed in the first place. Therefore, one appropriate attitude might be (as Wittgenstein suggests in the final parenthesis) to "give thanks to the Diety for our agreement."

Although there may be a touch of irony in Wittgenstein's point, his reference to magic ("as by a spell") or to the Deity should not be understood as simply arbitrary. It is, I believe, an instance of Wittgenstein's way of invoking the Durkheimian distinction between the Sacred and the Profane.[8] So when Wittgenstein here and elsewhere makes use of religious words and concepts, he is simply saying that the whole social fabric has a kind of sacred quality. That there are rules, that we agree, is something that cannot be disputed and that at the time exerts a binding force upon us. It is not that we cannot change the particular rules. We can even "make up the rules as we go along" (*PI* #83). But once the rules are there, we are obligated to follow them; maybe with thanks to the Deity!

When discussing "rules," etc, Wittgenstein often uses words like "rock-bottom," or "bedrock." I will cite a few examples. The first one is from *PI* #217:

"How am I able to obey a rule?"—if this is not a question about causes, then it is about the justification for my following the rule in the way I do. If I have exhausted the justifications I have reached bedrock, and my spade is turned. Then I am inclined to say: "This is simply what I do."

When we reach a certain point, we cannot proceed by giving reasons any longer, we just have to say: this is how we do it. The reasons we might be tempted to offer are not reasons at all. They do not support anything. They are like "ornaments" (compare end of paragraph quoted).

Let us now take a look at some related paragraphs in *On Certainty* (hereafter *OC*). In pages 94ff. Wittgenstein writes about his "world-picture" *(Weltbild)*. He says (in *OC* #94):

But I did not get my picture of the world by satisfying myself of its correctness; nor do I have it because I am satisfied of its correctness. No: it is the inherited background (der uberkommene Hintergrund) against which I distinguish between true and false.

When I think about the world, Wittgenstein is saying, I have certain convictions (for example, that no man has ever been far from the earth [*OC* #93]). These convictions *(Uberzeugungen)* are parts of my world-picture. I have not made any experiments, I have not tried to verify my convictions or argued for them. But I have not made them up myself either. They are "inherited." My world-picture is the background against which I accept some statements as false and others as true. But where does this "inheritance" come from? From the life I live together with others. It is society, or the social collectivity, that has given me my world-picture. Therefore, as Durkheim contended, it has a sacred quality. Wittgenstein does not say as much explicitly. But it is significant that he uses the word "mythology" immediately after. Like the word "magic," "mythology" points to what is presupposed by members of a society:

The propositions describing this world-picture might be part of a kind of mythology. And their role is like that of rules of a game; and the game can be learned purely practically, without learning any explicit rules. (*OC* #95)

Now as we know, we can make up the rules as we go along and change them. We might even have to purify thought from a misleading mythology. Therefore, the mythology is never, as it were, static, unalterable:

The mythology may change back into a state of flux, the riverbed of thought may shift. But I distinguish between movement of the waters on the riverbed and the shift of the bed itself; though there is not a sharp division of the one from the other. (*OC* #97)

Thus, even if some parts of the mythology might change, there is still a mythology (a riverbed) left. Going back to the "rock metaphors," Wittgenstein then concludes:

And the bank of that river consists partly of hard rock, subject to no alteration or only to an imperceptible one, partly of sand, which, now in one place, now in another, gets washed away, or deposited. (*OC* #99)

These mythologies, the inherited social forms, will always be there and form the background against which we distinguish between true and false; they do not have the character of philosophical *a prioris*—they are embedded in the language we speak together with our fellow human beings—"in our language a whole mythology is laid down."[9] They are, by the same token, embedded in our social practices. This is brought out in the following remarks:

Giving grounds, however, justifying the evidence, comes to an end;—but the end is not certain propositions striking us immediately as true, i.e., it is not a kind of *seeing* on our part; it is our *action*, which lies at the bottom of the language game. (*OC* #204)

And again:

I have arrived at the rock-bottom of my convictions. And one might almost say that these foundation walls are carried by the whole house. (*OC* #248)

One might "almost" say that the mythologies that carry my convictions are themselves carried by my activities as a member of a social collectivity ("the whole house"). But why the reservation? Because, though it might be said that "the *speaking* of language is part of an activity, or of a form of life" (*PI* #23), it is equally true that "to imagine a language means to imagine a form of life" (*PI* #19). To paraphrase: no society, no human collectivity can exist without a mythology that determines, as it were, what the members of the society *say* to each other. But it is also true that there would be no talking to each other if there did not exist *social* activities.

Another important point to be mentioned is that the word "belief" frequently crops up in these connections. Take, for instance, the following remark: "At the foundation of well-founded belief lies belief that is not founded" (*OC* #253). A well-founded belief (in German, *ein begründeter Glaübe*) is, of course, a belief you can give reasons *(Grunde)* for. But when we try to give reasons for our actions, our rule following, or our sayings, we often end up with no reasons at all. "This is simply what I do (or say)." We simply believe, that is, without reasons we accept the rules, agree upon them, and follow them. The rule as such "stands out in its glory." The social rule (or rules) can be likened, says Wittgenstein, to the office of a king.

What I have to do is something like describing the office of a king;—in doing which I must never fall into the error of explaining the kingly dignity by the king's usefulness, but I must leave neither his usefulness nor his dignity out of account.[10]

We have, then, in Wittgenstein's works, a view of our place in human society that has a religious or quasi-religious tone—which points to the sacredness of our social life. Without the social life, our agreeing, etc., there would be no life at all. The question now is, what is the relation between religion in the first sense, as a personal affair, and religion in the second sense, as a social affair?[11] Let us, for the sake of simplification, speak of the relation between a religion X and a religion Y.

Let us now take a look at some of the "grammatical remarks" related to both religion X and Y. It is "a grammatical remark" that neither utterances in the religion X category, nor those of the religion Y category can be verified, be given reasons for, or explicitly represented. If I hear God speaking to me, I simply hear God speaking to me. I might afterwards make a drawing of the situation in which God spoke to me, but then I am representing, not listening. The same holds for my "world-picture." My "world-picture" is the way I see the world. I may try to justify it, but somewhere along the line, my justifications come to an end, to the bedrock, the rock on which I stand and see things. To put it another way, a society's mythology cannot be questioned from within that society. Or if it may happen that the mythology comes into a state of flux, the changes will be almost imperceptible. After a while, the slightly rearranged mythology reappears, or rather, it appears that it had been there all the time. By way of illustration, we might think of that particular kind of mythology that is called "the American dream." The American dream may change imperceptibly, but there will always be an American dream. And people in the United States will go on looking at the rest of the world with the inherited background of this dream. It takes a European or an African (with dreams of their own) to ask for reasons or justifications!

The real problem is whether we can establish a relationship between religion X and religion Y at a deeper level. If not, we are left only with "family resemblances" (*PI* #s 66–67) between two kinds of discourse. Although that would be interesting enough, it would hardly justify discussing the two as compatible under one author. Why would Wittgenstein hold two such apparently diverse views of religion?

At the level Wittgenstein called "depth grammar" (in the sense in which I have used the term above) we must look at the forms of life in which the various discourses enter and from which they spring. In the first section of this essay I contended, with a little help from Kierkegaard, that the depth grammar of the Christian discourse confronts us with a choice: either you listen to God and do the works of love, or you do not. This means that there is a specific Christian way of life (or way of life of our religion X). There are grammatical remarks to be found in Wittgenstein that point to the task of being Christian. In a manuscript entry of 1937 he asks, "What is it that attracts also me to the belief in the resurrection of Christ; I toy, as it were, with the thought." So here, apparently, he is almost capitulating to a Christian "world-picture." He does not capitulate, though. He only toys. But a little further on he writes, "Only *love* can believe the resurrection. Or: it is *love* that believes the resurrection."[12] This is a depth grammatical remark that makes religion X a question of doing the works of love or not doing them. If someone (for example, Wittgenstein) does the works of love, he or she believes the resurrection. Maybe this was what Wittgenstein was hinting at when he said to Drury, "There is a sense in which you and I are both Christians."[13]

In his *Lectures on Religious Belief* Wittgenstein said the following:

A great writer said that, when he was a boy, his father set him a task, and he suddenly felt that nothing, not even death, could take away the responsibility (in doing this task); this was his duty to do, and that even death couldn't stop it being his duty. He said that this was, in a way, a proof of the immortality of the soul—because if this lives on (the responsibility won't die). The idea is given by what we call the proof. Well, if this is the idea, (all right).[14]

Here again we have a depth grammatical remark, and one that Wittgenstein endorsed in his own life. Malcolm wrote about him that he once suggested a way in which the religious notion of immortality could acquire a meaning, namely, "through one's feeling that one has duties from which one cannot be released, even by death." This is, of course, what he brought out in the passage above. Furthermore, as Malcolm notices, "Wittgenstein himself possessed a stern sense of duty."[15] It can come as no surprise by now that the "great writer" is none other than Kierkegaard. In *Either-Or* he lets Judge Wilhelm speak about himself as a little boy who is being told to learn his lesson and from there derives a first proof of the immortality of the soul.[16]

Now, is there anything like a duty to be found in religion *Y*? I think there is. Following Saul Kripke, we might say that the collectivity or community is under obligation to accept as its member every individual who follows the community's rules, who has grasped the concept, say, of adding.

The rough conditional thus expresses a restriction on the community's game of attributing to one of its members the grasping of a certain concept: if the individual in question no longer conforms to what the community would do in these circumstances, the community can no longer attribute the concept to him. Even though, when we play this game and attribute concepts to individuals, we depict no special "state" of their minds, we do something of importance. We take them provisionally into the community, as long as further deviant behavior does not exclude them. In practice, such deviant behavior rarely occurs.[17]

But these concepts or rules are embedded in the form of life that we share and thus also in the mythology or "world-picture" that makes up the inherited background of our rule following or acting. Nobody is in principle under obligation to share the collectivity's mythology, but if he or she does not, that person is no longer a member of that society. Conversely, as long as deviant behavior does not occur, that person *must* be counted as a member of that society or community.[18]

If these considerations carry some weight, there is more than a family resemblance between religion *X* and religion *Y*. They are related to each other not just as one cousin to another. An individual person may not have a cousin. But one cannot be a person without being a person in a society. One cannot follow a rule "privately" or only once in one's lifetime:

Is what we call "obeying a rule" something that it would be possible for only *one* man to do, and to do only *once* in his life? (*PI* #199)

The answer to the hypothetical question is, of course, negative. We might add that, therefore, religion *X*, even if it is a private affair, does take place in a community.[19] Whether or not this specific religious community coincides with the larger community, in which we all live our lives, is another question.

Before coming to a close I would like to examine briefly one important attempt at bringing Wittgenstein's insights to bear on modern social theory. I am referring to Jurgen Habermas, who in his latest works has introduced the concept of "life-world" as opposed to "system."[20] In modernity the system, whose components are power and money, constantly threatens the life-world. At the same time the life-world is indispensable to human beings for two reasons. First, the life-world constitutes the horizon within which we act, individually and socially. Second, it functions as a resource for our actions. If the life-world got totally destroyed or "colonized" by the system, there would be no human actions left. We would end up with something like Huxley's "brave new world."

As a horizon as well as a resource, the life-world has three components (as opposed to the system's two). We might schematize them as being (1) background assumptions (*Hintergrundannahmen*), (2) shared values, and (3) individual competencies. Thanks to the existence of the life-world with its three components, we never start to act from scratch, so to speak. We will always go in one direction rather than in another. At the same time, whenever we do start acting, we stand upon this capital of "cultural trivialities," as Habermas sometimes says. For all of these three components taken together (though in between only for the first) Habermas uses the term "background knowledge" *(Hintergrundwissen)*, relying on Wittgenstein, especially on *On Certainty,* for the general idea.[21]

Obviously, there are affinities with Wittgenstein's thought here. Habermas's thinking is apparently in full agreement with Wittgenstein's when he quotes, for example, *OC* #144, with approval:

The child learns to believe a host of things. I.e., it learns to act according to these beliefs. Bit by bit there forms a system of what is believed, and in that system some things stand unshakeably fast and some are more or less liable to shift. What stands fast does so, not because it is intrinsically obvious or convincing; it is rather held fast by what lies around it.

Even if Wittgenstein is far less explicit than is Habermas, the parallel between the "background knowledge" and Wittgenstein's concept of "certainty" is indeed striking. However, there is also an important disagreement, of which Habermas is not aware, but one that really jeopardizes his attempt at using Wittgenstein.

According to Habermas's evolutionary thought, religion has had its day. To an ever-increasing extent, it has left the field to language or to communication. Habermas's favorite term for this development could be translated as "the Sacred has turned linguistic" *(die Versprachlichung des Sakralen).* Whereas in former times (roughly, until the Enlightenment), the life-world depended for its functions on a religious setting, a religious world-picture, it now depends on language, that is, on communication. This means that we *can* in principle, and *do* in actual fact, thematize every bit of our three components and argue about them *pro et contra.* "Bit by bit there forms a system," says Wittgenstein. But every bit can be made the subject matter of a discussion.

To a certain extent, Wittgenstein would have no objections, or one cannot object on Wittgensteinian grounds. Some things are liable to shift. The hard rock *can* be altered, even if the alteration is an imperceptible one. The riverbed *can* be shifted. On the other hand, as we have seen, a whole mythology is laid down in our language, and so it cannot be removed without our social world collapsing altogether. Religion *Y* is as important and all-pervading as ever. Durkheim's distinction between the Sacred and the Profane is still valid.

Even if I am inclined to think that Habermas is basically right and Wittgenstein wrong, it seems to me beyond doubt that Habermas can use *On Certainty* only by a very selective reading of his work. Or, otherwise stated, Habermas and Wittgenstein agree only at the level of surface grammar.

In concluding, I will now go back to Wittgenstein and ask whether religion *X* and religion *Y* are complementary or whether you can adhere to the one (religion *Y*—as we cannot step outside our mythology) without adhering to the other. According to Malcolm, there was in Wittgenstein, in some sense, the *possibility* of religion, but no more than that.[22] If you look at the surface grammar of Wittgenstein's works, Malcolm is probably right. If you look at the depth grammar, I am not so sure. Wittgenstein rejected a lot of traditional Christian concepts, for example, the notion of a "creator"[23] or, as we have seen, "sin" as a scapegoat. He even claimed that the essence of ethical and/or religious talk is the tendency to get beyond the boundaries of language. But he also said of ethical (and/or religious) talk that "it is a document of a tendency in the human mind which I personally cannot help respecting deeply and I would not for my life ridicule it."[24]

When a person respects a tendency "deeply," he or she at least understands it and may be very close to sharing it. Nevertheless it is possible that we do have to make what in the English reception of Kierkegaard is commonly labeled a "leap of faith" in order to get from our religion *Y* to religion *X*. Also it is possible that Wittgenstein himself was not able to leap from the shared religion *Y* to the religion of Kierkegaard's "the individual" (*hin Enkelte*). Yet, on Wittgensteinian grounds, even religion *X* people must start from somewhere, namely from our shared religion *Y*. But the question whether there is such a thing as a shared religion *Y* any longer cannot be answered within the confines of Wittgenstein's work. Or to put it another way, on Wittgensteinian grounds the modern concept of "secularization" may not make sense!

NOTES

1. Søren Kierkegaard, *Works of Love*, trans. Howard and Edna Hong (New York: Harper & Row, 1964), p. 104f.
2. Søren Kierkegaard, *Training in Christianity*, trans. Walter Lowrie (Princeton: Princeton Press, 1947), p. 228f.
3. *Ludwig Wittgenstein under der Wiener Kreis, Schriften III* (Frankfurt: Suhrkamp, 1967), p. 111 (my translation).
4. Quoted by Rush Rhees in Brian McGuiness, ed., *Wittgenstein and His Times* (Oxford: Blackwell, 1982), p. 81.
5. Wittgenstein claimed he had never read *Works of Love*, see Norman Malcolm, *Ludwig Wittgenstein: A Memoir* (London: Oxford University Press, 1966), p. 75.
6. The concept of "theology as grammar" seems to be derived from Luther, maybe in particular from Luther's "De divinitate et humanitate Christi," seventh argument, *Weimarer Ausgabe 39, II*, p. 104f. (according to letter from "Institut für Spätmittelalter und Reformation," University of Tubingen).
7. On another interpretation, already demarcating the religious discourse from other kinds of discourse would be an instance of doing theology as depth grammar. However, the notion "depth" (deep, deeper, etc.) in Wittgenstein almost always denotes the personal or existential dimension. I have discussed the notion in my book *Wittgenstein og religionen* (Copenhagen: G. E. C. Gad, 1968), especially on pp. 136f. and 261ff. On my interpretation, "theology as grammar" is akin to "the grammar of faith." See Paul L. Holmer, *The Grammar of Faith* (New York: Harper & Row, 1978). Among the many discussions of *Zettel* 144 and 717, see especially Richard H. Bell, "Theology As Grammar: Is God an Object of Understanding?" *Religious Studies* 11 (1975): p. 313f.
8. Compare David Bloor, *Wittgenstein: A Social Theory of Knowledge* (London: Macmillan, 1983), p. 20 and throughout.
9. Ludwig Wittgenstein, "Bemerkungen uber Frazer's *The Golden Bough*," *Synthese* 17 (1967): p. 242.
10. Ludwig Wittgenstein, *Remarks on the Foundations of Mathematics*, 3d edition (Oxford: Blackwell, 1978), p. 357.
11. This is a question that, by the way, Durkheim also had to consider. See Françoise Digneffe, "A propos de l'origine de l'obligation morale: la perspective durkheimienne," *Revue philosophique de Louvain*, 83 (1985), p. 355–73.
12. Wittgenstein, *Ludwig Wittgenstein: Sein Leben in Bildern und Texten*, ed. Nedo and Ranchetti (Frankfurt: Suhrkamp, 1983), p. 163 (my translation). Also in Ludwig Wittgenstein, *Culture and Value*, trans. Peter Winch (Oxford: Blackwell, 1980), pp. 33–33e.
13. Rush Rhees, ed., *Recollections of Wittgenstein* (Oxford: Oxford University Press, 1984), p. 114.
14. Ludwig Wittgenstein, *Lectures and Conversations on Aesthetics, Psychology and Religion*, ed. Cyril Barrett (Oxford: Blackwell, 1966), p. 70. Compare also my discussion in *Wittgenstein og religionen*, p. 208f.
15. Norman Malcolm, *Ludwig Wittgenstein: A Memoir* (London: Oxford University Press, 1966), p. 71.
16. Søren Kierkegaard, *Either-Or*, trans. Walter Lowrie (Princeton: Princeton University Press, 1959; paperback ed. 1971), p. 274f.
17. Saul A. Kripke, *Wittgenstein on Rules and Private Language* (Oxford: Blackwell, 1984), p. 95.
18. As opposed to G. P. Baker and P. M. S. Hacker, *Scepticism, Rules and Language*

(Oxford: Blackwell, 1984), I find it impossible to give up the "community view" that is supported, *inter alia*, by *PI* #199.

19. As underlined by D. Z. Phillips, *The Concept of Prayer* (London: Routledge and Kegan Paul, 1965), chap. 7.

20. See especially Jurgen Habermas, *Theorie des kommunikativen Handelns 1–2* (Frankfurt: Suhrkamp, 1981) and *Der philosophische Diskurs der Moderne* (Frankfurt: Suhrkamp, 1985).

21. Habermas, *Theorie, 1*, p. 451.

22. Malcolm, *A Memoir*, p. 72.

23. Ibid., p. 71.

24. Wittgenstein, "Lecture on Ethics," *Philosophical Review* (1965): p. 12.

II. THE GRAMMAR OF THE HEART

8. Making Sense Morally

PAUL L. HOLMER

One of the uncomfortable facts about ourselves is that we all must live in a way that meets our own approval. A bad conscience is the awareness that we have not behaved as we should. The longer and more thoughtfully we live, the deeper such a view of ourselves becomes. Soon we no longer think only of this or that lapse or decision or deed that was wrong, we begin to evaluate ourselves as a kind of totality. The whole person comes into perspective, and we begin to regret what we have made of ourselves. We do not easily entertain our intentions, our motives, or our purposes, because after a while these too look ambiguous, unclear, and sometimes even wild. We want to do what we ought, but we also want to enjoy ourselves; we seek the good in the situation, but we also want to please everybody; we strive to serve God, but we surely never forget what we deserve from Mammon. When all this happens, our life becomes blurred again, and we can hardly bear the light of our own thought upon it. Furthermore, we become secretly wretched, our conscience gives us no peace, and the tasks of living get burdensome.

It does little good, then, to heed the advice that comes so easily: "Don't think so much about yourself!" "Get busy!" "Take it easy!" "Have a nice day!" We would like to oblige, but these suggestions do not seem adequate for what ails us. For we are beginning to discover the plain truth, that we are moral beings. We also have to make sense with our deeds and behavior, with our purposes, motives, and accomplishments. In a peculiar yet very detailed way, most of us discover that we are judges of ourselves, that we project ideals for ourselves, that we are accountable not only to others but to ourselves as well. Instead of not thinking about ourselves and not having self-concern, it seems necessary, rather, to have a great deal of concern and to be very thoughtful about what one is making of oneself.

Certainly all of us are sooner or later in this kind of situation. When we were very young, someone else took care of us, even deciding what we should do and when. But with maturity, that begins to change. We suddenly discover that we are responsible for our own existence, not only physically but morally. Now we have to decide whether we are going to be honest, courageous, temperate, lazy, and clean, and also godly. Eventually there is no one but oneself to depend on in these matters.

Before too long we all are cognizant of the fact that we do have to live a life of which we can approve. It is not enough merely to please others, for groups, societies, churches, and even families change, and they do not always speak with a common voice. Furthermore, in growing up most of us want desperately to be ourselves and not to be only what others will make of us. Everybody remembers a bit of rebellion, perhaps, when one wanted thoughts of one's own, a slant that was distinctive, some freedom to decide, and, surely, the liberty to explore all kinds of behavior. Rules and duties, expectations and laws, commands and what others wanted—all felt oppressive and onerous. Everybody seemed willing to tell us what was right, but we began to resent always being told what was right. We wanted to discover even that for ourselves.

No one is quite so bold as to think that one can afford to be in the wrong or to live preferring what is evil. Human rebellion never goes quite that far. What we protest is the fact that others, the society, the Church, and our elders decide what is right for us. Here we would like to be competent ourselves, make decisions, and bear the responsibility—so, at least, we say. What makes all this so momentous is that our daily happiness and the very worth of our lives is at stake. This is why both sides feel the issues so deeply; parents and legislators of human affairs know all too well where human waywardness can lead, and the young surmise all too quickly what dull compliance and conformity can do to their lives. Both want the right and the good, and in ways that often conflict.

The Bible speaks to this situation in almost a matter-of-fact way when it worries its readers about the need for justification. There is not much of an argument presented for that notion; instead, the common human situation of discovering that one requires a life that is right and righteous, that is happy and justifiable, is simply assumed. Surely this theme from both the Old and the New Testament has to do with the conception that a life can be invalid and simply not worth much of anything. But it proposes always that every life can also become valid and that its worth can be saved and established. Two appropriate factors can be noted here. One is that the Bible would not speak to the human condition at all if it were not that each person can discover for himself or herself this need for rightness. The Bible addresses a state of affairs for each person that threatens to break down, that is full of potential for disaster. It is made for seekers, for sojourners, for those who need justification and validity. And part of its content is plainly moral, telling us how laws and commands can meet the indigence of the human spirit. This acknowledgment of the human factor, the plain truth that each of us knows about himself or herself, is a constant factor, bridging the Bible and the everyday world we all know. All this, then, is the first of the two factors we want to note.

The other factor is a little more difficult to understand. The Bible, in contrast to perhaps our own unaided reflection and that of most moral teachers in history, also puts this whole business of the need for justification in a radically different perspective. It conceives of us all in the presence of a living God who is not just powerful and terrifying but also holy and good. Furthermore, this Bible dares to say that God's chief interest is not only the cosmos at large and the machinery of the universe but also the justification and validation, the saving, of humankind. What becomes my concern when I become most sensitive to myself and most intelligent about my prospects—namely, my prospects for rightness—is also God's interest in making the world, in manifesting God's own self in Jesus Christ, and in giving us access to grace and mercy. In a bold and declaratory fashion, the Bible asserts that while God is our maker and our judge, God is also our very justification and vindication.

This second factor brings us to the heart of both testaments, not least to the story of Jesus' birth, life, death, and resurrection, all of which combine to make possible a forgiven and utterly grace-filled life. We have already alluded to the notion that this new life engendered in us by the life of Jesus can be lived zestfully, even hopefully, lovingly, and happily. Some very powerful emotions can now replace the anxiety, dread, disappointment, and even despair that most of us otherwise succumb to in living a natural and civil life.

There is something like that available for us morally, also. Hence, we will now note how the acquisition of virtues will help bring some order and even a certain kind of style into our everyday living.

The notion of the "virtues" probably makes us think of something desiccated, prim, and uninteresting. For a variety of reasons, including some theological and religious ones, the very idea of a virtue has gone out of fashion. For example, recent popular notions about morality have been in the direction of thinking about self-expression, self-development, and, above all, about each person developing his or her own individuality in creative and pleasurable ways. That it cannot be wrong if it feels so good, looks so good, and, besides, if everybody is doing it—all these notions loom up as the modern style of living and thinking. But such notions are not actually modern at all, nor are they a peculiar feature of our scientific culture, our permissiveness, and the new freedoms. Instead, every person has had, and still has, the raw material, the flesh and blood impulses and pleasure drives, to act and to think in such ways. These ways are as old and as natural and, furthermore, as easy as any practices and beliefs that have ever been articulated. They do not arise because of the way societies and cultures are; rather, they arise because people are initially prone to doing their own thing and seeking immediate satisfactions before all else. People are and have been that way from the beginning of recorded time.

It is just this state of affairs that called forth the virtues in the first place and has made them look like the rational and sensible way to meet the needs of both our natural life and our social living. If everyone does his or her own thing, then it is very hard for the untalented, the poor, and the little ones of the world. Besides, if each does his or her own thing, so much depends upon health, youth, personal appetites, and all kinds of other accidental components of one's life. Very few of these stay constant, and a mode of life dependent upon them often has to be almost whimsical, momentary, and even inconstant just to stay appropriate. So a life that is going to be approved needs continuity, some character, order, and less change. No wonder, then, that Aristotle and Plato, among others who thought very hard about how to live a life, concluded that we needed some shape and symmetry, some form and organization, to our wants, motives, intentions, and drives, just to make living agreeable to ourselves.

For centuries the term "virtues" has been applied to the organized ways that all of us can modulate and control our changeable and restless lives. At the least we can say that virtues are not quite natural, not quite native. They are acquired, even learned. But what, actually, are they? Perhaps a contrast will be useful. If I come to someone's rescue when he or she is being accosted by a thug, an observer might say, "How brave! You could have run away." Indeed, it may have been easy to do just that, and I did not. There are two possibilities here. One is that my action was totally impulsive, almost an accident, and surely not a clue to the way I usually am. My disposition may actually be to avoid trouble, look the other way, and generally stay away from anything that is dangerous, uncertain, and difficult. I could say that I know myself to be cowardly. Maybe I cringe over the prospects, debate endlessly with myself, and seldom take any action I consider rash. Therefore, my action in aiding another person was not in character, for I was not brave and surely not courageous. Moreover, I am unlikely to do anything like that again.

The other possibility is more appealing. Suppose that my action was typical of me, so that others might say, "That's just like him— always taking risks for others." Then others begin to think differently about me. Then they have the right to say, "He is truly courageous." For being courageous and brave is not a matter of doing something once. When we speak of a person as being courageous, we mean that he or she is characteristically that way. A certain kind of invariableness is known about him or her; he or she is prone to be like that in every circumstance where there is peril or need. Doing something just once does not count for very much if one is asking whether a person is punctual, patient, just, or courageous. In all such instances, we have to be sure that the disposition of the person is established, and that a pattern of behavior is likely, before we call the person just, courageous, or patient.

What we mean by a virtue, then, is an acquired disposition or inclination that will make behavior predictable and regular. In earlier times, virtues were also described as habits—not meaning mechanical or thoughtless, routine or compulsive behavior but, rather, behavior that could be counted on. People who had the reputation of being wise about human existence got that reputation because they saw clearly what most of us have seen only dimly. They saw that everyone needed to have courage as a standing capacity and way of coping with the uncertain world, the future, and the flux around them. No one can foresee very much, so we all must be ready for whatever happens. Courage is a kind of readiness or self-preparation to manage ourselves when the world and society begin to shift around us.

It is almost as if courage is that kind of virtue, that kind of self-information, that matches up with the lottery-like character of the world. Even Christians, who believe in God's providence and abiding love, do not escape this random way of the world. Rain falls on the just and the unjust; accidents, war, death, and separations make for extensive dislocations and radically novel situations to which we must adjust. Obviously, without courage, one could scarcely live at all. If one is cowardly, cringing, and timorous, the world itself begins to look totally bleak and dismal. Small wonder, then, that the ancients thought courage was "cardinal," meaning that this virtue was primary and fundamental, one upon which all kinds of other factors depended. As important as we might think politeness might be in some circumstances, it is so only in some circumstances, whereas courage is important in all circumstances. Hence the latter has been thought to be, and is, a cardinal virtue, a kind of hinge, upon which all kinds of other concerns depend.

Of course, there are other fundamental habits that are needed. Precisely because we are so changeable—so likely both to hate and to love, to vacillate in enthusiasm depending upon humidity, heat, and health—all of us need a kind of personal monitor, a kind of control. We do get that in part by the fact that laws and customs, police and parents, restrain us from the outside. But this works only very crudely and only under some circumstances. Waxing hot and cold, wavering between lust and indifference, wobbling between drunkenness and abstinence, we soon become very unruly and wretched people. How much better it might be to have the command rising up from within!

It is not surprising that a physical life that will allow us to eat endlessly, to enjoy voluptuous pleasure, and to be avaricious for goods and money also allows us to become penurious and stingy, unable to love anybody at all, and finally even mean and thoughtless toward others. When one becomes aware of the extremes that are possible, then it also becomes clear, as it did to early moralists, that being temperate is a sheer necessity. Temperance is also an acquired disposition, an acquired preference for moderation and for the mean between the extremes. Rather than letting appetite, satiation, or boredom randomly dictate one's behavior, it seem right and sensible to moderate one's satisfaction from within. Temperance is a name for a regularized way of governing personal impulses and habits.

Something like this could also be said about learning to be just. Oftentimes we can improvise our behavior in a chancy way and come out right. But an action that takes place just by chance or only once is not a great credit to anyone. If I treat someone with respect when everyone else is doing the same, then my action will be a matter of accidental conformity to a social pattern. But if I treat another person with propriety in circumstances that are not to my advantage, then a kind of character is asked of me. Having character is a matter of being disposed, being likely, and being predictable when circumstances are not always conducive. For the very reason that the world is as it is, full of uncertainties and unpredictable, and because it often rewards the unjust and the rapacious, justice as a personality qualification is sorely needed. Courage, temperance, and justice are not just accidental points of view, useful for one time and not for another. They are not relative or pertinent to just one society, one epoch, or one culture. Instead, they are needed because of the way people always are and the way physical and social contexts are.

The possibilities for injustice are endless, and they keep cropping up no matter whether the government is democratic, fascistic, or anarchical. Most of us suffer injustices and also commit them. None of us is so fortunate as to be without the need to become temperate, courageous, and just. If we do not become these things, then our lives disintegrate and make no sense at all. Who among us could ever decide to be a coward? Certainly, being without virtues is not a state that we can be taught or that we entertain with a clear mind and full awareness of the consequences. Instead we lapse into vices, just as an architect lapses into a poor design. No one builds a poor structure by trying to do so. No one who knows what it means to think thinks badly on purpose. A building that does not succeed and thoughts that do not hang together bring their own penalties. So do badly conceived lives. Virtues are the very means of bringing lives into a kind of rightness, a kind of moral sense, and this is why they are so momentous to all of us. Once we have thought about the virtues, they become very hard to ignore. They look like the minimal essentials for a life that is expected to have desirable results.

A contrasting state for all of us is easily understood. One does not have to be an apostle oneself to see with Paul how absurd lives become when they are full of pride, envy, murder, strife, malice, deceit, gossip, and ruthlessness (see Romans 1). Long ago, thoughtful people—indeed, wise ones—also saw that there were some terrible vices into which we could fall and thereby wreck our lives. If you so lived that envy became highly characteristic, then all sorts of things would go wrong. Envy, after a while, also becomes a habit, a kind of regular feature. And a terrible thing about it is that it begins to destroy an aptness for gracious activity and just assessment of others. It destroys peace of mind by always making us think that others are happier or more fortunate. It puts us in the insidious state of wanting to erase all the differences. It whets our appetite for what others have and are, and it turns life into a pursuit of more vanities. An envious person begins to look differently after a bit, for envy is very difficult to disguise. Worst of all, envy does not stand up to our own gaze. If we start to examine ourselves when envious, we can hardly bear to look. This is why envy, when it truly becomes a vice and an established way of comporting oneself, diminishes a person considerably. One of envy's first features is that it hardly allows any thinking about oneself. Thoughtfulness becomes the enemy, and with the lessening of thought comes the lessening of the person.

Other vices are like this, too. For example, if we allow ourselves to become lustful or gluttonous, it is very hard to be satisfied with ordinary pleasures and ordinary food. Lust for the extremes breeds a dissatisfaction with the middle range of pleasures that is otherwise the norm. If two people love each other over a long period and are temperate, they can find satisfaction with small accomplishments, with continuing loyalties, and with faithful attention to, and tolerance for, personal eccentricities. But once a lover demands the extraordinary in every embrace, then nothing less than tingling sensations and maximal enthusiasm will suffice. So, too, with the appetites for food and drink. The person who loses the capacity to be pleased by ordinary food soon has to make extravagant demands. Everything has to be excessive and ever novel.

The world itself, its persons, its foods, its circumstances, is not so bountiful that it can keep up with such meretricious and restless desire. We become meretricious ourselves when, instead of finding satisfaction and rest, we create ever more and more exquisite desires. Then we become driven people, urged on in ceaseless pursuits, with no peace for our souls. One of the debilitating features of modern life is that this endless push for satisfaction is now available to large numbers of people. Thus it looks as if it is natural and the standard point of departure for the good life. When everybody begins to do it, this mode of life looks irresistible. Even Christians of our day have not dared to criticize or to evaluate this freedom that masquerades as the license to be creative and to develop one's personality. But such compliance is befuddling, and it has caused many people to lose sight of the plain fact that there are other moral criteria and that these criteria are not a consequence of dogmatism or arbitrary moral authority. Vices are as clear negative instances as virtues are positive instances. Both are standards by which to judge our behavior.

It is hard to imagine anyone choosing to be sick. If we find someone like that, we are certain that there is an equally strange explanation, for sickness is never, under ordinary conditions, voluntary. We cannot understand anyone who chooses to be wretched, for happiness is what we seek, not its opposite. In moral matters it is safe to say that we fall into downright folly when we believe that all standards are individual and that everyone's life has to be an essay into the morally unknown. On the contrary, who with clear thought and awareness of himself or herself could ever choose to be cowardly? Who could choose lust? gluttony? envy? folly? and sloth of the spirit? All these are vices, just as honesty, temperance, prudence, courage, and more are virtues. We do not have to invent such notions for ourselves, nor are we the victims of others' imposition of values. When we endorse virtues and eschew vices, we are merely acknowledging how things are with all of us. Once more, these make up that grammar of life that no one person has invented and no one culture has prescribed. They set the boundaries of sense for lives anywhere and at any time.

If a person refused to obey the rules that make up the grammar of a language, we would not quite know what to say. The fact is that to speak the language at all requires that one get tenses, word order, and a host of other things straight. One has no choice. We can say with confidence to those who balk at the grammar of a language, "You can learn it," "You must learn it," and "You will learn it." "Can," "must," and "will"! In learning a language, everyone can master the grammar because it comes with the words and their use. If people want words but not grammar, we can say that they must learn the grammar, for the words mean little or nothing until we get sentences, paragraphs, arguments, and discourse. The "must" thus takes care of itself. Surely, then, they will learn the grammar in spite of themselves. Before one recognizes it, the grammar is in the very command one has of the vocabulary and all the uses of words.

Moral life, when thought about in terms of the elementary virtues and vices, is a little like this. Contrary to what most people say, morality can be learned. There is an air of skepticism that pervades our society on such matters. We easily conclude that morals are relative; if we say that often enough and long enough, it looks as if morals and values are merely asserted in this circumstance or by this person or that group. We begin to think that morals are made up as we go along, that morals have no more authority than we choose to give them. Then we do become skeptical, and we are inclined to drift along without any decisiveness. We let circumstances push us, and we wallow in uncertainty instead of invoking the certainties we actually have already. This is the very way that a life becomes meaningless and random. Our life becomes like a word does if it has no grammar—it dangles there without connections and without meaning much of anything.

But virtues and vices are already there as a big part of the grammar of life; they are already laid down. That grammar is not an imposition upon one's freedom any more than the grammar of French or English is an unwanted burden. To know the grammar of life is like knowing the grammar of a living language; it enables and empowers one to make sense. In fact, it does not tell us what to do any more than English grammar tells us what to say, but it does tell us *how* to live just as the constructions of a language inform us *how* to express ourselves.

We can learn this grammar of life if we pay a little attention. Obviously, "can" implies that every one of us is able and has the capacity. Think about how we learn the grammar of our native language. Very few people can state the grammatical rules that govern their speaking and writing. Nonetheless, they do obey those rules; otherwise, no one could understand them at all. The ability to become grammatical in one's speech does not depend completely upon understanding grammar abstractly or being qualified to discuss the reasons for the rules in a cogent way. One does not need to be a grammarian in order to be grammatical. This is why we say that something as important as making sense of one's life is not completely dependent upon having a theory of morals or upon having all the theological nuances under command. The sense of our lives is sometimes contingent upon how we fashion ourselves emotionally and how we manage ourselves morally. If we can become temperate, courageous, and just, we go a long way toward making a life that bears up under the human traffic. If we avoid intemperance, malice, wrath, and gnawing envy among the many vices, we discover the grammar of life in actual situations where it is embedded and readily accessible.

But every person will and must discover the grammar of the language he or she speaks. Grammar is so much a part of our language that to absorb even the simplest ways of talking is already to imbibe the grammar. We take it in unwittingly and almost without effort. And a few experiences of not making ourselves understood soon conspire to force us to speak according to the rules. The business of living is not quite like that. We can neglect and

refuse the grammar of life for a very long time indeed. We sometimes will our downfall and make our own perdition. Most of us
also learn pride and try to make a virtue of our independence and
individuality. We refuse help and deny our need. This is why
human living after a while becomes so solemn (but also so sardoni-
cally absurd and ridiculous). It is as if we have to live with what we
have made of ourselves, and the prospect is seldom pleasing. We
can for a time make our own rules, and we do. This is why the
learning of the grammar of life, the way of virtues, often comes
slowly and after many trials and failures. Often it is pressed on us
by the vicissitudes of a lifetime. Sometimes, unfortunately, we
come to ourselves when it is too late.

We do get used to despair. Some of us become cynics and
pessimists and think that all of existence is a big joke. Or we derive
the silly consolation, which is the only kin available after a while,
that says this is the way life is—bitter, short, and pointless. So the
grammar of life indeed "can" be surmised. Whether it will be or
not depends upon one's clarity of mind about oneself.

There is one range of considerations we have omitted thus far
that deserves longer consideration than we will be able to give it
here. While I am not retracting anything said about how sense
(and we could also say significance, worth, and meaning) gets
integrated into one's life stream, something else has to be noted
about making sense of one's life before God. It should be patent
by now that one simple picture that we get from a superficially
conceived account is being sidestepped. That shallow notion is
that we first encounter some teachings, then ascertain whether
they make sense—for example, whether they are true, false,
meaningful, or relevant at all—then respond to them with our
emotions, will, and behavior. This way of describing human living puts the theory first; the abstract statement of facts, rules, or
duties is in the dominant position. Then the "sense" is supposed
to be chiefly in the teachings, while the rest—deeds, emotions,
and willing—is part of the application or the practice. Then we
get familiar distinctions like theory and practice, teachings and
use, abstract and concrete. Instead of all that, these pages have
declared that our lives themselves lose sense and quality when
we do not achieve the standing dispositions that are virtues, in

contrast to the vagrant tendencies that we call vices. The point is that people, not just words or teaching also have to make sense. Modification and managing of ourselves is a good part of the wisdom of the moralists as well as the wisdom of the Lord. When we put all the stress on teachings as the sense bearers, we tend to neglect the very qualities of our personal life that will truly ruin us if we do not give them heed.

Now we return again to a consideration of the differences that Christian teachings make. Making sense morally is something like a minimum natural requirement. However, there is a kind of difficulty that is peculiar to moral striving itself, and Christian literature writes that difficulty very large. Most of us are tempted by the thought of moral improvement to think that we can secure our own judgment of our rightness. We are prone to think that we can establish ourselves in righteousness and that we can overcome the wasting and gnawing sense of not being good enough by moral effort. All of us do want an established and certain guarantee of our worth, our validity, as persons. The more sensitive and concerned we are about ourselves, the more we yearn for that. Thus making sense of ourselves by the virtues—and the emotions—is not an optional and accidental matter at all.

But Christian teaching tells us plainly that doing the works of the law will not establish our righteousness and furthermore that God, who is the ultimate judge, will not be persuaded by our achievements either. This kind of teaching does not dangle loosely over human life. For it does appear to be the case that anyone who works hard on being virtuous finds the goal continually receding. What the Bible says in general about all of us can be discovered in particular about oneself. We are in a rather poor position to make our own righteousness. We can always criticize ourselves and see that often we have done good, not because we like goodness, but because we want the praise we get for it. Doublemindedness and duplicity can pervade our morals, too.

More than this, we can begin to despair about the possibility of moral success. Nothing fits a person so well, so exquisitely, as does guilt. Here, then, is another kind of emotion, one that is hurtful and pervasive. It can bring about the mood of despair and an ever-deeper sloth of the spirit, when no effort, not even an upright and upbuilding one, seems quite worth the cost. Guilt of a responsible sort occurs typically in those who care a great deal about themselves. Such guilt is not just a psychological peculiarity. It, too, belongs to the working out of a life.

Now, however, the Bible's teachings also can get a grip on each of us. For this guilt is part of what is implied by the notion that works—righteousness is not enough. The Scriptures flatter us with the thought that the eternal is already planted in our hearts, and our restlessness with both our unrighteousness and our righteousness is a token of the need for something more. And that something more is God. For the God of the law and the God of Jesus Christ are the same God. The New Testament is the story of how Jesus Christ is a kind of passive righteousness, a righteousness that is given and not achieved. That righteous God forgives us for our lacks and failures, our immorality as well as our morality. Righteousness is imputed to us; and, before God and ourselves, we no longer have to grovel in need or fester in guilt.

Right here, then, thinking about making sense of our lives takes on a different hue. The notion that righteousness can be imputed, that one can be passive and receive the fundamental kind of rightness, is certainly a formidable and difficult one to comprehend. But this much does ensue. The motive for becoming virtuous and good no longer has to be to please God or even to please oneself. Anyway, neither of these quite works. Instead, one can do all of this simply by making sense as one goes along. One's own life is more tolerable if one is temperate and courageous; one does not then sow more seeds of regret, fear, self-contempt, and dismay. Somehow, morality can start by being just that and nothing more.

Furthermore, Christians, too, have to be courageous just to get along in the everyday world. Likewise, no one is exempted from the need for temperance. And the presence of other people simply requires us, Christian or not, to be just and to give everyone his or her due. The issue is still that a life does not make sense unless the person begins to qualify himself or herself. We cannot let ourselves be completely uncultivated. Furthermore, we need the action made by our decisions and deeds—what Luther called "active righteousness"—just to stay alive. The need is natural and unremitting. But once one is a Christian, the works become a consequence of the new confidence, the new certainty, and the new righteousness that faith provides. Whereas previously our striving for virtues and our battle against vices augmented our own sense of worthlessness and despair, now it is as if we are free of having to use morals for nonmoral ends. We need no longer be in despair even if we fail, for the Christian gospel is the story of God's love, which justifies us when we truly believe and trust in God, not just when we succeed morally.

Therefore, there can be no diminution of concern for making sense of one's life. But it is now the case that morality is not expected to save any one of us. We do not ask so much of ourselves or of our moral efforts. Besides, there is another kind of germane consideration. Our world is full of people who are confused and frustrated by the existence of a certain kind of moral disagreement. Many of us are inclined to think that morals make no sense at all unless it is possible to reach an agreement on them. This happens because we tend to think that we are moral only when we are deciding issues of right and wrong, goodness and badness. Then we suppose that anyone's view is as good as anyone else's, which sounds as if morals do not amount to anything. But after thinking about it, we begin to understand that every one of us needs to be qualified in order to make his or her own way. Instead of being frustrated by the disagreements, we now see that, amid all the shortcomings of our moral views and the uncertainty of thinking about the world and its happenings in moral terms, we ourselves can still become moral. The world, too, needs people who will be temperate, kind, patient, and courageous amid its confusions and uncertainties.

Many times, whether Christians or unbelievers, we will be unable to see what we should do. We will be in doubt about whether we took the right decision or did the right thing for another person. It is not as if such questions have an answer in the mind of God and the task of faith is to find it out. No, the point is rather that living in such a world as God has made requires us to be decisive and to make up our minds, often right on the spot. This is why we have to be temperate, thoughtful, considerate, just, and ever courageous. As people we have to be prepared. And those virtues are like ways open to us that will enable us to make sense as we go along.

Christians have dared to think, too, that love is a new disposition that believing in God allows us to enjoy. Of course, charity as it is described in the New Testament does not quite seem to be what we would call a natural love or an attraction. It is more comprehensive; it accounts for enemies, aliens, strangers, and many others who are very difficult to love. Such a disposition looks like something that comes only when you can truly relax your striving and can have your solace in the thought that God already loves you, unlovely though you may be. When you have faith in such a God, it is as if the faith rooted in you allows that disposition to grow and to generate a new life. Furthermore, love gives you another source of motives to be kind, temperate, and without envy or avarice. Love itself is satisfying; it is often its own reward. All the other virtues become easier, almost as if they were fruits of God's Spirit in us.

These, then, are some of the considerations that bear upon our common human tasks. If we only had to make sense on paper, we could probably write out a fairly coherent proposal. But the human agenda is more important than that. Our lives can fail, and do; but they also can succeed, and do. If we have spoken at all correctly, we have described ways to make sense with our virtues.

9. The Many Faces of Morality: Reflections on *Fear and Trembling*

H. E. MASON

The role of morality in our lives and the passions it serves are much more diverse and often more obscure than most of us are ready to acknowledge. The common view of a conscientious and responsible person as someone moved by a sense of duty and ready to do what it would be reasonable to expect of a person in one circumstance or another is undoubtedly borne out to a degree in the lives of a wide range of people, and in its philosophical expressions it is marked by an attractive simplicity and directness. But, as Wittgenstein said of another form of commonsense realism, it skips the difficulties. It leaves us without a suggestion of the difficulties lurking in the notion of what it would be reasonable to expect of a person and with little acknowledgment of the varying ways in which social circumstances and the mutual understandings and misunderstandings of people in those circumstances figure in judgments of what can be reasonably expected.

Philosophical expressions of the common view tend to locate the task of determining the requirements of morality in general moral principles supposed to specify what a responsible person can be expected to do in any situation in which the person might find himself or herself. The hazards of that undertaking are well known and have been much celebrated. A reader of Wittgenstein can perhaps be forgiven for suggesting that the hazards in an excessive reliance on explicitly formulated principles should have been anticipated. But attempts to turn Wittgenstein's doubts about explicitly formulated principles to philosophical advantage are not without their own hazards. It is doubtless true, as a number of writers have recently observed, that in the course of moral deliberation and criticism, conscientious people do go on from case to case without apparent reliance on explicitly formulated principles. They use moral expressions in question in keeping with the place those expressions have in the language games that are their natural home.[1] But excessive reliance on the implicit regularity of moral deliberation and criticism has a tendency to obscure some of the very features of moral justification that distinguish moral discourse from other forms of discourse. The notion that there are language games that are constitutive of morality is in that respect not altogether dissimilar from the notion that there are general principles constitutive of morality. In their common expressions neither approach gives sufficient attention to the question whether the responsibility a person bears as a moral agent peculiarly distinguishes what justification is appropriate to moral judgments, that is, justifications linked with explicit moral principles or justifications found to be regulative within local and particular moral situations. In this essay I will explore that question, seeking help from some ideas to be found in *Fear and Trembling*.[2]

It is a little noticed merit of Kierkegaard's treatment of the idea of the ethical in *Fear and Trembling* that both the social context of moral responsibility and the deep conflicts that almost inevitably occasions are developed in a highly original and suggestive way. Kierkegaard gives Johannes de Silentio an idea of the ethical that is deceptively simple and hardly original: the ethical is the universal. But as that familiar idea is developed, it is given a rich and striking content. De Silentio's question whether Abraham was ethically justified in his silence before Sarah and Isaac is used to explore the idea that we have a responsibility to explain ourselves to those affected by our actions. The conditions of moral justification are thus located in the objections of the particular people affected by what we do. In the place of general moral principles we are supposed to look to reasonable ways of satisfying the objections brought against our actions by those likely to be hurt by them.

This picture of moral justification has a way of bringing moral questions down to earth. It stands against the idea that we can know what we can or must do in some *a priori* way without actually listening to those our actions are likely to affect. De Silentio's remarks about Abraham's responsibility to explain himself thus lead directly to a much more concrete conception of moral responsibility and an equally concrete notion of the rationality that figures in moral discourse. But they also lead to an unsettling picture of the psychological conditions of moral responsibility. De Silentio's idea of the ethical life is ostensibly used as a kind of foil for his exhibition of the singular isolation of a knight of faith before God, but as that contrast is developed, with one instance of isolation after another, most of them with no particular religious significance, it becomes clear that Kierkegaard is as much interested in exhibiting the psychological fragility of a form of conscientious concern that essentially depends upon mutual understanding. Discussing characters isolated in one way or another from the communities in which they live, he suggests a variety of ways in which, in the face of the resulting forms of misunderstanding, moral concern can become destructive. At the extreme it can become, as he puts it, demonic, but even short of that he suggests that there are many ways in which it has a tendency to destroy the forms of human solidarity it supposedly serves.

In *Fear and Trembling* Kierkegaard was not primarily interested in philosophical expressions of common moral views. His critical attention was fixed on eviscerating views of religious faith. But to explain the bearing of his notion of moral responsibility on philosophical expressions of the common view, I must say something about them. What is known and practiced as morality is a complex web of diverse and diversely related practices not readily susceptible to philosophical regimentation. Philosophical accounts of morality tend to proceed by generalization from prominent features of particular practices, treating one feature or another as essential to morality. The resulting untidy diversity of theory is doubtless due in part to the tendency to generalize from particular features of particular practices. Normally, a more balanced diet of examples would be the indicated prescription. But there is a deeper cause of the apparent partiality of moral theories. More than other parts of philosophy, moral philosophy aspires to serve our daily practice, thoughtfully developing common forms of criticism and justification. The principles and forms of argument it offers are commonly supposed to provide a more reasonable basis from which to consider things done in the name of morality. So conceived, its questions are not simply questions of what morality is or has been, but of what at its best it might become. Moral philosophy's theories are formulations of reasonable expectations and requirements and not simply accounts of things already in place. Moral philosophy is, that is to say, Socratic, listening to learn what morality is, but searching for a way of saying what it should become. Familiarity with Socratic exercises should remind anyone that they can take many directions.

The common view of morality that I mentioned at the outset of this essay doubtless arises with something of a Socratic intention, but in its philosophical articulation it leads to a bewildering thicket of perplexities. Consider a difficult moral decision. In most such cases it is easy enough to say what sorts of things might show up as reasons for taking one course or another and as easy to imagine what might be said in favor of the reasons offered. What is difficult is to know when and how the reasoning must come to an end. Regarded from a very natural point of view, any resting point will appear to be arbitrary. From that point of view, asking of a line of reasoning or a principle cited in its favor whether it is plausible or seems reasonable will appear little different from asking a water diviner whether he or she can feel water three feet under the ground. Against what is one's thought supposed to work in judging whether a principle is plausible or seems reasonable? What is there that resists any answer one feels inclined to give? I believe that de Silentio points us in the direction of the resistance that matters. To get out of the grip of these dizzying questions, however, we need some perspective on the use of principles in moral deliberation.

Suppose you are considering whether to help a neighbor you know to be in need of some help. You would like to be neighborly, or you owe this person a debt of gratitude. Your question is the deliberative question, "What should I do?" and any reasons to be considered will be considerations favoring an offer of help. They will be judgments to the effect that offering help would be a neighborly, even kind thing to do, or that it would be an appropriate expression of gratitude. Or they might be matters of fact making it clear that the action would be a neighborly thing to do or an appropriate expression of gratitude, that this person was actually in need of help, or had once helped you in a moment of need. To the further question of whether the facts cited would be sufficient to make the act an act of kindness or an appropriate expression of gratitude, the reasonable answer, that in the circumstances at hand they would be sufficient, cries out for elaboration. A principle doing the expected work would be hard to come by, but demands for further justification would not necessarily come to an end there. There might still be the question of whether, kind as it would be, the help you were ready to offer should really draw you away from your desk or your bench or your family or whether, in the case of the debt of gratitude, the thanks you were ready to offer should really be considered in a situation of fundamental political conflict. It takes little philosophical imagination to know how the lines of questioning might proceed, with the lines of reasoning accordingly extended. Simple deliberative questions can easily seem to lead ineluctably to a demand for justifying principles sufficient to decide any unsettling questions that might arise over a proffered course of action.

Many of the most prominent forms of moral philosophy can be regarded as offered to serve this natural and, in its way, practical concern to formulate principles adequate to justify questionable courses of action. Deliberation is taken as a generic feature of human practice, and the principles ruling in moral deliberation are the distinguishing characteristic of morality. The adequate specification of principles serving that purpose thus becomes the primary task of moral theory. Both contractarians and utilitarians, for example, conceive of moral theory in that way, with the ensuing controversies framed in terms of the adequacy of their respective specification of ruling principles, and focused on hard cases. The model of moral deliberation as ruled by general moral principles is taken as given, and arguments for particular specifications of those principles are supposed to turn on reasonable judgments of hard moral cases.

It must be said that the search for general moral principles sufficient to decide unsettling questions over particular courses of action can serve a Socratic purpose. Asking what principles would allow what we have done or propose to do is a way of calling those things into question. Furthermore, it facilitates a kind of reflective reconsideration of our lives and our practices. If we weigh the judgments we are inclined to make against those principles that allow or require them and go on to ask what can be said independently in favor of the principles, seeking a reflective equilibrium of judgments and principles, we may come to a better understanding of the general implications of both our particular actions and the practices in which we participate. That understanding may not determine particular choices, but, in its Socratic way, it doubtless clarifies some of the choices we face. It must also be said that the formulation and justification of relatively specific principles often play a critical role in moral argumentation. If just one farmer's roads are plowed by the county, a neighbor may rightfully demand the principles allowing that apparently special treatment. If some students are excused from class to go deer hunting with their fathers, students refused permission to engage in a political protest with their mothers may rightfully demand the principles allowing the difference in treatment. There is no dearth of comparable examples.

Despite these occasional virtues of the formulation of moral principles, whether general or relatively specific, the model of deliberation as ruled by principles is almost certainly misconceived. The idea that there might be principles capable of deciding any unsettling questions that might arise over a course of action misconceives both the role and the logical powers of principles, and it grossly underestimates the complexity and the diversity of objections that can be brought against the simplest piece of conduct. At one level the idea is simply a version of the idea that led Wittgenstein to ask

but what does a game look like that is everywhere bound by rules? Whose rules never let a doubt creep in, but stop all the cracks where it might?— Can't we imagine a rule determining the application of a rule, and a doubt which *it* removes—and so on?[3]

Wittgenstein's countering idea is that generally formulated rules may have a role, but they must play that role within the context of practices that are not themselves explicitly formulated in terms of rules and could not be so formulated. The difficulties of a person who did not know how to go on from one case to another in the use of an expression or the application of a concept could not be resolved through explicit instruction that did not in turn depend on that person's capacity to understand and apply that instruction. A principle, like a rule, is susceptible to explicit formulation. But, explicitly formulated, it "stands there like a signpost."[4] Like a signpost, neither a rule nor a principle can tell us how to take it, how, that is, to follow the instructions it offers.

There is another level of misconception in the model of deliberation and deliberated conduct as ruled by general moral principles. Principles are often cited in the face of particular objections, and explicitly formulated in terms of those objections. But while such principles may serve as a person's reason for acting as he or she does in the face of a particular objection, envisaged or actually pressed, they cannot normally be said to regulate the conduct "all the way down," as it may be put. A principle cannot provide an exhaustive reason for a particular action, and it cannot authorize an exhaustive reason. Consider some of the possibilities. (1) You object to something I propose to do. I take your objection to be salient and explicitly take it into account in formulating a principle justifying what I propose to do; other objections are noted but treated as insignificant, not of sufficient importance to show up in an explicit formulation of my reasons. (2) I acknowledge your objection and take it into account in an explicitly formulated principle justifying what I propose to do. In slightly different circumstances the principle would not be acceptable or would not even apply. My judgment of that figures in my justification of what I propose to do, but not explicitly. (3) I accept your objection and acknowledge that what I propose to do cannot be justified. But I go on to mention circumstances possibly excusing what I propose. A principle reasonably offered in such a case would have to grant the force of the objection while allowing that in the particular circumstances the action in question might be excused. In these and countless other ways the justifying use of explicitly states rules depends upon judgments of relevance and appropriateness that are not made explicit and could not all be made explicit. Happily, a degree of tolerance and mutual understanding often stands in the way of the otherwise unending conversations that might ensue. But that should not be taken to show that explicitly formulated principles have done all the work. Only a deliberative division of labor makes it possible for them to do the work they do in fact do.

This point can be made in another way. The sheer complexity of the considerations relevant to a particular moral question stands in the way of the model of deliberation as ruled by general moral principles. The simplest of moral questions will exhibit that complexity to a degree. Suppose you wonder whether you can ask a friend or neighbor to care for your dog while you are away on vacation. You have no right to expect this neighbor to do it, you may be told. You know that, but you wondered whether it would be an imposition to ask her to do it as a favor. Told that it would, you wonder why it would be an imposition to ask her to take the dog, but not an imposition to ask this same friend to feed the cat or water the plants. That is a matter of relative inconvenience and likely bother, you may be told. Granting that, you may wonder whether the friend might not welcome the opportunity to be of some help and even feel somewhat offended if she knew that, in the belief that it would be an imposition, you had refrained from asking her to care for the dog. If you were in serious difficulty your friend would surely be offended if you did not turn to her for help. True enough, it may be said, but that is only a matter of your own convenience and surely not a matter of serious difficulty. The ensuing judgment, that you could not ask her to take the dog, is one that might be questioned but not without some recognition of the force of all these diverse considerations. Even in a case of little consequence, the relevant considerations are both diverse and diversely related to the question at stake.

The diversity of considerations relevant to even the simplest moral decision stands against the idea that the question of what to do in a particular case must be ruled by uniformly applicable moral principles. Where a thoughtful and conscientious decision requires taking into account a variety of heterogeneous considerations, a general principle requiring or permitting an action of one sort or another in a complex situation can at most specify salient features of a situation. That they are the morally salient features of the situation depends, as the example illustrates, on an assessment of their weight in comparison to the various other considerations that might have been thought to be salient. Thus, even if a principle is cited in favor of one alternative or another, assessment of its moral force will depend upon judgments of relevance and appropriateness. It will do its work, that is to say, only within the context of practices in which there is some mutual acknowledgment of judgments of relevance and appropriateness. Appeal to a principle may in such a case be important and even critical, but its force will be local and not constitutive.

While acknowledging that general principles do on occasion serve a critical, if modest, role in deliberation and reflection over moral questions, it must also be said that principles play a much less prominent role in moral deliberation than the discussions of philosophers would suggest. Conscientious moral questions tend to be local and specific, focused on particular circumstances and considerations. We question the justice of a particular form of taxation or a particular institutional practice, and we question particular rights that are claimed or particular obligations proposed. Questions that are more global tend to arise out of and be supported by reference to particular doubts. Where particular doubts are raised they tend to be argued by reference to other judgments not questioned. Thus, for example, by contrast with an accepted form of taxation acknowledged as reasonably just, the justice of a proposed form of taxation is said to be doubtful. Where it is acknowledged that a person has a right to the disclosure of one sort of information, it is thought doubtful that he or she should be denied access to information of a somewhat similar kind. Moral questions do tend to be answered systematically, that is to say, their answers argued on a systematic basis, but the elements in the system are much more likely to be particular judgments and practices than general moral principles.

Moral instruction tends to bear out the view that relatively specific judgments determined by a variety of interrelated considerations play a critical role in the daily consideration of moral questions. In moral instruction, people may be taught some absolute proscriptions and some general precepts, but they soon learn that it is relatively specific judgments that they are supposed to take seriously: "A person in your position has no right to speak to her like that." "You have to give them an opportunity to object: that's the least people in those circumstances can expect." "It would be an imposition to ask anyone else to do that for you." "You're not being fair to them in making that judgment without hearing their side of the story." Wittgenstein's observation about empirical judgments is at least equally true of moral judgments: "We do not learn the practice of making empirical judgments by learning rules: we are taught *judgments* and their connection with other judgments. A *totality* of judgments is made plausible to us."[5] Not all judgments offered in the course of moral instruction are accepted, and not all that are initially accepted continue to be. But it would be a mistake to focus on the instances of rejection. We do come to accept a body of interconnected judgments about relatively specific cases, and in moral instruction, as in moral argument, cases loom large, with attention focused on similarities and differences supposed to make a difference.

Suppose that the practice of moral deliberation takes this form, with relatively specific judgments standing in the place in which we might have expected to find general moral principles. Within that practice, justification comes to an end with the mention of judgments and patterns of judgments accepted and acknowledged within the community in question. General principles play some role, but not the constitutive role commonly given them by moral philosophers. The notion of morality and of moral practices is not to be explained by citing constitutive general principles but by citing, instead, relatively specific judgments and patterns of judgments and describing their place within the practices of the community in question. Critical questions calling particular actions and practices into question arise and are conscientiously treated in their own terms, but they are not subject to more general or, one might say, more fundamental justification. To those demands for more fundamental justification that call the moral practices of a community into question, it will be sufficient to say that this language game is played. That has a dismissive sound, and it will, in fact, be intended that way. The alternative is to allow questions that may have a serious ring but that neither a critic nor a participant will be able to manage.

I believe that de Silentio's question of whether Abraham was justified in his silence suggests the appropriate constraint on moral practices and, for that matter, on the use of rules and principles employed within those practices. De Silentio's question serves as a reminder of a critical feature of the context in which questions of moral justification arise. Those moral theories that offer general moral principles to which our conduct and our practices are supposed to conform do not commonly address the question of whether there is anyone in particular to whom we owe an explanation for the things we do or propose to do. It is assumed in those theories that, if a piece of conduct satisfies the principles constitutive of morality, it will be justifiable however it affects particular people and whatever their objections may be. Those theorists who disallow the constitutive role of moral principles, and suppose instead that the regularities of judgment learned within appropriate language games play the critical role, are no more likely to give a special place to the question of whether there are people to whom we own special explanation for the things we do or propose to do. Having mastered the use of moral concepts within the language games in which they have their home, we are supposed to be able to apply them in problematic cases, judging whether a particular course of action would be unkind or unfair, or even wrong. Since the language games in question are constitutive of morality, it is sufficient that a questionable piece of conduct conform to the regularities of judgment embodied in those language games. Conduct that does conform is supposed to satisfy anyone's objections.

Why should the objections of those likely to be affected by a course of action have any particular standing in the consideration of its justification? De Silentio does not offer a direct answer to that question, but he does discuss a series of cases in which a person's silence in the face of people likely to be affected would be morally questionable. In the early pages of *Fear and Trembling*, [6] he offers a series of abortive attempts to reconstruct the story of Abraham's trial in a way that makes the story, as he puts it, humanly understandable. With the successive versions of the story, each an attempt to make sense of the story, but each equally unsatisfactory, de Silentio exhibits the difficulty Abraham might have been expected to encounter had he searched for an explanation of his undertaking that would have been reasonable to expect Isaac to accept. As the reconstruction proceeds, no thought is given to the possibility that there might be no need to explain the undertaking to Isaac. Nor can it be said that the successive versions of the story exhibit the need. It is assumed that a wish on Abraham's part to explain himself, even some recognition of a kind of obligation to do that, is a constraint on the intelligibility of the story and, furthermore, that his incapacity to explain himself is a critical feature of its unintelligibility.

De Silentio speaks more directly to an obligation of disclosure in his discussion of Agamemnon's sacrifice of Iphigenia.[7] It may be aesthetically preferable for Agamemnon to bear silently the pain of what he must do, and out of solicitude he may wish to shield Iphigenia from her harsh prospect as long as he can. But, as de Silentio puts it, ethics demands disclosure. Agamemnon must be tried by the tears of Clytemnestra and Iphigenia. De Silentio goes so far as to say that Iphigenia ought to be permitted to weep for two months at her father's feet, entwining herself around his knees. Why should Agamemnon submit himself to the argument from Iphigenia's tears? If there is, as de Silentio insists, a clear and overriding public purpose to be served by the sacrifice, what point can there be in that painful exercise? De Silentio says that Agamemnon must shirk no argument from outside. His justification must be tried in the face of the strongest objections, the objections of those who will be adversely affected. Their objections are not the only relevant considerations, but if the justification is truly overriding, it must be sufficient to stand in the face of those objections. De Silentio offers no suggestion how the objections are to be judged, and his interpretation proceeds on the assumption that the sacrifice might have been justified, Agamemnon's action heroic. But in arguing that Agamemnon's readiness to hear Iphigenia's objections is a measure of his heroism, De Silentio gives special standing to the objections of people likely to be adversely affected by an action.

This feature of moral deliberation must be familiar to everyone. If a private physician learns that a bisexual patient is unwilling to inform his wife that he is infected with the AIDS virus, the physician owes the wife an explanation of his own failure to warn her if she becomes infected. She may be ready to accept his explanation, but that seems unlikely if he simply stands on the rule that confidentiality must be maintained at all costs. In these situations a responsible person does not simply ask the abstract question of what is the ethical thing to do or the rational thing to do. Such a person asks how to explain himself or herself to those affected by such actions. He or she recognizes a responsibility to those affected in one way or another by what he or she does or fails to do and deliberates in the light of that. It is, of course, true that the responsibility goes in many ways. The physician must be ready to explain himself or herself to the husband as well as to the wife. But that is no more than a condition of the moral problem the physician faces. The fact that the responsibility can go in many ways is one of the factors that makes such a problem difficult. But the fact that a moral problem has no simple solution, or no solution at all, is no reason to reject it.

If responsibility can go in many ways, the task of justifying a course of action takes on a somewhat different appearance. The context in which justification is sought will determine the task of justification in a manner reminiscent of the way in which the context in which a scientific explanation is offered determines its task. What needs to be justified in a course of action will vary with the specific objections likely to be brought, just as the specific features of a natural phenomenon that call for explanation will vary with the specific perplexities at hand. Suppose that the physician does stand on the rule that a physician must respect the confidentiality of any information about a patient acquired in the course of normal duties. The physician's responsibility to the wife to justify this failure to warn her that she was in jeopardy will not allow the physician to simply cite the rule or affirm its importance. If the physician responds conscientiously, he or she will have to address the wife's objection, explaining, for example, the importance of abiding by the rule even in the face of a case with the difficulty of hers. The likely pattern of argument may seem little different from the familiar treatment of hard cases. But if the task of justification is framed by the physician's responsibility to explain himself or herself to the affected person, and set by the wife's objections, it takes on a different character. The justification must be thought of as offered to the affected person. If it is successful, it must be reasonable to expect this person to accept it and unreasonable of her to reject it.

In a fairly cohesive society such conditions might be satisfied. It is altogether possible that a person objecting to her treatment might find sufficient satisfaction in the justification offered to withdraw her objections. Or it might be beyond question that it was unreasonable of her to reject the justification. But it is important not to make too much of that. In describing the responsibility of consultation as a constraint on moral practices, I do not mean to suggest that it promises a decision procedure. That would be at odds with the degree of uncertainty conscientious and responsible persons often experience in the face of difficult moral questions. The question of whether it would be reasonable to expect an adversely affected person to accept a proffered justification, unreasonable of her to reject it, is, at best, a question of judgment. What force the constraint has does not lie in a promise to settle issues that appear beyond settling, but rather in its setting a task for justification that will, in many instances, broaden the range of consideration and sharpen its focus. What it stands against is a tendency to rely on principles, or practices in place, to the exclusion of a consideration of the objections that might be brought by people likely to be affected by a course of action.

I want to stress this last point. Kierkegaard writes in a way to suggest that moral practices are likely to be monolithic, the choices they allow lexically ordered. Agamemnon is said to have recognized in his action a higher expression of the ethical. But as Wittgenstein is reported to have suggested to O. K. Bouwsma, speaking of the treatment of pride in *The Brothers Karamazov,* the story might have been told in a way to make quite a different moral point.[8] Everyone knows that life is filled with choices, and most people know that the choices they make shape their moral lives. One person is fastidious about his work, but careless with his garden, and professes to be bored with politics; another devotes her life to political protest and ignores both her work and her family. One teacher is warm and welcoming to students but never returns their papers; another makes long and detailed and carefully crafted comments on their papers and then gives them all A's. There is no neat and telling way of ordering these choices, or even of saying which is ethical. There are doubtless stories to be told in each case, and the moral points will vary with the stories.

I have argued that moral questions and the terms commonly used to frame them must be understood within the practices in which they arise. If we were impervious to such things as insult and neglect, kindness might take on quite a different meaning or drop out altogether. But knowing what it is does not tell us what weight to give it where it conflicts with honesty or fairness or, for that matter, with tedium. Even within the shared life of a community, people of goodwill and common concern may find themselves in deep and continuing moral disagreement. The constraint I have described does not promise to resolve such disagreements but rather to focus them on an open consideration of the responsibility each bears to those affected by the actions and the policies in question. In doing that, it may introduce some telling considerations, but it is more likely to complicate moral questions and increase conflict than to eliminate it.

Mutual understanding is bound to play a critical role in moral deliberations subject to a constraint requiring that the objections of people likely to be affected by a course of action be heard. If I owe you an explanation of what I do, and that explanation is supposed to take your objections into account, some mutual understanding is indispensable. Commonly, that understanding requires a knowledge of circumstances and concerns, but it also requires some sense of the moral basis of the objection in question. Where there were commonly acknowledged moral principles, the moral basis of an objection would undoubtedly be easier to grasp as well as to judge. But if, as I have argued, principles can do their work only within the provenance of common understandings and practices well in place, and if there is some reason for doubt about the extent of those common understandings, the prospects may seem questionable. To complicate the matter, if there are forces working against common understanding, the prospects may seem even more questionable. Paradoxically, that is the picture de Silentio offers. It is paradoxical because de Silentio insists throughout that the paradigm of conscientiousness, the tragic hero, acts with the full understanding and support of the community.

In the course of his discussion of the question of whether Abraham was ethically justified in his silence, de Silentio offers a number of counterparts to Abraham, people isolated in one way or another from human community and in their isolation, tempted to a defiant and even demonic response to the community of fellow humans.[9] Subjected to a pity or a contempt that marks their difference, they respond with a defiance that establishes their isolation. Or suffering a guilt that stands in the way of an easy exchange of respect and concern, their attempts to explain themselves are, at best, ambiguous. De Silentio's discussion of these possibilities serves as a reminder of the fragility of a form of life that requires mutual understanding. Expecting understanding and not receiving it, or wishing to exhibit it and not being able to, a person may be driven to the most contrary expressions. The resulting defiance and motivated ambiguity can undo the most patient attempts at understanding. But while such possibilities can pose extreme personal and practical difficulties in particular cases, they cannot be said to provide reason to reject the constraint on morality requiring that a person be ready to explain himself or herself to those likely to be adversely affected by his or her actions. They only serve to underline the possibility that, in many instances, its acceptance will increase the difficulty and complication of acting in a responsible way.

What standing should be given to the constraint I have described? It is tempting to say that it is a critical feature of those practices in which questions of moral justification arise or, if you prefer, a feature of those language games. It does, in fact, seem self-defeating to claim justification for an action or a policy but refuse to hear the objections of those most likely to have complaints. But what sort of mistake would then be made by someone who stood defiantly on principle or clung desperately to established ways of doing things? The adverbs suggest what Kierkegaard would say: either life would be one of despairing narrowness, the defiance or the desperation exhibiting an anxious dread of a more expansive life. That description, it must be said, assumes a standing for the responsibility threatening a more expansive life. *The Sickness Unto Death* was published, it should be recalled, under a pseudonym, allowing a book that might seem "too strict to be edifying, and too edifying to be strictly scientific."[10] The adverbs are, in any case, ours. A person who stood on principle or observed established ways without giving a thought to those affected by his or her actions would be unlikely to agree that he or she did that defiantly or desperately. The stands in questions might, moreover, be taken in many quarters as paradigms of moral rectitude. That view may exhibit a failing, but where the view is widely shared, the failure can hardly be a failure to recognize and acknowledge crucial features of a common practice or language game in place.

It is useful in trying to place the force of a consideration to ask how it is encouraged in moral sensitivities and might be effectively introduced in moral deliberations. If we think of instances in which the range of acknowledged responsibility is extended, it is apparent that it almost always happens through the concern of a few people who dramatize the concern and exhibit the respect for adversely affected people that responsibility requires. The argument is an argument from concern and example and, more subtly, from a demonstration by concern and respect of who is worthy of concern and respect. Such arguments doubtless build on practices in place, but it would be an Hegelian exaggeration to say that they were no more than an articulation of those practices.

In *Fear and Trembling* Kierkegaard allows this form of moral argument but restricts its use to the knight of faith. The knight of faith is said to be a witness, never a teacher.[11] The idea, presumably, is that while a teacher must depend on some consensus in the course of instruction, a witness, standing alone, can do more than exhibit where he or she stands and what he or she wishes to communicate. The contrast is exaggerated. The knight of faith is said to follow a lonely path, narrow and steep, where the knight may walk without meeting a single traveler and where the knight may be a witness, but never a teacher. That description may apply to Kierkegaard's knight of faith, but there are circumstances in which it applies as well to a conscientious and responsible person. There must be many people who, out of concern and an enlarged sense of responsibility, have found themselves standing pretty much alone, with a feeling that they were following a lonely path, and most serious people must have had the thought at one time or another that they might find themselves following such a path. It may be true that not many of us follow a course without a single compatriot, but everyone ready to take a serious moral position must know that in the extreme case they may find themselves doing that. Standing alone or not, the argument for the responsibilities they recognize will be an argument from their concern and from what they do, exhibiting a recognition of those responsibilities. There are a great many circumstances in which standing for a moral position, giving voice to it, and acting on it, is the most that anyone can do.

NOTES

1. S. Lovibond, *Realism and Imagination in Ethics* (Minneapolis: University of Minnesota Press, 1983); J. McDowell, "Noncognitivism and Rule Following," in *Wittgenstein: To Follow a Rule*, ed. S. H. Holtzman and C. M. Leach (London: Routledge and Kegan Paul, 1981), pp. 141–62; D. Wiggins, "Truth, Invention and the Meaning of Life," *Proceedings of the British Academy* (1976): pp. 331–78.
2. Søren Kierkegaard, *Fear and Trembling*, trans. H. Hong and E. Hong, (Princeton: Princeton University Press, 1983).
3. Ludwig Wittgenstein, *Philosophical Investigations*, trans. G. E. M. Anscombe (New York: Macmillan, 1953), #84.
4. Wittgenstein, *Philosophical Investigations*, #85.
5. Ludwig Wittgenstein, *On Certainty*, ed. G. E. M. Anscombe and G. H. von Wright (Oxford: Blackwell, 1969), #140.
6. Kierkegaard, *Fear and Trembling*, p. 9–14.
7. Ibid., pp. 58–59 and 86–87.
8. O. K. Bouwsma, *Wittgenstein Conversations 1949–1951*, ed. J. L. Craft and R. E. Hustwit (Indianapolis: Hackett, 1986), p. 5.
9. Kierkegaard, *Fear and Trembling*, pp. 94–112.
10. Søren Kierkegaard, *The Sickness Unto Death*, trans. W. Lowrie (Princeton: Princeton University Press, 1941), p. 3.
11. Kierkegaard, *Sickness Unto Death*, p. 80.

10. Therapies and the Grammar of a Virtue

ROBERT C. ROBERTS

In 1966 Philip Rieff's *The Triumph of the Therapeutic*[1] began a tradition of social criticism the latest installment of which is Robert Bellah's *Habits of the Heart*.[2] In this literature, psychotherapy is taken to task as a corrupter of moral character—both of persons who engage therapists' services and of ones who, though never seeing a helping professional, imbibe a vocabulary that carries a "therapeutic" conception of human nature and psychic well-being. "Therapy" teaches us to be in touch with our feelings; to be assertive, not letting other people run our lives; to be "authentic"; to assess our relationships by an analysis of their costs and benefits to ourselves; to pursue the unfettered realization of our "potential"; to abjure "musts," "oughts," and "shoulds"; not to be "defensive" but instead "open" and "honest"; not to be rigid but constantly open to change and to have new experiences. The result, say the critics, is individualism, egoism, narcissism, manipulation of persons, superficiality, aimlessness, distrust, anxiety, and rootlessness, to mention just a few mishaps of character.

I agree with the critics that therapies have sometimes corrupted persons and that an analysis of their influence is an important philosophical, ethical, and theological task. But I propose in this paper a method for a more evenhanded and fine-grained assessment than the critics have hitherto produced. In the approach that I propose, therapies are not lumped together but considered one by one (usually with primary reference to the work of their originators) so as to maximize our likelihood of seeing their distinctive features.[3] Or, in another kind of case, the results of the therapeutic influence on a given world of thought are displayed rather precisely without regard to their exact therapeutic origin.[4] And they are assessed not from a generic ethical point of view but from a fairly definite ethical vantage point.[5] Further fineness of grain is achieved by individuating the "virtues" implicit in a therapeutic mode of thought and practice and by offering a method of seeing the deep structural features of these virtues, so as to compare them with their Christian counterparts.

This comparative "grammatical" undertaking will not only allow us to make a Christian-ethical assessment of therapies. It will also be of general interest to those who think about Christian ethics and spirituality, since the grammatical comparison will reflect light back on the ethical and spiritual contours of Christianity. And it may lead us to adopt some insights from the therapists, who after all are theorists of human nature and masters of human transformation.

VIRTUES-SYSTEMS AND THE GRAMMAR OF A VIRTUE

Virtues are traits of human fulfillment, completeness, well-being. Salient ones typically go by names such as "truthfulness," "courage," "equanimity," "patience," "fairness." Very essential to the concept of any given virtue is the patterns of action, emotion, and motivations typical of it and the circumstances in which actions and emotions exemplifying the virtue are appropriate. A virtue's connections to these constitute a part of what I call its "grammar."[6] But a more complete account of the grammar of a virtue requires reference to a certain context in which it is embedded, which I call a virtues-system.

A virtues-system is a system of thought and practice with the following dimensions: (1) a list of virtues; (2) a concept of human nature, an answer to the question, What sort of being is a human? (3) a system of diagnostic concepts that (a) identify forms of human failure or defect ("vices") and (b) explain them; and (4) a set of expedients for effecting change in persons, ultimately for engendering the virtues and eradicating the vices.

The stoicism of Epictetus (born A.D. 55) is a clear example.[7] (I shall alter the order of the four dimensions, for a more natural exposition.)

3. Epictetus notes that all the emotions of human misery (disappointment, anger, grief, fear, anxiety) can be diagnosed as

forms of frustration or the anticipation of it, frustration of being the desire of what circumstances withhold. Thus characteristic vices are covetousness, envy, resentment, obsequiousness. (This last is characteristic because the obsequious individual is afraid he or she will be frustrated if he or she does not show deference to the powerful.) In these vices we make ourselves victims by the "opinion" or "view" we take of things: "What hurts this man is not this occurrence itself—for another man might not be hurt by it—but the view he chooses to take of it (XVI)."

1. The stoic virtues, then, are forms of emotional independence, in which the individual views his or her circumstances as not ingredient to well-being. Well-being is instead a voluntary state of mind: by affirming my mental independence of circumstance, I become content, free, faithful to myself and others, self-respecting, objective, consistent.

4. Epictetus offers a number of exercises for eradicating the stoic vices and instilling the stoic virtues. He recommends that we reconstrue what we consider our *possessions as a trust:* "Never say of anything, 'I have lost it,' but 'I have restored it [that is, given it back].' Has your child died? It is restored (XI; see also XXIV, XXVI)." Other exercises are anticipating departure from some circumstance (VII), contemplating death (XXI), anticipating the worst scenario (XXII), turning attention away from circumstances and toward the state of one's own mind (XXX), and contemplating supposed models of the stoic virtues, such as Socrates and Zeno (XXXIII, L).

2. In this virtues-system, persons are conceived as highly individualized centers of free mental activity locked into a fatalistic system of nature to which they are characteristically tempted to "attach" themselves by their desires and unfitting construals.

Various forms of Christianity are virtues-systems. Let me expound a noneccentric form of Christianity, something that bids fair to be "mere Christianity."

1. In the New Testament, especially in the Epistles, we find lists of virtues, of which there are more than thirty distinct concepts. Here is a representative selection: patience (Ephesians 5, Galatians 5, I Corinthians 13, I Thessalonians 5), peace-

ableness (II Corinthians 13, Romans 12 and 15, I Thessalonians 5, James 3), peace (Romans 5 and 15, Philippians 4, Colossians 3), gratitude (Colossians 3, I Thessalonians 5), contentment (I Timothy 6:6–7, Philippians 4:11, Hebrews 13:5), hope (Romans 5, I Corinthians 13, I Thessalonians 5, I Timothy 4), generosity (II Corinthians 9), hospitality (Romans 12:13), obedience (I Peter 1), compassion (Colossians 3, I Peter 3).

2. In the Christian view, humans are fundamentally communal beings. They are made by God for a particular form of fellowship or "participation" with both God and their fellow humans known as "the kingdom of God." They have some say in the formation of this society, for they are agents, not just in a private mental realm, but in the physical and social world. People are essentially beings under the authority and grace of God.

3. Pride, envy, covetousness, idolatry, anxiety, gluttony, and licentiousness are some representative Christian vices. The occurrence of some vices can be partially explained by reference to other vices—for example, a person is envious because of his or her pride, or anxious because he or she is an idolater—but they are also partially explained sociohistorically, by reference to the Fall and by reference to present temptations and dark forces, evil spirits, principalities, etc., and by free choice.

4. Christianity has a number of practices that are prized, in part, for their power to effect change of character in people: fellowship, confessions, spiritual guidance, public worship, prayer, Scripture reading and interpretation, doing Christian works, meditation, and reading or hearing stories about "saints."

What I call the "grammar" of a virtue is largely a function of the relationships it bears to other items within its constituting virtues-system. For the logical structure (and thus the essential identity)[8] of the virtue is determined by the system in which it is embedded. Thus, for example, the grammar of stoic contentment can be displayed by noting the kind of "view" of things that it involves; what its characteristic counterpart vices are; what rationale or motive is given within the system for seeking contentment;[9] what similarities and differences, as well as dependency-relationships, there are between contentment and other stoic virtues like objectivity and self-respect; what the practices are by which contentment is cultivated; and what conception of the nature of persons lies behind stoic contentment. Remarks detailing these connections, similarities, differences, etc. are called, following Wittgenstein, "grammatical remarks." These intrasystem relationships can be highlighted, too, by *comparing* the grammar of stoic contentment with that of its Christian counterpart (or its Aristotelian, Freudian, Rogerian, or Buddhist counterpart). An important part of the procedure that I am recommending for assessing psychotherapies is such a comparative grammatical analysis.

My procedure turns on observing a formal parallel between Christianity and major psychotherapies, namely, that the latter are virtues-systems.

In the rest of this paper I illustrate the power of a grammatical analysis to produce a perspicuous Christian assessment of therapeutic thinking. The first illustration shows how my approach can penetrate below the surface of thinking that has been influenced by the "therapeutic mentality." I have selected a popular book in the genre of Christian spirituality or ethics, Lewis Smedes' *Forgive and Forget.* [10] The "therapeutic" influence on this book is quite generic and, as far as I can see, cannot be traced to any particular school of psychotherapy. My second illustration is Albert Ellis's rational emotive therapy.[11]

FIRST ILLUSTRATION

Smedes' book is an argument, in therapeutic terms, that forgiveness is a virtue. If you understand what forgiveness is, you will see that it plays such an essential role in mental well-being that to reject it as a virtue is to call into question the value of mental health. But the argument requires that Smedes present a particular conception of forgiveness, and the one he offers is interestingly different from and at odds with that of classical Christianity.

Forgive and Forget, especially in the first fifty pages, invites reading as a series of grammatical remarks about forgiveness, of which the following are a sampling:

1. You cannot forgive events, nature, or systems but only persons.
2. You can forgive someone only if he or she wrongs *you*, not if he or she only wrongs somebody else.
3. You cannot forgive someone for a hurt you do not acknowledge.
4. Forgiveness is only for unfair hurts, not for such things as just punishments and painful therapies; it is for "hurts we don't deserve."
5. It is fitting to forgive someone for causing a hurt even if he or she is not blameworthy for it; it is enough that "we *experience* the hurt as an unfair assault (p. 9)."
6. The emotion of which forgiveness is the dissolution is hatred, directed toward people, not toward evil.
7. Forgiveness is a reconstrual, in newly benevolent terms, of the person forgiven, a seeing with "the magic eyes."
8. The purpose of forgiveness is the healing of the forgiver; it is to claim our "right to be free from hate (p. 12)."
9. The characteristic motive for acts of forgiveness stems from this purpose: it is the forgiver's desire to be healed of hate.
10. Forgiveness cannot be performed for a hurt the forgiver does not remember.

The kind of forgiveness Smedes expounds both overlaps with Christian forgiveness and is significantly different from it. The similarities and differences are revealed by comparing the grammars of the two virtues. I shall call Smedes' concept of forgiveness the "therapeutic" concept and the other the "Christian" concept.

I can illustrate my point by considering remarks (1) and (10) above. The first is clearly an overlap between Christian and therapeutic forgiveness, while the last indicates a difference. Smedes tells of refusing to forgive a friend for a wrong the friend committed against him, on the grounds that Smedes couldn't remember it.

If he had brought back old pain by bringing back my memory, I should have forgiven him. But as it was, I could not really forgive him; I could only love him, and by loving him, heal the separation that he felt, though I did not. (P. 39)

But if a friend convinces me that he or she wronged me (thus fulfilling the condition laid down by remark (3), why should my inability to remember the injury, and thus feel the alienation, be a reason for not forgiving that friend? Why can I not just accept his or her account of the wrong as authoritative and pronounce the friend forgiven? I submit that in the Christian context my failure to remember would not constitute any such impediment to forgiveness. It does impede therapeutic forgiveness, however, because of the connection between forgiving and healing: I can't hate somebody for a wrong I don't remember, so if forgiveness is always a way of healing myself of hate, it can't have any application to wrongs I don't remember. But in Christian forgiveness, the connection with healing is not so tight.

The Purpose is to Heal the Forgiver

Explication of the grammar of a virtue often involves reference to the kind of motive necessary or characteristic for acts exemplifying the virtue. The clear drift of *Forgive and Forget* is that the characteristic motive for forgiving is the forgiver's desire to heal himself or herself of hatred. Smedes notes that sometimes forgiveness leads to reconciliation with the offender, so we can suppose a forgiver might fittingly desire this; but this motive of forgiveness receives much less emphasis than the other.

The motive of self-healing, while not inconsistent with Christian forgiveness, is not paradigmatic. It is hard to imagine Saint Paul exhorting his readers to forgive one another "for each of you has a right to be healed of your hate." It is typical of him to tell them to forgive one another because Christ has forgiven them and in doing so they will be like Christ, or for the sake of harmony in the church, or because in forgiving one another we will become fit for the kingdom of God or ready for the judgment day. In other words, when asked for a rationale for forgiveness, Paul does not speak in *therapeutic* terms, but instead in terms of what is *fitting*, given certain beliefs about the history of God's actions, the character and actions of Jesus, the nature of the church and the coming kingdom.

In an age when people are focused on their own physical fitness and psychological well-being as the noblest and most basic motives for every action, the Pauline rationale for forgiveness will be far less persuasive than the therapeutic one.

FORGIVENESS AND BLAMEWORTHINESS

It seems to be a grammatical feature of Christian forgiveness that it is unfitting to forgive somebody for a hurt for which that person is not blameworthy. It is not enough that the person *seem* blameworthy to me, nor even that I with full conviction *believe* the person to be blameworthy. For forgiveness to be fitting, the person has to *be* blameworthy. If I falsely believe the person to be blameworthy and go through an ever so rich, agonizing, and healing psychological process of forgiving that person's "wrong," still what I have done is at best second best. What is fully appropriate is not to *forgive* the person but to *understand the situation better*.

Just as the connection of forgiveness with the healing is tighter in therapeutic than in Christian forgiveness, we might expect the connection with blameworthiness to be looser. For, through false belief or irrationality, we often *feel* wounded by people who are not in fact blameworthy and thus are inclined to work up a hatred of them that is in need of healing. If the main point of forgiveness is the healing of the forgiver, it seems natural to proscribe forgiving in these cases, too.

At this point Smedes becomes unclear. He recognizes a connection between blameworthiness and forgiveness, but construes it in ways that weaken the concept.

When Bob hung himself, he did not tell anybody what his motives were. Did he have to end his life? Is he to blame for the awesome pain he left behind? Should his wife forgive him? I cannot tell. Only she can tell. (P. 9)

Why say, "Only she can tell"? What makes *her* any special authority on whether Bob is blameworthy? Maybe her status as wife makes her unusually privy to his inmost thought. But it is possible that his therapist or his lawyer has even more insight into his motives. One suspects that whether Bob is "blameworthy" is, for Smedes, not finally an issue about Bob's mental life but about his wife's, and it is for this reason that she is an authority. One suspects that the issue is not really Bob's blameworthiness, but how strongly inclined his wife is to blame him.

Smedes tells us that in deciding whether forgiveness is appropriate we need to "see the difference between feeling the pain that comes from our vulnerability and the pain that comes from being the butt of an unfair attack" (p. 9). Again, the statement is teasingly ambiguous. He seems to be saying it's important to recognize a genuinely "unfair attack." But then the discrimination he prescribes is one between kinds of *feelings of pain*. But surely, if we want to know whether a person is blameworthy, we do not assess the feelings that person has caused us. We *would* do this, however, if we were trying to decide whether to perform an act of therapeutic forgiveness.

The unfairness of hurt is one of the things that makes it an appropriate occasion for forgiving, says Smedes. But unfairness, as he understands it, does not require blameworthiness.

Pain is unfair when we do not *deserve* it, or when it is not necessary. . . . The unfairness of the hurt often lies in the experience of the victim, not in the intention of the one who causes it. (Pp. 9, 12)

Many cases of undeserved and unnecessary pain are not blamable on anyone (an uncle takes your son fishing, and, despite every safety precaution, your son drowns); so this criterion clearly does not make blameworthiness necessary. And many blameworthy actions fall short of being intentional (disasters perpetrated through negligence); so in denying that actions need be intentional to warrant forgiveness, Smedes does not deny my claim (that it is unfitting to forgive somebody for a hurt for which that person is not blameworthy) but a much stronger and less plausible one—indeed a straw man, thus skirting the question we want to ask. To sum up my impression: Smedes is sufficiently attracted (or confused?) by the traditional concept of forgiveness to feel that he ought to work in blameworthiness as a necessary condition of appropriateness. But given his project of a therapeutic concept of forgiveness, he understandably hesitates to do so and finally seems to allow that it is enough that "we *experience* the hurt as an unfair assault" (p. 9, his italics).

Forgiving God

If in Christian forgiveness it is appropriate to forgive somebody for something only if the person is blameworthy for it, then it will make no sense to forgive the Christian God for anything. Smedes acknowledges the grammar: "You may react automatically: God cannot be blamed for anything, so he cannot be forgiven for anything (p. 83)." But our reaction is "automatic" (and presumably unreflective?) and does not deter Smedes from writing one of the longer chapters in the book on "forgiving God."

Would it bother God too much if we *found our peace* by forgiving him for the wrongs we suffer? What if we found a way to forgive him without blaming him? A *special sort of forgiving* for a special sort of relationship? Would he mind? Let us try; let us talk a little, reverently but honestly, about forgiving God. (P. 83, my italics)

My point is that Smedes has indeed found "a special sort of forgiving," not just in this chapter, but throughout the book. This chapter, which may appear odd on first sight, is not odd given the grammar of the therapeutic forgiveness.

So we have before us two overlapping but incompatible concepts of forgiveness, two virtues with different grammars. Therapeutic forgiveness can take God as its object because it only requires that the forgiver *experience* God's acts as unfair. Christian forgiveness cannot take God as its object because it requires that the forgiven one be blameworthy. I do not deny that someone can *think* he or she has forgiven God with Christian forgiveness, but this requires confusion, either about forgiveness or about God. But to think one has enacted therapeutic forgiveness of God requires no confusion, since this kind of forgiving makes grammatical allowance for us to "forgive him without blaming him."

WHAT THE MAGIC EYES SEE

Smedes tells us that forgiveness is a reconstrual, in newly benevolent terms, of the forgiven one, a seeing with "the magic eyes." This is one of the many respects in which the therapeutic and Christian forms of forgiveness overlap. They are both "re-visions" of the offender.

But a distinctive belief informs the vision of the offender in Christian forgiveness, a belief not present in the forgiveness outlined in *Forgive and Forget.*

As we forgive people, we gradually come to see the deeper truth about them, a truth our hate blinds us to, a truth we can see only when we separate them from what they did to us. . . . For the truth about those who hurt us is that they are weak, needy and fallible human beings. . . . They are not *only* people who hurt us; this is not the deepest truth about them. (P. 27)

In the Christian view, the deepest truth about every offender is not that he or she is a "weak, needy, and fallible human being" but that he or she is a forgiven sinner, one for whom Christ died. And not this only, but that he or she is one for whom, *along with me,* Christ died. We are in a common predicament. In God's sight we are in need of being died for, and because Christ did so we are adopted daughters or sons. That the forgiven one is a child of God, in cosmic community with the forgiver, is what is "seen" by the person who most deeply experiences offering Christian forgiveness.

It might be thought that such a particular, historical belief cannot form part of the grammar of any virtue. "Grammar," surely, is a rough synonym for an informal sort of logic; and logic makes no reference to historical events. Normally this would be true. But the doctrine of righteousness through Christ's atoning death for sinners is the hub of the Christian view of the world, the axis upon which everything else turns. And the virtue of forgiveness is especially close to the hub. So in this case, like it or not, a particular historical belief is essential to the grammar of a virtue, and every exposition of Christian forgiveness must give a central place to this belief, just as every instance of distinctively Christian forgiveness involves envisioning the offender in the light of the cross. To put this in the terms of the Christian virtues-system, the historical fact that Christ died for sinners becomes an essential feature of human nature.

SECOND ILLUSTRATION

I turn now to a bona fide psychotherapy, the rational emotive therapy (RET) of Albert Ellis. This therapy is of interest as more than an academic illustration, for it seems to be increasingly adopted and adapted by Christians.

The RET virtues-system is as follows:

1. The central virtues are rationality, self-transparency, mutuality in relationships, responsibility, self-acceptance, equanimity, and a sense of humor.
2. According to Ellis, the human being is a pleasure-seeking,

"rational" (that is, satisfaction-maximizing) individual, part of whose pleasure no doubt comes from his or her interactions with others. The relation to others, however, is not part of human nature; others play the role of *occasions* for individual satisfaction and fulfillment.

3. People get anxious, depressed, and have low self-esteem because they have what Ellis calls "nutty ideas": they tell themselves they "must" have certain things, be a certain sort of person, succeed in specified ways, please others, meet the standards set down by others.

4. So Ellis teaches the client that the belief that he or she "must" succeed in specified ways, "ought not" to be immoral, "should" please others is irrational—that while it might be *nice* to achieve things and please others, the really *important* thing in life is to remain relatively undisturbed and to please oneself.

Because of space constraints, I am going to select just two RET virtues for comparative grammatical analysis; so let me give a quick overview of RET virtues. "Rationality" is a disposition to believe only propositions that can be backed up empirically, not to commit logical fallacies such as overgeneralization when deriving beliefs from evidence, and generally to seek beliefs that promote in oneself such other virtues as mutuality, self-acceptance, and equanimity. Ellis's ideal person is roughly a consistent logical empiricist and a pragmatist of an enlightened hedonist variety. Self-transparency is a general awareness of the influence that beliefs have on one's emotions and behavior and a particular awareness of the bad influence that particular beliefs may have. Thus it is the capacity to "troubleshoot" therapeutically for oneself and is basic for responsibility. RET responsibility is willingness to admit that your nutty emotions, behavior, and beliefs are of your own choosing, and it is willingness to undertake strategies for self-improvement. Mutuality is the ability to maximize your satisfactions insofar as they depend on other people's attitudes and behavior, through maximizing the satisfactions that others experience in relation to yourself. Self-acceptance is the disposition not to rate yourself globally nor to generalize ratings of your particular performances, attitudes, and traits to ratings of your "self." Equanimity is the ability to remain relatively undisturbed and emotionally level in a wide variety of potentially upsetting circumstances. A sense of humor is the ability to see and appreciate, from the perspective of RET rationality, the comical character of your own nutty beliefs.

Let us turn to a grammatical examination of two of these virtues: equanimity and self-acceptance.[12]

MUSTURBATION AND EQUANIMITY

Much of the emotional disturbance, according to Ellis, is a consequence of making unreasonable demands on oneself, one's associates, and one's environment: "What we normally call 'emotional disturbance,' 'neurosis,' or 'mental illness,' then, largely consists of demandingness—or what I now refer to as *musturbation.*"[13] Thus if I believe that I *must* succeed at lovemaking, or *must* get the job I'm interviewing for, or *must* not make a fool of myself in the seminar, I set myself up for experiencing failure as horrible, awful, terrible, catastrophic, and unbearable. I make myself anxious about the prospect of lovemaking, interviewing, and seminar participation, thus increasing my chances of failure. Then when I do fail, I experience despair and loss of self-esteem. It would be much healthier, says Ellis, to believe that while it would be *nice* to succeed in these areas, it is certainly not required; and while it is no doubt *disappointing* to fail, it is hardly catastrophic. Ellis advises that we adopt a *generally* nonmusturbating view of ourselves and the world:

All awfulness or awfulizing, as far as I can see, makes . . . nonsense— because it goes *beyond* empirical reality and invents a *surplus* badness or greater-than-badness to add to the obnoxious element in human living that, because of our choice of basic values (again, surviving and remaining reasonable happy while surviving), actually exist [*sic*].[14]

If we can learn to see *all* our goals as attractive and even important but not required, then we will have the RET virtue of equanimity. We will be emotionally flexible and adaptable, relatively content regardless of what happens. (Since I want to focus on the RET virtues I give this trait a name—something that Ellis does not do. He usually refers only to the vices, such as musturbation, awfulizing, and can't-stand-it-itis, to which this virtue corresponds.)

Another virtue that can be called equanimity is evident in the writings of the apostle Paul. It, too, is an adaptability to varied and potentially distressing circumstances. "Give thanks in all circumstances" (I Thessalonians 5:18, RSV), he says, and "I have learned, in whatever state I am, to be content. I know how to be abased, and I know how to abound; in any and all circumstances I have learned the secret of facing plenty and hunger, abundance and want" (Philippians 4:11–12, RSV). "We are afflicted in every way, but not crushed; perplexed, but not driven to despair; persecuted, but not forsaken; struck down, but not destroyed" (II Corinthians 4:8–9, RSV). "So we do not lose heart. Though our outer nature is wasting away, our inner nature is being renewed every day. For this slight momentary affliction is preparing for us an eternal weight of glory beyond all comparison, because we look not to the things that are seen, but to the things that are unseen . . ." (II Corinthians 4:16–18, RSV). "So we are always of good courage . . ." (II Corinthians 5:6a, RSV). One can detect in these utterances a trait contrary to what Ellis calls "can't-stand-it-itis." Paul has, in his psychological repertoire, the capacity to "stand" a lot of adversities, sufferings, setbacks, and failures, without losing his "cool"—indeed, without losing his *joy!* And an element of this is a kind of nonmusturbation: he does not *demand* that things go his way.

Undoubtedly, demandingness is both a source of unpleasant emotions and, for the Christian, in many cases highly inappropriate spiritually. The Christian ought not to ascribe ultimate significance to such things as sexual performance, succeeding in a job interview, and making a good impression in a seminar. If highly upset over failure in such areas, the Christian betrays spiritual immaturity; were he or she to mature, Christian equanimity would prevent these circumstances from upsetting him or her. The Christian ought to be able to treat these goals with a light touch, out of respect for a more appropriate order of priorities. And it seems that a Christian can even parallel the rational emotive therapist in explaining *how* such attitudes are distortions. The Christian can agree that it is just silly to be ultimately concerned over success in a seminar. If you think critically about the rationale for giving the seminar this degree of significance, it becomes obvious in both the Christian and the RET conceptual schemes that it just doesn't *have* this much significance.

So the Christian and the rational emotive therapist can agree that musturbating in this context is irrational. But their reason is only partly the same. Ellis's rationale is that catastrophes don't exist; nothing is ultimately appalling:

The very worst thing that could happen to me or any other person would presumably consist of our getting tortured to death very slowly. But even that would not be 100% badness—for we could always get tortured to death *even slower!*. . . No matter what you desire, even the moon, you can always conclude in the end, "Well, I just don't seem to get what I want, and maybe I'll never get it. Too bad! I'll just have to live without it, for now and probably forever."[15]

By contrast, the Christian's main rationale for not musturbating is that something else is of such great importance that success in a seminar pales to insignificance by comparison. Not that nothing is of ultimate value, but that something is so much more wonderful and important than seminars and orgasms that the latter get decisively "put in their place." For one with the eternal destiny of a child of God, to "catastrophize" over a job interview is to get things out of perspective, to say the least. For somebody who stands in the noble line of apostles, prophets, saints, and martyrs, "awfulizing" over failure to get an erection is more embarrassing than the failure itself. For one who seeks first the kingdom of heaven—who has only one master whom one loves with all one's heart—"musturbating" over a seminar looks downright comical!

Kierkegaard has sketched the grammar of Christian equanimity in this way:

What the natural man catalogs as appalling—after he has recounted everything and has nothing more to mention—this to the Christian is like a jest. Such is the relation between a child and an adult: what makes the child shudder and shrink, the adult regards as nothing. The child does not know what the horrifying is; the adult knows and shrinks from it. The child's imperfection is, first, not to recognize the horrifying, and then, implicit in this, to shrink from what is not horrifying.[16]

In other words, the mature Christian has gained equanimity in little things like job interviews by getting them into a perspective where, by comparison with what is truly momentous, they are seen as relatively unmomentous. This momentous Christian project Kierkegaard calls becoming a "self": "It is Christian heroism—a rarity, to be sure—to venture wholly to become oneself, an individual human being, this specific individual human being, alone before God, alone in the prodigious strenuousness and this prodigious responsibility."[17]

Christianity raises the stakes by conceiving life as an arena where a person's acceptability before God is at issue; life is a matter of life and death. Such a view of life is, as Kierkegaard remarks, "strenuous," with the potential for producing or heightening "disturbing" emotions like anxiety and despair as well as the happy passion of faith. Ellis proposes that we avoid anxiety and despair by lowering the stakes, by adopting a less strenuous view of life, by making our highest goal not heaven and the love of God and neighbor but "surviving and remaining reasonable happy while surviving"[18] or leading "a longer, pain-avoiding, and satisfaction-filled life."[19]

RET equanimity is thus very different from Christian equanimity. Although both virtues are dispositions not to be "disturbed" by a certain range of things, the two visions of human nature and destiny projected in them are mutually inconsistent. Thus the attitudes themselves have different grammatical structures. Christian equanimity has its background in a Christian "heroism," a passionate pursuit of "the prize of the upward call of God in Christ Jesus" (Philippians 3:14, RSV), a transcendent valuing of human life. RET contentment is achieved precisely by *eschewing* all prizes of upward calls and reducing one's life goals to manageable, obviously attainable ones—by telling oneself that nothing is of ultimate value. The Christian who is clear about the grammar of RET equanimity will judge that to possess this "virtue" is not triumph and health, but spiritual death. Lacking anything that corresponds to the passionate response to an "upward call," the RET virtue of contentment seems to belong to what Kierkegaard calls "the philistine-bourgeois mentality":

The philistine-bourgeois mentality lacks every qualification of spirit and is completely wrapped up in probability. . . . Bereft of imagination, as the philistine-bourgeois always is, whether alehouse keeper or prime minister, he lives within a certain trivial compendium of experience as to how things go, what is possible, what usually happens. In this way the philistine-bourgeois has lost his self and God.[20]

SELF-ACCEPTANCE

Another main source of upset, according to Ellis, is self-evaluation and self-justification. This he sharply distinguishes from rating one's *performances,* which is a legitimate activity, necessary to lead a "rational" life. People strongly tend to let their evaluation of their performances stain their evaluation of their selves. (Indeed, Ellis believes this tendency has a biological basis.)[21] Thus, if I perform an awkward act, I tend to think myself an awkward person; if I do a culpable act, I tend to rate myself as a guilty person, thus feeling overall guilty and depressed. People don't get emotionally disturbed as a result of believing they have performed badly, but only as a result of the further belief that they are therefore bad people. So if we can get them to stop with the former kind of belief, leaving their "selves" a complete evaluative blank, we will eradicate a lot of anxiety and depression.

Ellis draws a strong contrast between self-acceptance and self-esteem:

Self-acceptance means that the individual fully and unconditionally accepts himself whether or not he behaves intelligently, correctly, or competently and whether or not other people approve, respect, or love them. Whereas, therefore, only well-behaving (not to mention perfectly behaving) individuals can merit and feel self-esteem, virtually all humans are capable of feeling self-acceptance.[22]

Here Ellis needs help understanding his own position. He refers to the "feeling" of self-acceptance as though it is something positive, not just an evaluational blankness about oneself. And if I read his therapy right, he does want people to feel good about themselves. It would not really be human flourishing to feel nothing one way or the other about ourselves, but only to have feelings about our performances.

A feeling, on Ellis's view, is a function of a belief or self-statement. But Ellis has instructed us not to believe anything, one way or the other, about the value of our "selves." So how can one have a feeling of self-acceptance? If Ellis wants to retain his implicit and commonsense view that self-acceptance is a "positive" feeling and still deny that it is based on any belief about one's self, he must give up two things: his blanket rejection of self-esteem and his belief that feelings are all grounded in beliefs.

One kind of feeling of self-esteem is a function of the belief that one is performing well or has good traits, and Ellis is right that a person with this kind of self-esteem risks hating himself or herself if the conditions of self-regard cease to be fulfilled. But there is another kind that he should not reject and that is, in fact, what he often refers to as self-acceptance. This is a precognitive "sense of identity" or "feeling of personal security" that derives not from anything one *believes* about oneself, but instead from experiences of being unconditionally regarded by significant others, such as parents (largely long ago in forgotten childhood) and friends. One strongly *construes* oneself as having worth but without this construal being, or being based in, any beliefs about oneself. So there is a self-acceptance that is a positive feeling of worth but is not based on any fallacious (or valid) inference from beliefs about one's performances. I speculate that Ellis has this concept, though he is not forthcoming about this because of his view that all feelings are based in beliefs. The "self-acceptance" he officially countenances, which is the erasure of all evaluative beliefs from one's self-concept, is parasitic upon this precognitive self-esteem. It is only because a person already has some such self-esteem that the process of abandoning self-evaluative beliefs can bring about the feeling of self-acceptance that he mentions in the above quote.

What then is the RET virtue of self-acceptance? It would seem to be a *precognitive self-esteem protected against the overlay of cognitive self-rejection or self-condemnation by a systematic abstinence from all propositions of global self-assessment.*

Let us now evaluate this RET virtue. The first step is to find a counterpart, a Christian virtue as similar as possible to RET self-acceptance. In looking for counterparts it is permissible to pick virtues that are not named, but only exemplified in the New Testament. But when we turn to the New Testament for a virtue resembling self-acceptance, we seem to find nothing exemplified. The modern preoccupation with issues of self-love/hate, self-acceptance/rejection, self-esteem/downing seems strangely absent. The New Testament thought-world is not a world without selves, but it is short on self preoccupation. Krister Stendahl has argued that, contrary to the standard Western interpretation since Augustine, the apostle Paul did not struggle with a guilty conscience nor did he think of the gospel as an answer to any such "subjective" or "psychological" problem as self-rejection, self-hatred, or self-condemnation.[23] In the Gospels we find some examples of self-condemnation, but it is this, rather than a subsequent self-acceptance, that is commended (see Luke 7:36–50 and 16:9–14). It appears that the point of commending self-condemnation in these cases is not as a stage in the process towards fully liking or accepting oneself, but as a recognition of sin for what it is and thus a certain clarity about what the kingdom of God is and what acceptance or forgiveness by God is. Indeed, we find a great deal in the New Testament about God's acceptance of sinners, at the same time that we find nothing about their acceptance of themselves.

It would be hopeless for twentieth century Christians to be so rigidly biblicist as to reject any virtue in the family of self-acceptance just because the New Testament has none. Whether the concern is biblical or not, self-esteem issues are inescapable for us, and, in the light of the gospel, it is incredible to think that self-condemnation, for which there is such abundant biblical warrant, should be the last word. Besides this, the New Testament contains conceptual materials, such as forgiveness, reconciliation, the love of God, being a child of God, and others, that have a clear bearing on Christian self-acceptance. So it seems right to *construct* a virtue-concept on these lines.

The conceptual materials I just referred to will be beliefs and images concerning who believers are. Distinctive about the Christian virtue of self-acceptance are the *terms* in which the person accepts himself or herself. These beliefs will be evaluative ones such as that I am a sinner, that God loves me and nothing can separate me from God's love, that I am destined for an eternal weight of glory, that I have rebelled against God and am helpless apart from grace, that God has adopted me along with these others to be God's child.

Implicit in the New Testament are two different modes of self-evaluation, which we might call the imputation mode and the responsibility mode. In the imputation mode a person is evaluated, apart from performances, by relationship to someone—cither to Adam, in which case the individual is a sinner (a member of a race of sinners), or to Christ as one justified by his blood and saved by him from the wrath of God (Romans 5). In the responsibility mode a person is evaluated on the basis of performances. Because the person has scorned some of God's children, refused them succor in time of need, and committed other identifiable sins, he or she is a sinner (Matthew 25). The more deeply a self-condemning person comes to construe himself or herself in these terms and at the same time to rejoice in the positive self-evaluation (forgiven, accepted, adopted as son or daughter), the more Christianly self-accepting he or she is.

Thus we see a stark grammatical difference between Christian self-acceptance and RET self-acceptance. To accept oneself on the RET model is to avoid all terms of self-evaluation, so that the only feeling of self-acceptance left is whatever precognitive self-esteem one possesses. On the Christian model, it is to adopt some definite *terms* of self-evaluation and consequently to feel a variety of "rejoicing" emotions such as gratitude, hope, and peace, now focused, in a way somewhat different from New Testament examples, on oneself. A therapist who succeeded in Ellis's strategy of getting the client to forswear all global self-evaluations would also have precluded the client's development of Christian self-acceptance.

This is a significant point at which Ellis's psychotherapy resists Christian integration. However, much of the actual use of RET disputation of self-evaluations might be compatible with Christian practice. A person who insists on deprecating one's self because one makes insignificant social mistakes needs to see that such mistakes hardly makes one an overall jerk. Much of the therapy with some individual might turn out to be correcting this sort of mistake. But in addition to this ground clearing, the Christian therapist will have some global self-conceptualizations to promote, and these will be central to the formation of self-acceptance.

CONCLUSION

No virtue is an island. Each virtue gets its character from the surrounding geography of concepts and practice—what I have called the virtues-system—to which it belongs. Applying Wittgenstein's idea of conceptual grammar to virtues allows us to see deeper differences between traits that, because they go by the same name or issue in often similar behavior, look deceptively the same.[24] Most of the psychotherapies that have proliferated in the twentieth century are virtues-systems. This is why they effectively compete with the traditions of Christian and civic virtues that we have inherited from earlier ages. The social critics of therapy, speaking out of those traditions, are right to raise a cry of alarm about these powerful new systems of self-understanding and personal formation. I have suggested that the concept of the grammar of a virtue can refine the practice of assessing therapies. It can help us to represent more perspicuously just where and how the therapies diverge from our orienting tradition—and also help us to be more open to features that can be borrowed from them, and confident that in so borrowing, we are not putting in jeopardy the virtues upon which we refuse to compromise.

NOTES

1. Philip Rieff, *The Triumph of the Therapeutic* (New York: Harper & Row, 1966).
2. Robert Bellah et al., *Habits of the Heart* (New York: Harper & Row, 1985). Other books in this tradition include Alasdair MacIntyre's *After Virtue* (Notre Dame: University of Notre Press, 1981), Christopher Lasch's *The Culture of Narcissism* (New York: Warner Books, 1979), and Paul Vitz's *Psychology as Religion* (Grand Rapids: Wm. B. Eerdman's Publishing Co., 1977).
3. See the analysis below of Albert Ellis's rational emotive psychotherapy.
4. See the analysis below of Lewis Smedes's *Forgive and Forget*.
5. Mine is Christianity; the method allows for others, requiring only that the assessment be done frankly from *some* definite vantage point.
6. My use of this term for the ruled and connected and context-hewn character of virtue-concepts derives from Ludwig Wittgenstein. My initial attention to the idea and subsequent concentrated use of it are due to the incitement of my teacher, Paul L. Holmer. See Holmer's book *The Grammar of Faith* (San Francisco: Harper & Row, 1978).
7. My references are to *The Enchiridion*, trans. Thomas W. Higginson (Indianapolis: Bobbs Merrill Company, 1948).
8. "*Essence* is expressed by grammar. . . . Grammar tells what kind of object anything is." (Wittgenstein, *Philosophical Investigations*, part 1, #371,373)
9. Some virtues are directly exemplified in actions, while others are not. Stoic contentment and Christian hope are examples of virtues that are not directly exemplified in actions. For virtues that are directly exemplified in actions (for example, Christian compassion or Aristotelian courage), the range of motives proper for such actions is an important determinant of the virtue's grammar.
10. Lewis Smedes, *Forgive and Forget* (San Francisco: Harper & Row, 1984). The material in this section is excerpted, with revisions, and with permission, from my article "Forgiveness as Therapy," *The Reformed Journal* 36 (July 1986).
11. For an application of this approach to the psychotherapy of Carl Rogers, see

my "Carl Rogers and the Christian Virtues," *Journal of Psychology and Theology* 13 (1985): pp. 263–73.

12. The account of these two virtues is excerpted, in revised form, from my article "Psychotherapeutic Virtues and the Grammar of Faith," *Journal of Psychology and Theology,* forthcoming.

13. Albert Ellis, *Handbook of Rational-Emotive Therapy* (New York: Springer Publishing Co., 1977), p. 27.

14. Ibid., p. 25.

15. Ibid., pp. 23, 26.

16. Søren Kierkegaard, *The Sickness Unto Death,* trans. Howard Hong and Edna Hong (Princeton: Princeton University Press, 1980), p. 8.

17. Ibid., p. 5

18. Ellis, *Handbook,* p. 25.

19. Ibid., p. 110.

20. Kierkegaard, *Sickness,* p. 41.

21. Albert Ellis, "The Biological Basis of Human Irrationality," *Journal of Individual Psychology* 32 (1976): pp. 145–68.

22. Ellis, *Handbook,* pp. 101–102.

23. Krister Stendahl, "The Apostle Paul and the Introspective Conscience of the West," *Harvard Theological Review* (1963): pp. 199–215.

24. It may also possibly allow us to see deeper similarities between traits that look superficially different.

11. Inspiration and the Heart

PATRICK SHERRY

In recent times consideration of the concept of inspiration has been confined within a limited compass. Christian theologians have been mainly concerned with the question of Biblical inspiration; and since the authority of Scripture (especially its truth) has been an important issue for nearly two centuries, they have often had a very intellectualistic view, seeing it as divine instruction or dictation or as an illumination of the mind. Secular writers have subsumed the question under what has come to be called the "psychology of creativity" and have sought to investigate the sources of originality among artists, writers, and creative scientists. In so confining the areas of discussion, people have ignored Wittgenstein's advice to feed on a wide diet of examples[1] and have thus impoverished the concept. A further impoverishment is seen in the way in which people try to fit inspiration into an oversimple explanatory pattern (and here I include both the appeal to the concept of inspiration as an explanation of creativity, and the further question of explaining inspiration itself). There is a widespread tendency, both among religious and secular writers, to see inspiration as a psychological process, the antecedents of which must be traced back either to divine intervention or to unconscious mental processes. Since, however, so many of the relevant factors are, it seems, as yet unknown, inspiration comes to take on the character of an explanatory "black box" or "something I know not what." Thus, Rosamund Harding concludes her fascinating study of the operation of inspiration amongst artists and scientists with the following definition:

Inspiration may thus be defined as the result of some unknown factor accidentally met with operating on the mind of the man of science or artist at that particular moment when it is pent up to a certain tension. . . .[2]

Such a definition is inadequate for many reasons; but the main weakness to be noted now is that it says nothing of the *quality* of the ideas or products that lead people to describe them as "inspired." Her definition would cover the emergence of the trivial and the mediocre as well as the brilliance of genius.

My purpose in this essay will be to try to provide a fuller and richer concept of inspiration and then, in the light of this, to look briefly again at the question of explanation. I think that the two topics mentioned at the beginning, biblical inspiration and artistic or scientific originality, are but fragments broken off from a larger whole. My strategy in enlarging the concept of inspiration will be to look particularly at some other areas of life, namely ethics and the emotions, and to argue that there is something that might be called "moral inspiration" or "inspiration of the heart."

ON "INSPIRATION"

Before I look at these particular areas, however, I need to make two very fundamental points about the nature of the inspiration that are often ignored: first, the term "inspiration" means literally "blowing upon" or "breathing into" and is not a technical concept either in psychology or in theology; and second, as I have suggested in my comment on Harding's definition, it is used to express a judgment about the quality of things, especially with regard to beauty, goodness, and truth, as well as about their provenance. In both these respects the term "inspiration" is somewhat like that of "enlightenment."

My first point can be verified by consulting dictionaries and by comparing the use of Greek and Latin terms like *epipneō, epipnoia, inspiro, inspiratio,* and *afflatus.* It should also be remembered that inspiration is closely related to another rich and important concept, that of "spirit," which originally meant "wind" or "breath" in Greek, Latin, and Hebrew. In many biblical passages there is a deliberate play on words, for example, John 3:8 ("the wind/spirit blows where it wills") and John 20:22. If, as I have argued elsewhere,[3] the Bible often envisages the spirit of God as a power that "blows through" or permeates people, giving or heightening certain capacities particularly by producing a change of heart, then it would seem that inspiration was originally seen as an empowering of this kind. Unfortunately "spirit" has become a dead metaphor for most people by now, so that many contemporary philosophers and theologians are content to define it in terms of immaterial substances or incorporeal persons without any seeming awareness of its historical background and wealth of connotations. "Inspiration," too, is perhaps going the same way: it is often nowadays used as a synonym for encouragement or incitement. This fact and the dead hand of psychologists may do for it what philosophers and theologians have done for "spirit"! But here the living experience of poets and artists may at least slow down the process of banalization: Shelley, for instance, was well aware of the metaphorical character of the term when he mentioned inspiration in his *A Defence of Poetry* and said, "[T]he mind in creation is a fading coal, which some invisible influence, like an inconstant wind, awakens to transitory brightness."[4]

This consideration means that we should not look for an exact definition of the term; nor should we look for a single essence of inspiration, either in religious or secular contexts; nor should we assume that there is a single mode of operation: sometimes inspired people have felt seized by an external power,[5] sometimes it is more like sudden clarity of perception. In any case, as I shall show, the term has been employed much more widely in the past than in recent usage. So, again, there are good reasons for resisting its narrowing.

The second point that needs to be made at the outset is that to describe someone or something as inspired is usually to pass a favorable judgment on their quality.[6] This is so even in the case of trivial or derivative uses of the term, as when we talk of making inspired choices or guesses. An "inspired choice" by an employer is finding an unexpectedly brilliant performer for a job. And by someone shopping for presents, it is finding just the right gift. Conversely, to describe someone or something as "uninspired" is to criticize them as boring, mediocre, or unimaginative. To adopt a strategy of "Buggins' Turn" is to risk an uninspired choice in promoting employees, as to buy pens, after-shave lotion, and so on may be to betray a lack of inspiration in buying presents. Usually, however, we speak of inspiration when more serious issues are afoot, particularly with regard to outstanding examples of truth (both in the case of scientific discovery and in that of biblical inspiration), beauty, and goodness. Here it is not just a matter of passing a favorable verdict, but of expressing one's wonder. To describe a work of art as inspired is to convey a sense of the mysterious or miraculous, as well as to praise its excellence. Such judgments are often passed by artists on their own work when they recognize that they have surpassed themselves by doing something unforeseen and unplanned. In his *Critique of Judgment,* Kant remarked that the creators of works of genius cannot describe or indicate scientifically how they bring about their products or how they come by their ideas. A creative genius has not the power to devise works at will, nor can the genius give others precepts to enable them to produce similar works. The use of the term "genius" in such contexts is, Kant surmised, probably derived from *genius,* in the sense of "that peculiar guiding and guardian spirit given to man at his birth, from whose suggestion these original ideas proceed" (#46, translated by J. H. Bernard).

Sometimes the judgment that someone or something is inspired may be made retrospectively. Again, it is a matter of expressing wonder when discerning extraordinary quality. Thus, in one of the best treatments of the question of biblical inspiration, *Confessions of an Enquiring Spirit,* Coleridge wrote:

in the Bible there is more that *finds* me than I have experienced in all other books put together; . . . the words of the Bible find me at greater depths of my being; and . . . whatever finds me brings with it an irresistible evidence of its having proceeded from the Holy Spirit.[7]

Whereas many Christian apologists have inferred that the Bible must be true because God has inspired it, Coleridge seemingly proceeds in the opposite direction and discerns the Bible's inspiration in its quality of spiritual depth. More recently, Karl Rahner has related the question of the inspiration of the Bible to its canonicity: he argues that the early Church selected just the canon it did because that canon seemed to crystallize the authentic apostolic faith.[8] Here, too, there is an appeal to the retrospective nature of judgment about the importance of the Bible, though of a different kind from Coleridge's appeal.

WIDENING THE CONCEPT

Later on in the same work, Coleridge called for a widening of the concept when he distinguished between the narrow sense of inspiration as "inspired revelation" and a wider sense of the term where "the writer speaks or uses and applies his existing gifts of power and knowledge under the predisposing, aiding and directing actuation of God's Holy Spirit" (p. 77). He saw the latter kind of inspiration as something that all Christians might hope and pray for, to be related to the presence of the Holy Spirit in all true believers. A similar distinction was made about the same time by Søren Kierkegaard, in a passage in his *Journals* written in October 1834. There he said that inspiration means either exclusively the activity of the apostles as they were writing the New Testament or something extended over their whole lifetime:

We find no basis in the New Testament for the former view; on the contrary, what is referred to, the communication of the Holy Spirit, is something which must be regarded as being stretched out over their whole lifetime.[9]

Elsewhere he explained how the communication of the Holy Spirit might transform the lives of contemporary believers. In his discourse "It is the Spirit that Giveth Life,"[10] he described the Holy Spirit as the "life-giving spirit" and said that the new life that is given involves a death: death to selfishness, the world, and earthly hope. The Comforter only came after the horrors of Christ's passion and death; but still the Comforter came. And the Comforter comes now, bringing faith, hope against hope, and real love. But the work of the Spirit, the Comforter, in us is often uncomfortable, for we are treated like horses driven by a skilled coach driver who stretches them.

Here, then, we have inspiration subsumed under the communication of the Holy Spirit, the life-giving and transforming spirit. This proposal is, I think, correct. It is in accord with the meaning of the term; and it is not a novel proposal, for if we look back over the centuries, we find that earlier generations of Christians had a far wider understanding of inspiration than our contemporary one. Saint Thomas Aquinas, for example, used the term *inspiratio* of the gifts of the Holy Spirit, that is, wisdom, understanding,

knowledge, counsel, piety, fortitude, and fear of the Lord (in
Summa Theologiae 1a2ae.68.1). He said that they come through
divine inspiration and that they dispose people to become readily
mobile to this inspiration. Elsewhere, although he employed the
terms *inspiratio* and *inspirare* relatively rarely, he used them of faith,
repentance, good intentions, devotion, and holy desires, as well as
of prophecy and—very rarely—of Scripture.[11] Similarly, several
early Christian Fathers, countering the view that inspiration was
limited to the Jewish scriptures, claimed that it was now found in
the Church; they spoke of it in connection with, for example, the
work of elders, prophets, and preachers, the building of churches,
and the election of bishops.[12]

It is hardly surprising that the early Christians used the concept
of inspiration so widely, since they would naturally let its use be
molded by the related concept of spirit. Now in the Bible, this
term, too, is used very widely. When used of the spirit of God, it
expresses the way in which God "blows through" or "breathes
into" the world. It is used of God's creation (Genesis 1:2, 2:7), but
usually of more specific, outstanding endowments, for instance,
Samson's strength (Judges 14:6), the skill, perception, and knowledge of the craftsman, Bezalel (Exodus 35:31), the inspiration of
prophets (Numbers 11:25, Ezekiel 11:5), the gifts already mentioned with reference to Aquinas (Isaiah 11:1f.), the charisms and
fruit of the Spirit listed by Saint Paul (I Corinthians 12:8–11; Galatians 5:22), and the guidance of the early Church (Acts 8:29, 9:31,
13:2).[13] The particular connection that I would like to bring out,
however, is that made between the Spirit of God and the human
heart. Ezekiel sees the Spirit of God as creating a new heart:
removing the heart of stone and giving a heart of flesh instead
(Ezekiel 36:26f.). Similarly, one of the few references in the Old
Testament to God's "Holy Spirit" associates it with the creation
of a "clean heart" and with repentance (Psalms 51:10f.). The New
Testament writers often speak of the Spirit as being located in
human hearts (Romans 5:5; II Corinthians 1:22; Galatians 4:6) and
as leading to wisdom and understanding (I Corinthians 2:12–15,
12:8) and to works of love (Galatians 5:22, Ephesians 3:16f.). The
presence of the Spirit is seen as essentially linked, too, with repentance, prayer, and faith (Acts 2:38; Romans 8:15f.).

It should be pointed out here that the biblical writers did not make the kind of contrast that we make between the head and the heart, sometimes treating the latter as the source of irrationality. For them the heart was the person, the seat of reason as well as the will and emotions, which is aware of God's presence and determines conduct, but which may also be the source of the evil intentions that make a person unclean (Matthew 15:18–20). Hence, Christian tradition can speak not only of "hardness of heart" but of "blindness of heart."[14] In one of his sermons, Saint Bernard used the striking phrase "cleansing the eyes of our heart," something produced by prayerful contemplation and leading to great joy in the Spirit of God (*De Diversis* 5:4–5).

INSPIRATION AND THE HEART

I need to go on now to say more about why it is still appropriate to speak of inspiration in this way. So far my approach has been mainly historical: I have shown that the term "inspiration" has been used much more widely in the past than in the present and that in the last century two writers, Coleridge and Kierkegaard, advocated contemporaneously the restoration of a wider usage. But my appeal is not merely to history. I want to go on to give an argument showing why the usage *should* be widened and to provide some illustrations from the moral and emotional life. Such examples are needed because, if we simply equate inspiration with the presence and guidance of the Holy Spirit, we fail to explain why the term has acquired its particular connotations of creativity and imagination.

My argument is one from consistency, and it is this: We already use the term "inspiration" of that enhancement of people's capacities whereby they create things of beauty or perceive and formulate outstandingly striking truths. So, by analogy, we should also use the term of that enhancing of people's capacities in which their emotional and moral range is extended. Such enhancement gives rise to particular creative moral actions or to the perception of new patterns of goodness—or to both these things. In these circumstances it seems appropriate to speak of "moral vision" or of "moral imagination" (to borrow a term of Sabina Lovibond's).[15] Let me give some examples to illustrate what I have in mind.

The enhancement of capacities here may involve the recognition of new kinds of claims laid on us—something that may be challenging and, as Kierkegaard remarked, uncomfortable; or it may involve an awareness of the possibility of new forms of emotional response and of new kinds of relationship with others. Such an awareness and inspiration of the affections is described by Dante in his encounters with Beatrice:

I must tell you that whenever and wherever she appeared, I, in anticipation of her miraculous greeting, could not have considered any man my enemy; on the contrary, a flame of charity was lit within me and made me forgive whoever had offended me. And if, at this moment, anyone had asked me about anything, I could only have answered, my face all kindness: "Love."[16]

As an example of particular inspired actions, we might instance Christ's forgiveness of his tormentors from the cross (Luke 23:34). There is a medieval English hymn, "The Seven Words," that begins:

Jesus, he stood with mournful cheer,
His friends he saw exceeding few;
His foes he shrove with sudden grace,
Saying, "They wis not what they do."[17]

This, I think, captures exactly what I would call an inspiration of the heart. Christ's forgiveness would have been totally unexpected, given his painful situation and the natural human desire to exact vengeance on enemies; hence it came to them as a "sudden grace." Yet it was not a transitory feeling: for he *did* something ("his foes he shrove"), and this action went with an intellectual judgment that they did not know what they were doing. Furthermore, his action established a pattern of goodness and has served as an inspiration for subsequent generations—somewhat in the way that an "inspired" work of art may be said to inspire those who appreciate it. It was, one might say, an exercise of moral vision, one that opened up new possibilities of feeling and response for others. Although it was a single action, it was an expression of a disposition to love one's enemies, as taught earlier in the Sermon on the Mount (Matthew 5:44).

This example suggests that moral inspiration has both particular and general aspects. Although the inspiration may come on a single occasion, it is to be related to a virtue, moral principle, or value, and may, therefore, serve as a pattern of behavior for others subsequently.

Sometimes, however, the general aspect of moral inspiration is realized not through particular actions but through perceptions or insights. I have suggested that such moral perceptions or insights are analogous to the "inspired" realization of truths in other fields, for example, science. It may be that the inspiration appropriate to Proverbs and some other biblical "wisdom" literature was of this kind. But as an example of such a perception, I would instance the antislavery law passed by the Grand Council of Dubrovnik in 1417, which imposed penalties on slave traders

. . . since it must be held to be base, wicked and abominable, and contrary to all humanity, and to redound to the great disgrace of our city, that the human form, made after the image and similitude of our Creator, should be turned to mercenary profit, and sold as if it were brute beast.[18]

Such insights may come to people in a variety of ways. Often they are sparked off by particular events—perhaps the city fathers of Dubrovnik had actually witnessed examples of the degradation of slavery. Sometimes there is a move from one general truth to another as a matter of consistency. Thus, to choose a more contentious example, Dorothy Day drew an analogy between nuclear warfare and the Holocaust when she asked the challenging question: "If it is wrong to herd people into ovens, then is it not also wrong to hurl ovens at people?" Similarly, Karl Marx drew an analogy between slavery and the working conditions of early industrialization that Jacques Maritain described as "the great lightning-flash of truth which traverses all his work . . . this intuition pregnant with Judeo-Christian values."[19] Lastly, there may be a move from the general to the particular, as when reading or hearing a moral insight serves as a source of moral inspiration to the individual. Thus, Jesus' parables, which might themselves be described as inspired and as expressions of moral imagination, evoke insights in their hearers and readers with regard both to what must be done and to our present conduct (we may realize that, like the priest and the Levite, we have often passed by on the other side). Similarly, reading works like Kierkegaard's *Purity of Heart* and *Works of Love* may make us embarrassingly aware of our lukewarmness and double-mindedness, our evasions and self-deception; such works expose our moral sickness and suggest remedies. So, again, there is an analogy with the inspired work of art that continues to inspire its beholders.

My use of the terms "insight" and "perception" seems to suggest that moral inspiration involves the discernment of the *truth* of moral judgment, that my account is wedded to a "cognitivist" view of moral judgment. This is indeed so. But Sabina Lovibond rightly points out that such a stance does not preclude the development of moral imagination, whereby people come to see things from an unfamiliar point of view, and that moral realism need not limit one to a constricting conservatism that takes account only of strict obligation and "unimaginative" notions of virtue (loc. cit.). More to the point here, a cognitivist account of moral judgment does not require one to discount the emotions. I have already made the point that the biblical concept of the heart does not exclude intellectual judgment. In recent times many people have questioned the common disjunctions made between the head and the heart, the reason and the passions, cognition and affection. They have pointed out that emotions are ways of attending to the world and seeing things, or, as Robert Roberts describes them, "concern-based construals."[20] Thus gratitude involves seeing something as a gift and, therefore, believing that it is such, whilst anger and indignation express unfavorable judgments about their objects, judgments that may be assessed as reasonable or irrational, justified or hasty and unfair. Similarly, our affections and commitments express implicit intellectual judgments about the worth of their objects. As Jonathan Edwards put it elegantly, "Holy affections are not heat without light."[21]

One commonly noted feature of inspiration is that it comes suddenly and unexpectedly and is apparently not under our control. Of course, people have recommended various techniques for producing it: Schiller kept rotten apples in his desk; he and Grétry immersed their feet in ice-cold water; Balzac worked wearing a monastic gown, whilst de Musset and Guido Reni preferred magnificent costumes; and the aesthetician Baumgarten advised poets seeking inspiration to ride on horseback, to drink wine in moderation, and, provided that they were chaste, to look at beautiful women.[22] But more often, artists have been advised to wait and to prepare for the coming of inspiration by getting on with their work, being open and observant, reading widely, and so on. Thus, Rosamund Harding shows that, although Tchaikovsky called inspiration a "supernatural and inexplicable force," he also counseled the need to work regular hours whether or not one feels inspired, saying, "We must be patient, and believe that inspiration will come to those who can master their *disinclination*" (op. cit., pp. 12, 35). Similarly, in his classic study, *The Road to Xanadu: A Study in the Ways of the Imagination,* Livingston Lowes used Coleridge's notebook of 1795–98 to lay bare the ideas and wide program of reading that formed the soil from which both *The Rime of the Ancient Mariner* and *Kubla Khan* grew. Lowes quotes the mathematician Henri Poincaré as saying, "The unconscious work is not possible, or in any case, not fruitful, *unless it is first preceded and then followed by a period of conscious work.*"[23]

The question naturally arises, then, of whether there are states of mind that provide fertile soil for moral inspiration and, indeed, of whether we can cultivate them to prepare ourselves for such inspiration. Later on in his *Journals,* Kierkegaard wrote, "Just as one does not begin a feast at sunrise, but at sundown, just so in the spiritual world; one must first work forward for some time before the sun really shines for us and rises in all its glory. . . ."[24] Of course, it might be replied that inspiration is, in theological terms, the communication of the Holy Spirit, which is wholly gratuitous. But at least there seem to be ways of being open to inspiration; and in the case of moral inspiration, one might say, putting it sententiously, that inspiration requires aspiration. Here I am thinking of a cluster of related qualities: purity of heart, sensitivity, honesty about one's failings and a desire to overcome them, living with a certain sober tone, humbly awaiting wisdom and guidance, and so on. Those who are faced with difficult choices, say with regard to marriage or careers, know that it is often necessary to wait—not in the passive sense of doing nothing, but in the active sense of remaining attentive and open to guidance or advice and willing to act when the appropriate *kairos* comes. To be *un*inspired here is to be self-satisfied, to simply settle in a routine or follow the crowd, and to show a lack of openness to new truths or to anything that may disturb one's complacency. Of course, inspiration is such that it may "blow through" our defenses. But we can resist our good impulses, something akin to what Saint Paul calls "quenching the Spirit" (I Thessalonians 5:19). Such betrayals are often accompanied by a feeling of heaviness, a dampening of the spirits. Acceptance of inspiration, on the other hand, is often accompanied by joy or at least by a sense of the rightness of things.

Acceptance of moral inspiration in all the ways that I have mentioned, namely, the raising of one's moral and emotional capacities and the consequent creative moral actions and perception of new patterns of goodness, eventually produces that change of heart, that remaking of the person, to which Christianity aspires.

INSPIRATION AND EXPLANATION

Having given two arguments (one historical, the other by analogy) for enlarging the concept of inspiration, it remains for me to see if such an enlargement throws any light upon the questions of explanation that I raised at the beginning about what sort of explanation an appeal to inspiration provides and whether we can explain inspiration itself.

Recent religious treatments of inspiration largely confine themselves to biblical inspiration, whilst secular ones tend to treat the concept as a psychological or cognitive one, describing the sudden occurrence of good ideas, something that is apparently not under our control. Secular writers recognize that as a matter of history the concept of inspiration is originally a metaphor with religious connotations, but they wish to "demythologize" it by subsuming it under the study of creativity and, in some cases, by replacing the appeal to God or gods with the concept of the unconscious.[25] Many of them realize that it is difficult to explain creativity in terms of any "covering law" pattern of explanation. As Ian Jarvie puts it, "Creative achievements are unique events; explanatory progress is made only with repeatable events. Hence, there is something inexplicable about creativity."[26] He remarks that purported explanations of creativity are suspect because, if they were successful, they would explain it *away*. Another contributor to the same volume, Larry Briskman, presses the point further when he argues that if we could explain creativity in terms of covering law, we would be able to deduce its attainment from the presence of certain conditioning factors and also provide a kind of recipe for being creative.

He concludes that the most we can explain is the *possibility* of creativity.[27]

At the moment there seem to be two main models of explanation of inspiration or creativity that are prevalent, one secular and one religious, both of which have a psychological slant. The first, associated particularly with Arthur Koestler, sees creativity as the discovery of hidden similarities and the connection of previously unconnected frames of reference. Thus, Koestler recommends what he calls "bisociative" thinking and says that "the creative act consists in combining previously unrelated structures in such a way that you get more out of the emergent whole than you have put in."[28] The second, religious model, sees inspiration in terms of God's working through our psychological processes. William James appealed to such a model when he explained religious experience on the hypothesis that on the "hither side" the source of saving experiences is the subconscious self, but that on the "farther side" their source is God.[29] The model has been applied to biblical inspiration by writers who eschew talk of divine dictation or the supernatural communication of divine revelation, preferring instead to construe such inspiration in terms of God's increasing a writer's level of spiritual insight or intellectual vision.[30] Roman Catholic writers often appeal here to the scholastic notions of "secondary causes" and "instrumental causality"; they describe inspiration in terms of the Holy Spirit's working through the ordinary psychological apparatus of the inspired writer (sometimes distinguishing this process from the pagan notion of "possession," in which the faculties of the writers seemed to be suspended as they went into a trance, and assimilating it rather to the concept of grace).[31]

Now if I am right in extending the concept of inspiration to the realms of ethics and the emotions, both models turn out to be inadequate (though not wholly erroneous). Koestler's model of explanation has the general weakness of failing to reckon with a point that I made at the outset, that describing someone or something as inspired is often an expression of wonder or of admiration for sheer excellence. His recommendation of "bisociative" thinking gives us a recipe for producing novelties, which may or may not turn out to have the qualities of excellence that are desired. More specifically, his approach seems inappropriate in many moral and emotional contexts: Are Jesus' words of forgiveness from the cross indeed an example of bisociative thinking?

The religious model is attractive to many people today because the appeal to the notion of secondary causes conveys some idea of how God may work through the ordinary course of events without intervening miraculously, and so it seems to avoid theological crudity. It is also eirenic, for it sees religious and secular explanations of inspiration or creativity as complementary rather than as rivals: for psychological explanations are seen as attempts to delineate the nature of the mental processes through which the Spirit of God communicates. The trouble is, however, that in practice, the model turns out to be either too limited or too general. It is too limited when the concept of inspiration is restricted to biblical inspiration (as it is, for example, by Luis Alonso Schökel, who regards "inspiration" as a technical term, standing for a charism pertaining to language).[32] Once, however, such a dictatorial limitation of the concept is rejected, because it ignores so much later usage, the model becomes too wide: it does not by itself help us to distinguish inspiration from other ways in which the Spirit works through us, for instance, in religious experience, guidance, and assistance. We would need to go on here to convey the notion of creativity and to make specific connections with the concepts of goodness, beauty, and truth.

The inadequacies of both models stem, I think, from the fragmentation of the concept of the inspiration that I noted earlier: both have been developed to cover particular areas, the one scientific creativity, humor, and art; the other, the Bible. There is often, too (particularly in the case of the secular model, perhaps because of its preoccupation with the suddenness and unexpectedness of creative ideas), a tendency to regard inspiration as a psychological process. Wittgenstein's misgivings about labeling understanding, intending, and so on as "mental processes" (compare *Zettel* 446, for example) should be borne in mind here. But more specifically, Livingston Lowes made an important point when he concluded his remorseless and wide-ranging study of the sources of Coleridge's inspiration by saying that he could merely lay bare the way in which the poet's creative genius had worked on his material through processes that are common to humankind; but in his case, those processes were "superlatively enhanced" (op. cit., p. 431). If one were interested merely in psychological processes and their genesis, one could as well do a study of William McGonagall as of Coleridge!

I do not propose now to suggest a further model; indeed, as my citations from Jarvie, Briskman, and Lowes indicate, I am unclear about what an adequate *theory* explaining inspiration would be like—can we explain excellence? We need to ask now whether even the fullest psychological account could ever explain the *quality* of the content of inspiration and whether religious appeals to inspiration are ever simply attempts to find a causal explanation.

I suggest, in conclusion, that what is characteristic of a religious view of inspiration is that it is put into a wider pattern of explanation involving an appeal to something like Aristotle's notions of final and formal causes. If we restrict ourselves to the question of whether God intervenes directly in our psychological processes or works though secondary causes (or does both), we are limiting ourselves to the level of efficient causes. But a religious account of inspiration also considers its purpose and the relationship between its content and the nature of God. Its purpose is seen in terms of our salvation or, more widely, in terms of our mirroring God's creativity through moral vision, scientific research, and artistic creation. Similarly, its content may be related to God's nature, for the three activities mentioned may also be seen as ways in which we dimly reflect God's perfections. Thus, beauty can be regarded as a reflection of God's glory, our goodness as a sharing in God's goodness, and our perception of truth as a sharing in God's wisdom and knowledge. Inspiration then, is seen as one expression of God's creativity, understanding this, not just in terms of God bringing creatures into being and sustaining them, but also in terms of God communicating divine qualities to them and having a purpose for them.

If this suggestion is correct, then the wonder and admiration that, as I remarked at the beginning, inspiration evokes may be seen as part of our wonder at the manifoldness of creation. Talk of wonder perhaps reminds us of Plato's saying that philosophy begins in wonder (*Theaetetus* 155 D). But it may also remind us of the psalmist, who, like Kant, wondered at the starry skies but went a step further and exclaimed, "The heavens declare the glory of the Lord"—only now we are thinking not of the heavens above but of the Spirit within.

NOTES

1. "A main cause of philosophical disease—a one-sided diet: one nourishes one's thinking with only one kind of example." (Wittgenstein, *Philosophical Investigations*, trans. G. E. M. Anscombe, [Oxford: Basil Blackwell, 1968], pt. I, #593).

2. Rosamund Harding, *An Anatomy of Inspiration*, reprint of 2d ed. (London: Frank Cass, 1967), p. 102.

3. See my *Spirit, Saints and Immortality* (London: Macmillan, 1984), chap. 2.

4. *Shelley: Selected Poetry, Prose and Letters*, A. S. B. Glover, ed., (London: Nonesuch Press, 1957), p. 1050.

5. Thus George Eliot told J. W. Cross that "in her best writing there was a 'not herself' which took possession of her, and that she felt her own personality to be merely the instrument through which this spirit, as it were, was acting." (Cross's *Life*, vol. 3, pp. 421–25, cited in Harding, *Anatomy of Inspiration*, chap. 2).

6. Wittgenstein points to a possible exception to my generalization when he remarks, "Is this the sense of belief in the devil: that not everything that comes to us as an inspiration comes from what is good?" (*Culture and Value*, trans. Peter Winch, 2d ed. (Oxford: Basil Blackwell, 1980), p. 87. But I think that we have enough on our plates now without contending with the devil too!

7. Samuel Coleridge, *Confessions of an Enquiring Spirit*, ed. H. StJ. Hart (London: A. and C. Black, 1956), p. 43.

8. Karl Rahner, *Inspiration in the Bible* (New York: Herder and Herder, 1961).

9. Søren Kierkegaard, *Søren Kierkegaard's Journals and Papers*, vol. 3, ed. Howard V. Hong and Edna H. Hong (Bloomington and London: Indiana University Press, 1975), #2854, p. 265.

10. This discourse forms part 3 of *For Self-Examination*.

11. For references, see appendix 5 of the Blackfriars edition of the *Summa Theologiae*, vol. 24 (London: Eyre & Spottiswoode, 1974), pp. 131–36.

12. For references, see A. C. Sundberg, "The Bible Canon and the Christian Doctrine of Inspiration," *Interpretation* 29 (1975): pp. 352–71. There is, of course, pagan usage to be considered, which by this time, was variegated. Quintilian, for instance, speaks of an orator inspiring his hearers by his power (*Inst. Or.* II. v. 8).

13. See further my *Spirit, Saints and Immortality*, pp. 17–22.

14. One of the sayings attributed to Jesus in the Oxyrhynchus papyri ends ". . . my soul grieveth over the sons of men, because they are blind in their heart." See Bernard P. Grenfell and Arthur S. Hunt, *Sayings of our Lord* (London: Henry Frowde, 1897), pp. 11f.; compare Ephesians 1:18, "having the eyes of your hearts enlightened."

15. Sabina Lovibond, *Realism and Imagination in Ethics* (Oxford: Basil Blackwell, 1983), #45. See also Stanley Hauerwas, *Vision and Virtue* (Notre Dame: Notre Dame University Press, 1981).

16. Dante, *Vita Nuova XI*, trans. Mark Musa.

17. No. 344 in *Cantionale*, ed. John Driscoll, S.J. (London, 1947), p. 404.

18. Rebecca West, *Black Lion and Grey Falcon* (London: MacMillan, 1955), p. 243.

19. Jacques Maritain, *True Humanism*, trans. M. R. Adamson (London: G. Bles, 1938), p. 39.

20. Robert Roberts, *Spirituality and Human Emotion* (Grand Rapids: W. B. Eerdmans, 1982), p. 95. See, more generally, Mary Midgley, *Heart and Mind* (New York: St. Martin's Press, 1981).

21. Jonathan Edwards, *A Treatise Concerning Religious Affections*, ed. John E. Smith (New Haven: Yale University Press, 1959), p. 266. What Edward goes on to say about "a sense of heart" (pp. 272ff.) is also very relevant to my theme.

22. See H. B. Levey, "A Theory Concerning Free Creation in the Inventive Arts," *Psychiatry* III (1940): pp. 229–93.

23. Livingston Lowes, *The Road to Xanadu: A Study in the Ways of the Imagination* (London: Constable, 1933), p. 62.

24. Kierkegaard, *Journals and Papers*, vol. 5, #5100, p. 39.

25. See, for example, Arthur Koestler, "The Three Domains of Creativity," in D. Dutton and M. Krausz, eds., *The Concept of Creativity in Science and Art* (The Hague: M. Nijhoff, 1981), p. 17; also his *The Act of Creation*, Danube ed., (London: Hutchinson, 1969).

26. Ian Jarvie, "The Rationality of Creativity," in Dutton and Krausz, *Concept of Creativity*, pp. 109–28. I quote from p. 112.

27. Larry Briskman, "Creative Product and Creative Process in Science and Art," in Dutton and Krausz, *Concept of Creativity*, pp. 129–55.

29. William James, *The Varieties of Religious Experience*, lecture 20 and postscript.

30. See M. R. Austin, "How Biblical is 'The Inspiration of Scripture'?" *Expository Times* 93 (1981–82): pp. 75–79, for examples. Coleridge similarly distinguished "between the divine Will working with the agency of natural causes, and the same Will supplying their place by a special *fiat*" (*Confessions*, pp. 72–73).

31. See Rahner, *Inspiration in the Bible*, especially pp. 6of.; and James T. Burtchaell, *Catholic Theories of Biblical Inspiration since 1810* (Cambridge: Cambridge University Press, 1969), especially chapters 1, 4, and 6.

32. Luis Alonso Schökel, *The Inspired Word: Scripture in the Light of Language and Literature* (New York: Herder and Herder 1965), p. 45.

12. Religious Affections and the Grammar of Prayer

DON E. SALIERS

Magister Adler's religious enthusiasms were given a prominent place in Kierkegaard's *Authority and Revelation* and a considerable critique:

> Now, as we have seen, it was Magister Adler's advantage that he was deeply moved, shaken in his inmost being, and that hence his inwardness came into being, or he came into being in accordance with his inwardness. But to be thus profoundly moved is a very indefinite expression for something so concrete as Christian awakening or conversion. . . . To be shaken is the more universal foundation of all religiousness; the experience of being shaken, of being deeply moved, the coming into being of subjectivity in the inwardness of emotion. . . . [But] one does not become a Christian by being moved by something indefinitely higher, and not every outpouring of religious emotion is a Christian outpouring. That is to say: emotion which is Christian is checked by the definition of concepts, and when emotion is transposed or expressed in words in order to be communicated, this transposition must occur constantly within the definition of concepts.[1]

The language of religious faith is the language of emotion. Among religious believers, it is often said that the language of faith is "the language of the heart." This is no accident. Believers picture religious language *in use* as giving expression to deep inner experiences. The evidence is in how believers speak: "Out of the depths, I cry to you, O Lord" or "Create in me a clean heart, O God" or "Rejoice in the Lord. . . ." Scripture describes and enjoins the emotions, feelings, and attitudes requisite for the religious life: joy, peace, sorrow, guilt, contrition, and compassion. How natural to regard the real phenomenon of faith as something "inner," perhaps inchoate, and the language of religious belief as the public instrument by means of which faith expresses itself.

Philosophers and theologians who wish to have something more than metaphors and images have sometimes said that the assertions of religious beliefs are best understood as disguised expressions of emotion, attitude, or feeling. Those of a more angular persuasion may say flatly that statements of religious belief are nothing more than expressions of emotion and sentiment masquerading under the form of statements about how things are. More subtly, others have proposed that theological utterances express a possible self-understanding and nothing more.

A considerable amount of discussion and debate in contemporary philosophy of religion and among theologians as well has shown that brash generalizations about the language of religion being "emotive language" are hopelessly inadequate, if not plainly false. Still, the language of prayer and worship—the central "religious" activity—seems peculiarly susceptible to such analysis. Theologians have given tacit support to the idea that in understanding the language of worship we must attend to the rudimentary expression of religious feeling. The venerable tradition springing from Schleiermacher and Otto is one of the main, though not the only, sources of such tacit support.

Yet the same way of regarding the language of prayer and worship may result from a theologian's preoccupation with the defense of "truth" in "theological propositions." In attempting to ward off some philosophical attacks on the notion of religious assertions, the apologist may be tempted to give away a great deal by drawing a fairly sharp line between an expressive language of piety, prayer, and worship, and the "truth-bearing" language of theology. The general contrast between assertive and expressive functions of language in religion seems plausible when one's eye is toward common ground with other *kinds* of assertions or other general types of human belief. The purified truth-claim candidates are to be precipitated out of the vast admixture of religious utterances in prayer and worship. After the refining process, the remainder of the language can be seen as the language of poetry, suggestion, image, and expression.

This essay is an attempt to show why such a plausible contrast will not do. We have, in effect, already alluded to two large sets of issues. One centers on conceptual relations between beliefs and emotion in the language of prayer and worship. In order to make clear *how* it is that the language of faith is the language of emotion—or, better, to show the way in which it is—we need to examine some of the special features of the "logic" of such emotions. In so doing we must speak of the grammar of praying. The other set of issues has to do with the relation between "expressing" and "asserting" in religious discourse. Drawing a sharp line between theological assertions and the language of worship and prayer is conceptually inadequate and even falsifying to the task of explicating theological truth-claims. In this essay, the first set of issues will be primary.

There are many circumstances in which it is important to call attention to the *difference* between how things are and how we feel about them or between what we believe and the attitudes and emotions we have toward the particular features of the world picked out of the belief. Yet such a contrast easily becomes a "systematic" distinction when philosophers and theologians become self-conscious about the language of religious belief. Most arguments supporting skeptical conclusions concerning the meaningfulness and truth of belief in God try to show that the language of faith does not say anything about how things are, even though ordinary believers intend it to do so. This point characteristically includes the assumption that there is a general distinction for all thought on these matters between the belief and the emotion that accompanies the belief. This, in turn, draws its plausibility from the notion that believing and knowing are radically different sorts of mental activity from having an emotion, though both go on "in the mind." Furthermore, a picture holds us captive: religious belief in God is something "inner," while language and judgments about what is real are "outer" phenomena.

Suppose someone says that she believes that handguns are quite dangerous but that she does not fear them. In fact, when she picks one up she appears quite calm. We find this reasonable, though we can expect her to treat the gun gingerly. Here, it seems is a relatively clear case of the logical separability of belief from emotion. Having the belief is certainly not the same as having the appropri-

ate emotion. But if someone claims that all mad dogs are frightening and vicious, yet says he never fears them, we begin to wonder.
If he yawns and dozes off when one actually appears, we begin to
detect a difficulty about his "belief." We may think that the person
is either masking or controlling some inner fear. Or, he might not
really believe that mad dogs are frightening in the way his initial
remark seemed to imply. (Suppose he knows a special trick for
calming such beasts.) These considerations show that, in a range
of ordinary cases, certain emotions are signs of belief. Moreover,
the object of such emotions in such cases is clearly being characterized in the very description that, we say, articulates the relevant
belief or beliefs.

Consider yet another case. Gary is anxious because he believes
that, at his death, God will reveal the truth about his life to him.
He is afraid of dying. Linguistically, his belief that God demands
the truth is expressed in his exclamation that he is anxious. Here
it is difficult to imagine the belief being a mental act separable from
the anxiety, though it is obviously separable from the occurrence
of certain physiological sensations and "inner episodes" of being
anxious. But the emotion in this case, in light of the manner in
which we are considering it, is ingredient in his self-assessment
that shows the belief about God and his existence.

The kind of cases we wish to explore have more affinities to the
third of these just cited. In other words, our point is to show how,
in certain paradigmatic instances in the language of worship and
prayer, emotion and belief are not separable into "inner" and
"outer." To put it positively, in such cases, articulating and practicing certain beliefs in the language of prayer requires their being
formed in specific patterns of religious affection. This having of
the emotion is not to be understood simply in terms of "feeling
the emotion" as such. Central to understanding prayer language
is the conceptual tie-up between descriptions of what is believed
to be so about God and the articulation and expression of emotions that take God as their object. More precisely, the language
of liturgy and prayer provides us with cases in which emotions are
both formed and given expression in language that asserts what is
believed about God and about the believer in relation to God.
Religious affections, as I shall refer to them, are those deep patterns of attitude, emotion, disposition that are part and parcel of

the Christian understanding of God and the world. They are more than a matter of subjective response, to be understood as belonging solely to the psychology of religious behavior. Nor are religious affections the exclusive subject of ascetical and pastoral theology; they are essential to fundamental theology.

How is this so? Whatever else it may include, the Christian faith is a pattern of deep emotions. It is gratitude to God for the creation of the world. It is awe and holy fear of the divine majesty, repentant sorrow over our sinfulness, joy in God's steadfast love. To live a life characterized by these emotions is precisely to confess faith in God and to believe in God. The relationship between being a Christian and possessing a pattern of such emotions is so intimate that if someone lacks the particular gratitude formed in giving thanks to God, this particular holy fear, or this particular pattern of repentance in confessing sin before God, that person can be said not to have been characterized by Christian beliefs. Moreover, to say that one loves God while hating one's neighbor is—while it may be explained psychologically—a misunderstanding of what the love of God entails. This is a sign of contradiction— both in faith and in theology. Such an intimate relation between religious belief and the having of certain emotions is not peculiar to Christianity, but how it gets peculiar to Christianity is precisely seen in an analysis of the way in which Christian prayer both forms and expresses particular patterns of emotion.

All serious moral and religious ways of life have to do with the acquiring and the ordering of our gratitudes, our loves, and our patterns of desire. Some religious traditions may well aim at the cessation of all human emotion in the name of a greater good, as with the stoic traditions, for example. In every religious way of life the notion of patterning the passion and the emotion, and having some control over the unruly passions, is emphasized. Such control over the unruliness of our lives most always involves the requiring and the refinement of other emotions, which, as Kierkegaard suggests, are checked by concepts. Thus, in certain traditions love is to drive out fear and hatred, humility to replace envy and greed, trust to quell anxiety. But these are given a local habitation and a name in the exercise of such emotion capacities in prayer and in becoming prayerful in our lives.

To pray, to worship God, is necessary to understanding how language about God is ruled.

In coming to live a certain way we simply live into and acquire certain emotions in very specific ways by learning to value certain things in life and to perceive the world in certain and definite ways. In this sense, one could say that a general possibility of religious affections is natural to all humanity. Here the opening remark from Kierkegaard has saliency and point. It does appear that there is a kind of foundation—he says "universal foundation to all religiousness"—simply in reflecting on the fact of how we are in the world as persons. That is to say, we do not first, as it were, get clear on how the world is and then adopt the corresponding emotions or beliefs. Rather, the very coming to understand how things are is itself emotional, passional. This, I think, is very close to what Kierkegaard wants to suggest about a general foundation.

Yet something more is clearly involved because, in taking up a particular patterning of the emotions, we take a certain way of life that, in fact, views how things are in a certain way. Hence, how things are with God and the world is portrayed in the Christian community by the scriptural narratives, by the events narrated, by the features of God picked out in the practices of common worship and devotional life. The particularity of such emotions has to do precisely with the objects toward which they are directed and not with their experienced inner phenomenon as such. Left to our own devices, we may learn joy and grief and gratitude in relation to a wide range of things, including our own death, our own malleability of the will, and the corruptibility of the flesh. But the Christian theologian's task is to trace how it is we come to have gratitude for our creation, preservation, and the redemption in God or to learn how it is we ourselves become subject to confession of sin and turning and emendment of life. Why? Because of what we see in the life, in the word and act of Jesus Christ. One learns to grieve over wrong, to rejoice in mercy and justice, not in general, but specifically because the world is described and given in and through the way in which the biblical narrative goes. In this way the grounds for having particular sets of emotions become crucial for theological reflection. The essential feature of the ordering of the Christian affections is that they make God and God's acts their object and their ground and are continually formed and activated in prayer and worship.

Some familiar language from the Psalms may provide a useful touchstone:

> Have Mercy on me, O God,
> According to Thy steadfast love . . .
> According to Thy abundant mercy,
> Blot out my transgressions.
> Wash me thoroughly from my iniquity,
> And cleanse me from my sin.

> As a hart longs for flowing streams,
> So longs my soul for Thee, O God. . . .

> O Lord, Thou hast searched me and known me,
> Thou knowest when I sit down and when I rise up.
> Thou discernest my thoughts from afar. . . .

What interests us here is the manner in which descriptions of God are logical features of the language of aspiration, desire, and longing. These are not untypical cases of liturgical language. Time and again, the emotion of the believer (reverence and awe, joy in God, remorse over disobedience, and so on) are specified and made clear by language attributing things to God. The believer discovers, as it were, what constitutes belief about God in and through the articulation of the appropriate emotions. In the standard collect form of prayer, for example, the petition is always dependent upon the characteristic of God singled out in the open ascription. "Almighty God, unto whom all desires are known and from whom no secrets are hid, cleanse the thoughts of our hearts by the inspiration of your Holy Spirit that we may perfectly love you and worthily magnify your name."

The language of prayer and liturgy trains us in the emotions precisely by ascribing what is believed about God to God, usually in the vocative mode. In coming to have the affections of gratitude or sorrow over one's sins, we are reminded of who God is, creator and redeemer. The world and all the things in it are perceived and remembered in a certain way in the language of common prayer. In regarding God, the object of our thanksgiving *via* the language, we show our beliefs. This is merely to say that one of the most ubiquitous ways in which we express emotion linguistically is by describing the world—by characterizing it in certain ways. It is not simply a matter of using words to refer to emotions or to name our inner feelings.

The language of prayer and liturgy not only "expresses" emotion in these ways, it forms and critiques and refines the emotions as well. This point is often only dimly recognized in the discussions of the conceptual relation between emotion and religious beliefs. How does the language of the liturgy form and refine the emotions of the believer? An adequate answer to this question would begin to encompass the inner logic of the Christian life itself. We can only suggest a rude outline for one emotion complex in the remainder of this essay.

The language of prayer and worship articulates the fundamental emotion concepts of the faith. It does so by bearing directly upon the way in which the believers are to regard and assess themselves, persons, events, objects, and other features of their experience. It is common, but quite misleading, to think of religious conversion as a prior episode that one must undergo in order to "understand" the language of worship. Having certain "inner" experiences seems a necessary condition for validating the use of language by someone in worship. More helpful for our inquiry is the fact that the ongoing practice of worship is a continuous rehearsal of the central concepts—both those that must be exercised in understanding the doctrines and those more directly characterizable as "emotional concepts." The intention to *mean* what one says is not given with "conversion" in the sense that it is a recallable mental act. Rather the intention to mean what the language about God says, and thereby to have the requisite emotion capacities, is found in the rule-keeping activity of believing worship itself, over time. Thus, only when a *life* becomes prayerful can the criteria of authenticity be determined.

We thus describe worship as a rule-keeping activity. This is not a mere matter of keeping the language, though it is one consequence. Rather, it is a rule-keeping activity in which the emotions and beliefs are continuously being shaped and refined. Since this could only occur if the connection between our ways of seeing, our attitudes, and our emotion capacities are brought into play, we can say the rule-keeping activity of worship is a continuous shaping of *persons.* It is not simply a matter of shaping either just the feelings or just the intellect and hence the beliefs and judgments.

But more than this, liturgical utterance itself is a form of religious behavior. It is part of the rule-keeping activity of believing. Being able to say and to mean "We bless thee, we worship thee, we give thanks to thee" is as much religious behavior as nonpropositional rejoicing, being thankful, or repenting. An analogy with Wittgenstein's treatment of pain behaviors suggests itself. We tend to think of the situation of such liturgical utterances on the model of "inner" states and external descriptive language. But we must ask: to what does this language give expression? Certainly not antecedently introspected states, as though we first looked into our soul and then reported what we felt. If this account of prayer and worship is on target, then the question "How does one know that he feels grateful or sorrowful?" is misplaced. The question of doubting whether or not one *really* has such inner states before saying that one is forgiven or thankful does not arise in the way in which the standard model inclines us to think. The placement of Christian emotion is not given either by reference to the priority of inner sensation. Rather, the praying in worship just *is* the emotion behavior. Of course, self-deception is always possible. The awareness of self-deception, or of disengenuiness (play acting in prayer), itself becomes a necessary piece of self-knowledge. Hence the capacity of praise and thanksgiving is distinctively checked by *repentance*—capacity for acknowledgment of sin.

The peculiar character of this logic is shown in the fact that it is expressive of emotion to describe the object of the emotion, namely God or God's actions, in light of the beliefs the language trains one to hold. The Christian concept of God thus comes to function in the believer's description of the world and his or her life precisely in the exercise of the appropriate emotion capacities in addressing and being addressed by God in worship. Prayer, in all its forms, but particularly in its common liturgical forms, is thus an exercise of the grammar of believing, precisely by disclosing the rules that link speaking of God and *to* God with how we are to live.

We turn now to a more detailed examination of the relation between belief and emotion in a specific instance. I propose to clarify some of the key features of the emotion complex of sorrow and remorse over one's sins in light of the logically required belief that human beings are sinners before God. This case is not to be taken as a paradigm for all other instances, but it may illuminate key aspects of the line of reasoning I have just been sketching.

The emotions articulated in the Psalms and in the liturgies of the church are obviously mutually related to beliefs. This can be discerned in the shape of explanations of the emotion. "We rejoice in God because. . . ." "We repent and we are sorry because. . . ." In such expressions the relevant belief is expressed. There are reasons for having certain religious affections. In some instances the *thought* that we are sinners before God is the occasion for the emotion. Depending upon what aspects of the situation we are interested in highlighting, we may describe the having of the emotions as an exercise of the belief, or the exercise of the belief as manifested in the having of the emotion. Yet it still seems that we ought to have independent access to the object of the emotion in order to avoid hopeless circularity in explication. Do we have an independent descriptive access to the object, namely, "sin before God"? After all, can there not be emotions based on false beliefs? Might all of religious worship be based on false belief? Might we have fears and sorrows and hatreds and passion for an illusion? The answer to the last three questions is "Of course." The answer to the first is more complex. But the latter three need not be conflated with the former.

In order to get a clearer picture of the issue of independent descriptive access to the object of the belief, consider a standard nonreligious case for comparison: (a) "Arthur is full of remorse because he broke his promise"; (b) "Arthur is full of remorse because he believes he broke his promise." Remorse does involve the belief that what one has done has been wrong in some manner and that one is moved toward making amends. This standard case allows us to contrast (a) and (b) by virtue of citing the thought as the occasion of his remorse in the second instance and his action as the occasion in the first. If, in fact, Arthur has *not* broken his promise but only believes he has, then the remorse can be changed or removed by correction of the "false" belief. We could say, "Arthur, you did not promise that."

Of course, in both cases, Arthur's being full of remorse entails his believing that he has broken the promise, and much else besides. This believing is not some temporally antecedent mental act that thereby produces the emotion. At least that is not what interests us here. Rather, the sign of his believing that he has broken the promise is his being full of remorse. The fact that he could be mistaken does not take away this logical connection. It shows that an emotion such as remorse is belief-dependent in a special way. The nature of this belief-dependency is not explicated by a casual account, even if a casual account can be given.

The occasion of such an emotion is clearly the belief that something has been transgressed. Further, such beliefs are logical ingredients in the having of the emotion. They provide the background for describing the object of the emotion. Yet we are familiar in life with the case in which a person may know that a promise is broken and yet experiences no remorse at all. There may be other factors, including weariness of breaking promises to the point of cynicism or moral defeat. Or a person may have what he or she takes to be a justifying reason for having done so in the particular instance. "Yes, I realize I broke the promise, but I did it to save her." Generally, we agree that the cognizant promise-breaker who suffers no remorse also suffers from a defect in character. We attribute the lack of an emotion that is belief-dependent in this way to a moral flaw. For our purposes, we should say that a certain kind of conceptual capacity is missing. The consequences for our lives are extraordinarily deep (and, in most cases, pervasive and *subtle*).

There appears to be a peculiarity in the case of religious emotions, particularly those ranging in the sphere of remorse. While first-order theological statements speak of emotions such as guilt, remorse, and sorrow when a person is convicted of sin, it characteristically relates these to God's holiness and to the requisite emotion of the sinner. Thus, in the prayers of confession we speak of being "heartily sorry for these our misdoings, the remembrance of them is grievous unto us." We may be admonished to confess sins with a "humble, lowly, penitent, and obedient heart."

The occasion for "feeling" the affection is the thought or the assertion of sinfulness. It may be specifically occasioned by a parable or a reading or by a sermon; but it is descriptively embedded in prayers of confession. The object of such emotions as sorrow and remorse, however, is not simply the thought of the belief that one is a sinner before God. Rather, one expresses remorse to God because he or she judges himself or herself to be such. The concept "sin before God" has a grammar that includes seeing the truth about one's past and present act and being. The occasion of the remorse and sorrow is the exercise of the belief that one is sinful.

Let us return to the set of suggestions made a moment ago. The idea of what the object of an emotion is can be best explicated by finding what is common to the beliefs and desires bearing upon that particular emotion. In the case of emotions articulated in the confessional context of prayer and liturgy, the thought is made clear by the use of the concept "sin before God" in citing instances. The thought that we have sinned and broken our promises to God is the occasion for remorse and sorrow. To repent of one's sins is to exercise the emotion capacity of sorrow and remorse and to turn in a new direction. One desires to make amends. It is not only the thought that we have on past occasions sinned, but the belief that sinning before God that articulates the object of the emotion.

Ordinarily emotions of this sort exhibit an ambiguity with respect to their object. That is, one might "feel" guilty over the thought of having broken a promise when, in fact, no promise has been broken. But in our case, the guilt and the consequential remorse are not based on a "false" belief. In fact, we learn (if we come to understand the language of authentic prayer) that there can be no mistake about our being sinful, even in the face of no consciously remembered acts. The concept of sin is such that it entails the object of the emotions or sorrow, remorse, and repentance. One learns about God or the place of God's forgiveness by becoming penitent. Of course, one can utilize the words without "meaning" what is said. That, however, is a different kind of point about the truthfulness of the utterance, not about the nature of the object of these emotions.

Here we discern that a belief not only provides a necessary condition for the occasion of this range of emotions, but that it is also a reason for these emotions. The office of confession, or the act of confessing one's sins in the liturgy, is a special human gesture in which the belief is stated in the idiom of "expression." What is expressed is not so much the feeling states of the believer (this may vary considerably from time to time and from believer to believer) as the personal capacities of self-judgment and the person's relation to God. The accompanying feelings of remorse and the affective tone of the desire are not to be denied. But the point is that they are not separable from the concrete self-understanding of saying the words and meaning them. In the Christian context one learns to pray to, and hence live in the presence of, the One who searches the human heart and who "desires truth in the inmost being."

For the moment I am bypassing the interesting question of whether it is necessary to undergo or to "experience" certain standard feeling states in order to have truly confessed. But a few remarks are in order.

If we persist in regarding the applicability of the term "emotion" in the religious activities of worship and prayer solely with respect to episodic states of feeling "inside" the person, we will have missed an essential feature of religious affections. Religious affections are conceptually dependent upon beliefs and upon the capacity to assess oneself in light of a belief-laden description of the world. In liturgy, outside of bare incantation, there can be no purely "expressive" language if we mean by that "language that nonconceptually gives expression to the feelings."

Perhaps a qualification is needed. We might say that we are speaking only of "rational" religious emotions. I hesitate to use this awkward phrase because it is liable to immediate if not systematic misunderstanding. Its awkwardness derives from the fact that we persist in categorically contrasting emotions and thoughts or emotions and beliefs. Yet this is precisely why we need the qualification. In the liturgical domain we see why the conceptual account renders the awkward phrase necessary.

If this analysis of the emotions of sorrow and remorse over sin is near the mark, we may now discern the analogies between such cases as a child's believing and fearing that the fire will burn and the faithful person's believing and being penitent. Whatever inner episodes of feeling may occur, such inner episodes are simply not the kind of phenomena that can be said to constitute the regulative expression of the beliefs. The disposition to feel a certain way is characteristic of having an emotion. But the rulishness (the "grammar") that connects the relevant belief and the emotion does not, in order to be normative, depend upon the occurrence of "feeling the emotion" in certain standard ways. Even more, the manifestation of the emotion need not require special "feeling behavior."

Now if someone asks, "What determines whether one *truly* comes to regard oneself as a sinner?" or "How does one do this?" this appeal to particular experiences may be in order. We may read again Augustine's *Confessions*. A person who *never* felt remorseful or sorry may be in a disadvantaged position to say with any certainty that he or she believes himself or herself to be a sinner. The point is simply that there are no normative sets of "feelings of remorse" that could be normative in the sense required by the logical tie-up between beliefs and penitential emotion capacities.

In order to understand the biblical concept of God, a community of faith must enter into a pervasive patterning of the affections of gratitude and praise, of holy fear, and of repentance. The theological claim inherent in the grammar of prayer is this: Because God has created, we respond as creatures. In exercising the primordial affection of gratitude in relationship to repentance, of holy fear and joy, even in the midst of the suffering and in the midst of our own complicity, we come more and more to learn of our own interiority in relation to God's ways. Without those qualifications we know not God. We may have knowledge of ourselves and extraordinary, precocious introspective powers, but we will not know God because we have not learned to address our existence to God. Without prayer we cannot, as Augustine observed of the Eucharist, receive our *own* mystery in return.

The Eucharistic prayers of the church that developed in large measure along the pattern of extended Jewish *berakoth*, or prayers of blessing and thanksgiving, provide another range of examples. The structure of those prayers reveal dispositions that are patterned in the very reciting of God's works. To praise God is not a matter of recalling past events (covenants, Exodus, life of Jesus) and gaining interior feelings that are somehow correlated to something antecedently believed. Rather, what is remembered and recited is part and parcel of a present encounter in the utterance of praise and thanksgiving. "It is right always and everywhere to give thanks to you." The language of address, therefore, both forms and expresses the life-orientation of all who are drawn to address the God of Jewish and Christian Scriptures. What is believed about God cannot be explicated until it is seen in the logic of its enactment, the grammar of its formation of persons who approach their God in fear and trembling, in memory and hope. It calls forth deep emotional patterns that receive creation as a gift. Without life, such prayers may settle into linguistic routine, mere "habit"; but without the *habitus,* no depth of feeling is possible. While there are differences between thanksgiving and praise in Jewish and Christian prayer, they are nevertheless mutually involving. The offering of thanksgiving to God for "your goodness and loving kindness" is directed to show forth God's praise. What begins as thanking God for specific things construed as gifts ends in praising God for God's own mercy and goodness, hence for God's glory. Then and only then can we understand what Saint Irenaeus had in mind when he said, "The glory of God is the living human being."

In the classical eucharistic prayers of the first centuries, praise of God's glory governs the opening prefaces and gives way to thanking God for the mighty acts. Such praying shows the ruled mutual reciprocity of the patterning of the affections and a way of knowing God. All this is embryonically present in a child's simple prayer of thanks. As religious faith matures in its understanding of God and the awareness of human existence, this simple gratitude for small things intermingles with and learns more and more of the incomprehensibility of God to human reason.

Praise and glory for God's own being reveals to us not only the distance between ourselves and God but who God is for us; that this God should be *for us* is a wonder that strips all affections of their presumption. C. S. Lewis has a typically trenchant discussion of his struggle to understand why praise of God was so important. He admits that he was at first put off by the thought that God should demand doxology. It distressed him that in addition to gratitude, reverence, and obedience, he also had to participate in what he called a "perpetual eulogy of God." It seemed to Lewis that God must be above such demands. But he had overlooked the fact that all deep enjoyment overflows into praise unless it is deliberately suppressed. This is a fact in human life. Lovers praise the beloved, citizens their heroes, religious believers their saints. In all of us such enjoyments end in an overplus of praise. Furthermore, Lewis observed that the most loving and attentive people praised most while the cranks and malcontents praised least.

Theology, then, can be seen as a way of understanding the One addressed in prayer, and this involves reasoning at full stretch. It involves a logic, it involves clarity in reflecting on the concreteness of the grammar of prayer in response to the "Thou" of God.

Theology belongs to a mode of understanding deeper than knowing by discursive reason alone. Since prayer is communion and dialogue, always involving a relatedness in passion between those who pray and God who responds, between God who acts and those who respond, theological thinking must exhibit the very nature of the relationship in which it approaches its object. Hence, there is an essentially religious character, as distinct from purely discursive character, that theology must retain even in its task as reflective knowledge about God. This does not mean that theology is nothing more than quoting Scripture or skimming the top of prayers—even good Anglican collects—to find an antecedent theology. Put simply, theology must respect its object in such a way that it does not just dispute. As Saint Bernard of Clairvaux once said, "It is finally sanctity which comprehends if the incomprehensible can, after a certain fashion, be understood at all." Theology approaches its task by respecting and participating in the language of the vocative. This, I think, lies behind Karl Barth's assertion, "Theological work must really and truly take place in the form of a liturgical act, as invocation of God, and as prayer."[2]

Many contemporary people who find religious matters embarrassing in a world "come of age" find religious believing in God as emotional and therefore dismissible. Such views have, in fact, got half the truth. Believing in God involves the emotions, but it is often said that the judgment of believers about what is so in the world is distorted, emotionally biased, beclouded. But is it a matter of having clouded judgments about one's self, or is it a matter of taking refuge in illusory claims about the world to believe that God is the searcher of hearts? There are many who seek comfort in self-delusion, and much will be perpetrated in the name of God and the Bible and in the name and under the accidents of religious belief in Lynchburg, New York, or Teheran, or in some wild hankering after end-time news in 1999. God can and always will be at the disposal of human devices to become a *deus ex machina* for supporting what is already comfortably believed or what is already emotionally arranged in our lives. But these are recognized as abuses precisely because of the logic of the vocative and the grammatical features of authentic common prayer. The tie-up between believing that we are sinful and that God can forgive us and the capacity to repent seems anything but self-delusory.

In the case of religious emotions such as we have described, thinking and describing are not just casually related to how we feel about the world and what emotions are forthcoming in our lives. Rather, the relation would be one of coherence in the *person*. The having of religious emotions connected with confessing what one is before the God who forgives and who searches and knows the heart, as well as the gross behavior, is in fact the believing. But this is a remark directed toward showing the peculiar logical tie-up in light of another consideration: a person's life ought to be coherent with what a person says. *One* of the ways to seek illumination concerning the truth of religious beliefs about God is to examine the characteristics of "truthfulness" in holding such beliefs. For the person's discernment of what is so in the world cannot be abstracted as "general truths" outside the personal capacities required for "seeing" what is so. Prayer and worship allow us to become "grammatical" in such personal capacities as gratitude, awe, contrition, hope, and compassion.

Clarity of respecting conceptual connections between religious believing and emotion in prayer and prayer structure is certainly not to be confused with emotional clarity about our life before God by virtue of being a pray-er. What little clarity I have gained, or I have shed here, is not to be confused with the self-clarity that comes from saying and meaning the words of the psalmist: "Search me, O God, and know my heart; try me and know my thoughts, and see if there be any wicked way in me, and lead me in the way everlasting" or in the words of the hymn, "I'll praise my Maker while I've breath, and when my voice is lost in death, praise shall employ my nobler powers."[3]

NOTES

1. Søren Kierkegaard, *Authority and Revelation* (New York: Harper & Row, Torchbooks, 1966), p. 163. See also the larger context of these remarks, pp. 162–65.

2. Karl Barth, *Evangelical Theology: An Introduction* (New York: Holt, Rinehart & Winston, 1963), p. 164.

3. "I'll Praise My Maker While I've Breath," words by Isaac Watts (1674–1748); alt. by John Wesley (1703–1791); paraphrase of Psalm 146. *The Methodist Hymnal* no. 9, (Nashville: The Methodist Publishing House, 1964, 1966).

13. "Heart Enough To Be Confident": Kierkegaard on Reading James

TIMOTHY POLK

The Apostle James must be dragged a little into prominence—not in behalf of works *against* faith; no, no, that was not the Apostle's meaning, but in behalf of faith.[1]

That which he emphasizes is that as God's all-powerful hand made everything good, so He, the Father of lights, still constant, makes everything good in every moment, everything into a good and perfect gift for everyone who has the heart to humble himself, heart enough to be confident.[2]

How curious to suggest that a person might be both humble and confident at once! More curious still to suggest that the one is a precondition for the other. The world has never much favored humility, except in slaves. Nor does it easily imagine a confidence based on anything other than prowess, with all its potential for domination. The appearance of humility in persons wise to their own prowess, the world's reasoning goes, can only be an appearance. A tasteful restraint, perhaps; humility it is not. The world of mass-produced individualism, full of self and empty of humanity, has like its mirror image, totalitarianism, no heart for humility. And its displays of confidence ring pathetically hollow; often they are akin to terror, simultaneously suffered and imposed.

Like the virtues of humility and humility's confidence that it sponsors, the Bible is ever more marginal to such a world. For of course the Bible speaks of God, the ultimate in marginalia, and of faith to people who have "gone beyond." Even the church has largely gone beyond; the process of debiblicization has been scarcely less effective within mainstream Christianity than it has without. Kierkegaard's Christendom could feign familiarity with its canon; only the evangelical right can do that now, and a few peripheral others. The choices appear limited to using the Bible in privatistic pietism or as a social bludgeon or not at all. Many prefer not at all, their disregard ranging from obliviousness, through timid bewilderment and embarrassed incredulity, on to sheer contempt. And with the disregard comes drift: a loss of the language of faith that guides our practice of it, and the consequent formlessness of the practice. The tragedy is, to lose the stomach for Scripture is to lose the heart for Christian living.

If the Bible has been marginalized, how much the worse for one of its already most marginal entries, the Epistle of James to which the title quotation refers. Bad enough the Epistle should speak commendingly of *works,* and so become an automatic item of orthodox offense. (If Luther is known in no other respect than this, generations of Protestants know at least to despise James's "Epistle of straw," although they do not know the Epistle.) No, in its endless moralizing it should even go so far as to pronounce against *doubt,* that staple of critical inquiry, the culture's intellectual foundation. (If faith is understood in no other respect than this, generations of Christians know at least to embrace their doubt and chant, "I believe! Help my unbelief!"—although they do not know the Gospel of Mark.)

But the Epistle goes further still, as Kierkegaard cites it, saying that "every good gift and every perfect gift is from above, coming down from the Father of lights with whom there is no variation or shadow due to change" (1:17). Thereby it proves itself either perfectly banal ("If there is a God," common sense tells us, "of course it's the good things that come from God") or horribly banal ("What good things!" a more critical sense demands). In either case, it raises doubts as to its worthiness of being read, this letter which had as its purpose overcoming doubt.

Yet Kierkegaard would champion James, deploying the Epistle of straw against a state Lutheranism for which "justification by faith" had come to justify quietism and grease the skids of the free market. More specifically, he champions James 1:17, "every good and perfect gift . . ." in his "edifying discourse" of that title, suggesting that the problem is less with it than with the way it is being read. Indeed, he suggests that the problem is with the doubter who reads it, that what it takes to read it is a humble and confident heart. He even goes so far as to say how one might get such a heart. That would be a lesson worth learning.

So in this essay I shall champion Kierkegaard, moreover, the exegetical Kierkegaard of the biblically based (and academically marginalized) *Edifying Discourses*, "Every Good and Perfect Gift" in particular. For I would champion him as neither so much an "essential thinker" or a "premise thinker" but a biblical thinker, a rare thing in a world bent on going beyond faith and the Bible. And if he also proves to be an essential thinker, as of course he does, then I would propose it is because he thought with and through the biblical premises, some of which I wish to explore in these pages, such as the concept of the canon and the rule of faith.[3] But most important is the logic of the heart, which Kierkegaard finds diagramed in the Epistle of James.

JAMES AND THE LOGIC OF THE HEART

It is not only the mis/nonreading public that has been unkind to James; the scholarly discipline has done its part, too, in this as in so many of its ventures earning Kierkegaard's undying enmity. With several notable exceptions,[4] the general impression gained from the literature is that while the Epistle poses some interesting historical problems, it is theologically quaint, if not boring. Relatively "superficial and undeveloped," we hear from one of the more balanced commentators regarding James's appropriation of Christianity.[5] Its ethics are, "from the point of view of conceptual pattern, the simplest in the New Testament," we hear from another.[6] It is that conceptual pattern, or lack of any, that seems to be at the heart of the problem: "the author moves from one subject to another with only a loose train of thought discernible." "Eclecticism" and "lack of continuity" are the key characteristics.[7] This view reaches its nadir in Dibelius's judgment that the Epistle's genre, *paraenesis,* is one so epigrammatic, so lacking in larger structure that it is an exegetical mistake to try to interrelate its parts, that is, to interpret in context![8] And if there is no larger structure, "there is no 'theology' of James,"[9] nothing to think about, except historical curiosities.

Now *paraenesis* is essentially moral admonition, first-order language of the "heart." Part of Kierkegaard's appreciation of James, distancing them both from Dibelius, must have been James's appreciation for a certain pathos in *paraenesis,* for the pathos of the heart. James introduces the metaphor early in the letter. In 1:22 we are told that hearing the word without doing it is *self-*beguilement, while 1:26 claims that thinking one is religious while operating with a loose tongue is deception of the *heart.* In both cases there is a hiatus between thought and action, a fatal inconsistency between the faith avowed and that practiced, a doubling of motive and objective that amounts to duplicity and proves the first terms (thought and faith) counterfeit. When it comes to "the word" and the knowledge of God that the word hopes to effect, any hearing that is hearing only and not a doing is a mis-hearing. As for "religion," unbridled speech (compare showing partiality in 2:1–16, speaking evil against another in 3:10 and 4:11–12, and boasting in 4:13–16) reveals the religion as "vain" pretense and "impure" (1:26f.). At stake are the God-relationship (one's standing "before God," 1:27) and the integrity of the human being (the salvation of the soul, 1:21), which of course are mysteriously, dialectically, related. The great weight, the pathos, of the metaphor "heart" is that it is used precisely here, in relation to this foundational mystery of self- and God-relatedness and the wrenching human tendency to dissolve the mystery by delusively dissociating knowledge from action. For James, the heart stands for the human self in our capacity either to become whole "in faith" (1:6) or to fragment ourselves in tragic self-deception. It is no accident that in the discourse, as in the title quotation, Kierkegaard makes everything depend upon the heart.

To see the pathos of the heart is also to see that there is a logic to it. What Kierkegaard recognized was that James's *paraenesis* was not a random prose scoring of the ancient vice-and-virtue lists, but a mapping of moral equivalencies and oppositions in which receptivity and doubt head the chart. To wit, 1:5–8 says that while God gives generously to all, the doubting *(diakrinomenos),* doubleminded person *(dipsuxos)* who does not "ask in faith" will not receive. It is not that God does not give, but that the doubter is unreceptive. Faith is linked to receptivity as doublemindedness is linked to doubt. Verse 21 then speaks of receiving the gospel with meekness. Receptivity, now virtually a synonym for faith, is humble. No other posture makes sense before the God who gives generously to all, the Giver of every good and perfect gift, of life and salvation itself.

Next, 3:13 identifies this meekness, faith's humility, with wisdom, which in turn is qualified as divine or true to the extent that it is not tainted by envy (that is, "jealousy," vv. 14–16), but rather is "pure" (v. 17). Envy's close conjunction with pride and arrogance in 4:5–6 negatively mirrors wisdom's conjunction with meekness.[10] The dichotomy between the two pairs is emphasized both by the wisdom saying that culminates the indictment of 3:13–4:6, "God opposes the proud but gives grace to the humble," and by the admonition that completes the call to conversion in 4:7–10, "Humble yourselves before the Lord and he will exalt you."

Again, humility appears in a posture of receptivity before the God who gives grace and elevates the lowly. And just as receptivity was seen to be opposed to doublemindedness (that is, doubt, uncertainty, *diakrinomenos*) in 1:6–8, so now the pure heart, one without envy, is also "without uncertainty" (*adiakritos*, 3:17b); and the purification of the heart, for example, of envy, is clearly implied by 4:8 to be a matter of purging oneself of doublemindedness: "purify your hearts, ye doubleminded ones" (the ground text for Kierkegaard's *Purity of Heart Is To Will One Thing*).

The equivalence of doublemindedness and doubt or uncertainty is central, though perhaps not as obvious as that between doublemindedness and hypocrisy. The latter James illustrates in the accusing observation that "from the same mouth come blessing and curse" (3:10), and he sees it rooted in a disposition to "show partiality" (2:1–13) toward the rich and against the poor. Further, it is clear that the duplex attitude and behavior he calls "partiality" not only violates the "royal law" of Leviticus 19:18 ("You shall love your neighbor as yourself," 2:8f.) but represents the abandonment of "the faith of our Lord Jesus Christ, the Lord of glory" (2:1). And *that* of course means to have misconstrued the "Father of lights" (compare "glory"), preferring one's own fractured and darkly unstable purposes (doublemindedness, 1:6–8) for the constancy (singleness, purity) of God "with whom there is no variation or shadow due to change" (1:17). The human partiality that violates the integrity of God is therefore already rooted in a refusal to trust in, and in an uncertainty toward, the goodness of God—or, in a word, in doubt. Doublemindedness is by nature doubting, and doubt is doubleminded. Of course, neither is open to a purely cognitive repair, as if certainty would come with more information, for, remember, they are both a matter of the heart, that is, will: "Purify your hearts, ye doubleminded ones" (and "purity of heart is to will one thing").

Clearly, Kierkegaard saw in James an understanding of the human heart and the human dilemma that was far from superficial. It is no accident that in the title quotation, which appears precisely midway in the discourse, Kierkegaard corrects a misunderstanding of James 1:17 by calling for "heart enough to be confident." Like James, he knows how meaning itself can be a function of the moral life; it, too, is a matter of the heart. Nor, obviously, is it an accident that immediately following the call to confidence comes an analysis of doubt, the confident heart's antithesis. And though astonishing, it is finally no accident that in the quotation's paraphrase of 1:17, James's distributive syntax, "every good and perfect gift is from above," has been radically revised into the totalizing "He . . . makes *everything* good in every moment." To see why this would be a faithful reading of James will be one goal of the close reading to which we now turn.

THE ANATOMY OF DOUBT

It seems almost as if what Kierkegaard has in mind with his revision of James's words is the program Climacus set for himself in the *Postscript,* that is, to make matters more difficult.[11] At least, that is how he projects doubt responding, having it say "that the words [of James 1:17] are difficult, almost mysterious" (p. 40). There follows doubt's own way of reading the text in which it turns what Kierkegaard has just identified as a problem of the heart into a metaphysical question:

But how is this possible . . . either to determine what it is which comes from God, or what may rightly and in truth be called a good and perfect gift? Is then every human life a continuous chain of miracles? Or is it possible for a man's understanding to make its way through the interminable ranks of derived causes and effects, to penetrate all the intervening events, and thus find God? (P. 40)

Wittgenstein might have cited this operation as one of wrenching words out of their native habitat to place them in a foreign one (philosophy) in order to make a problem for oneself.[12] Kierkegaard, following James, would call it sin.[13] In the meantime he continues to demonstrate how doubt reads, and in the process we see doubt anatomized, depicted in its demonic ("cunning and wily," "unobtrusive and crafty," pp. 39f.) enterprise of not just rendering the words useless (compare "loose and idle," p. 29), but worse, of putting them to "lip" service, to the work of self-deception and hypocrisy. The metaphor of the heart anchors the depiction:

[Doubt] had changed the apostolic exhortation into mere words . . . ; it tore them out of the heart and left them on the lips. (Pp. 40f.)

Kierkegaard had mentioned "idle words" at the opening of the discourse. It was an apt phrase for anticipating the present dissection of doubt's workings, described in our next paragraph as "those anxious meditations in which thought exhausts itself but never makes any progress" (p. 41). Aptly enough, the phrase and the subsequent description again anticipate Wittgenstein, who no doubt would have characterized those same workings as "an engine idling," "language . . . on a holiday."[14] Doubt of this speculative, endlessly cerebral sort *is* idleness. Hence the satanic imagery; doubt is basic equipment on the devil's playground. But to reengage the gears of reality and get back to work, Wittgenstein would have agreed with Kierkegaard, the words would have to "find a dwelling place in the heart of man" (p. 41).

Finding the words a "dwelling in the heart" means more of course than merely adding feeling to thought, so as to have "heartfelt" thoughts, and it means something qualitatively different from sentimentally conjuring up feelings *about* the words, "so beautiful, so eloquent, so moving" though they may be (pp. 29, 49). The expression refers to appropriation as a mode of reception. Whereas the careless reading forfeits appropriation by hastily abandoning the words, thereby proving its understanding defective (p. 31), sophisticated doubt simply worries them to death. But appropriation demands that the words be put to practice; the thought must involve itself in action. Reality being unremittingly situational, thoughts and words must get situated in the sorts of real activities that pertain to their subject matter. They must get enacted so that the relevant concepts get exercised and the reader gets capacitated in order to begin even to apprehend the reality of which the words speak.[15] Otherwise, with the words "left on the lips," doubt defeats understanding and the reader remains an inert victim trapped in a realm of abstraction. And needless to say, the subject matter, God and God's good gifts, never comes into view.

Now, invoking Wittgenstein these several times is useful if only to help clear the "heart" talk that epitomizes the discourses from the taint of romantic pietism and epistemological naiveté, as if in the discourses Kierkegaard himself had "gone on holiday," taking leave of his rigor. Then again, Wittgenstein would be the first to point out that Kierkegaard need not go begging for philosophical legitimation. The language game is not one of generating new theories of knowledge but of explicating scripture, and clearly it is *James*'s "epistemology," shared by all the biblical writers, that has shaped Kierkegaard's thinking and that he here mirrors with compelling credibility. And that biblical epistemology, never detachable from its ethics, is one in which knowing is always a function of doing, the knowledge of God always a matter of obeying God.

For ancient Israel it was axiomatic that one obeyed *in order* to know God, while disobedience was both the sign that God had been forgotten and the means of the forgetting.[16] The classic instance of the use of the heart metaphor to express the behavioral component of this knowledge is Jeremiah's new covenant passage: "[The Lord says] . . . I will put my law within them, and I will write it upon their *hearts* . . . and they shall all *know* me, from the least of them to the greatest" (31:33–34 RSV). To take Torah to "heart," to have it "in" the heart so as to do God's will, as it were, by second nature, is knowing God at its most intimate. Clearly, the metaphor of the heart is no less appropriate to the Bible's epistemological discourse than is that of the "mind" to an Enlightenment one.

James, with his insistence that hearing God's word entails doing it, stands squarely within the same tradition. Faith, he argues, which is nothing if not the (at least incipient) religious command of the concept of God, is sterile so long as it remains at the level of mere intellectual assent: "So faith by itself, if it has no works, is dead. . . . You see that faith was *active* along with [Abraham's] works, and faith was completed *by* works . . ." (James 2:17, 22). Once again, any thought about God that remains at the level of thought is not about God. There is a discipline to knowledge, the biblical authors recognized, and the discipline constructs a certain form of life;[17] it etches a distinctive pattern into the "habits of the heart."[18]

Naturally, a recognition so reflexive is fraught with implications for the lives of the authors themselves. It is no surprise, then, that the question of authorship should arise again as the logical next step in doubt's assault.

If a concept is mastered in the use of it, one would think, surely its learning begins with the *teacher's* use of it. Hence, the lives of the tradition's paradigmatic teachers, the prophets and the apostles, had long been acknowledged as performing a modeling role, and from the Bible's oral stages down through to its canonization the depiction of those lives underwent a shaping—Mosaic in the first instance, cruciform in the second—in order to render them as guides to the interpretation of their words. A canonical conception of apostolicity has its hermeneutic function in just this context, and Kierkegaard had already put the conception to canonical use in his first paragraph in order to support confidence in the Scripture:

These words . . . are by an apostle of the Lord, and insofar as we ourselves have not felt their significance more deeply, we still dare have confidence that they are not loose and idle words, not a graceful expression for an airy thought, but that **they are faithful and unfailing, tested and proved, as was the life of the apostle who wrote them.** (P. 29)

But therein also lies the conception's vulnerability: the truth of the rendering can be challenged. Doubt, ever ready to subvert the word's hearing, can question its authenticity. Kierkegaard proceeds to show us how:

Was an apostle of the Lord perhaps *not* responsible for these words? . . . Was it their intention to confuse men? (P. 41)

So now doubt entertains the possibility that the words were pseudonymously authored or demonically inspired. Apparently, part of doubt's cunning is to project its own heartless reception of the words onto their sending—self-deceivingly, of course, as such projections typically work.

The hermeneutical issue here is the vexed question of how authorship bears on the meaning of a text.[19] As one might expect of Kierkegaard, the relationship between the two, though deemed significant, is somewhat less than direct and depends less on objective historical facts (who the author was and what he or she meant), or even on a rendering of the theological facts, than on the disposition with which the supposed facts and interpretive rendering are perceived. Moreover, that disposition has immensely creative (and destructive) meaning-making potential, and not just for the text but for what count as the facts behind the text as well. In doubt's case, the facts prove no sure defense against suspicion.

Again, it is clear that for Kierkegaard the shape of the life that authored the words, the disposition of the heart from which they sprang, is significant as a clue for how the words may be heard. The authorial heart does *not*, however, dictate how they *must* be heard, as if only one meaning, an "original" one, and that embedded "in" the text, were possible; it only suggests certain possibilities, likely construals, by modeling a set of purposes and practices that constitute a use. But doubt suggests possibilities, too ("Could it be this way, my hearer?"), by applying its hermeneutic of suspicion to the manner and motives of the text's composition.[20] Now just how insidious we see it to be depends on how we construe Kierkegaard at this point, for his text is open to possibilities as well.

For instance, we could easily take the first question ("Was an apostle of the Lord perhaps not responsible for these words?") in a purely historical sense. In that case, the doubt at work would be the principled doubt of historical inquiry: If as the evidence seems to indicate the apostle James did not write the "letter" (in fact, more a sermon than a real letter) attributed to him, the scholar asks, what Hellenistic Jewish-Christian of the late first century did, and what party interests was he or she promoting against which adversaries? Two centuries of historical criticism attest how corrosive of the ability to hear Scripture as the Word of God such methodological doubt can be.

The problem was not lost on Kierkegaard. In "The Mirror of the Word," the "newer science" takes its place among other forms of erudition as a means by which "I transform the word into an impersonal entity" (*FSE*, p. 61) so that, whatever else it has become (for example, evidence for the history of Christianity), it is not God's Word that I am reading.[21] To begin to restore the ability to read it as such, the suspicion needs to be redirected—against itself, that is, against the doubt, which is to say, against one's own self: "Seriousness consists precisely in having this honest suspicion of thyself, treating thyself as a suspicious character" (*FSE*, p. 68), for methodologically disinterested doubt turns out not to be so disinterested after all:

All this interpretation and interpretation and science and newer science which is introduced with the solemn and serious claim that this is the way to understand God's Word—look more closely and thou wilt perceive that this is with the intent of defending oneself against God's Word. (*FSE*, p. 59)

Even a principled doubt can be an instrument of evasion and self-deception. That is to say, Kierkegaard doubts its principles.

So returning to "Every Good Gift," we see that taking the question in an historical sense leads to a critique of historical criticism and the form of doubt thought proper to it. But that in turn suggests another way of construing our question. Yet what other than an historical sense could the question have, so straightforward it seems: "Was an apostle of the Lord perhaps not responsible for these words?" However, given the mythopoeic form of the questions that follow it—

Were perhaps those spiritual hosts beneath heaven responsible for them [Ephesians 6:12]? Was there a curse which rested upon them, so that they should be homeless in the world, and find no dwelling place in the heart of man? Was it their intention to confuse men? (P. 41)

—another sense seems likely, a suprahistorical sense. Given the context, the question puts in doubt not so much the name of the author as the spiritual power and authority behind him or her, and the allusion to Ephesians clearly implies a demonic power and authority. From this perspective it matters little who the human writer(s) happened to be in fact, whether the historical James or a later figure or community; doubt suspects the quality of the inspiration. This is radical doubt, with which its historical-critical cousin (or guise) seems almost trivial by comparison, for by its very nature, its target being spirit, there is no amount of historical information that can relieve it. It is fundamental doubt, challenging the ordinary Christian understanding of the concepts "apostle" and "Lord," implying that the confidence they are intended to inspire is bogus. Ultimately, of course, it is religious doubt, impugning the very goodness of God by suggesting that "God does tempt a man . . . by preaching a word whose only effect is to confuse his thought." (P. 41)

What antidote can be found for so resistant a poison? The words of Scripture, instead of being instrumental to the love and knowledge of God, have through doubt become the occasion for making God the enemy. How does the exegete-expositor remedy such misuse? (And if misuse, is it not misinterpretation?)[22]

We have reached a climactic moment in the discourse. Kierkegaard has brought us to the very point at which three previous forms of misreading (pp. 29–34) have culminated, namely, in "the error of thinking that God would tempt a man, [which is but a variant of] the error of believing that God would allow Himself to be tempted" (p. 39). And that is precisely the same error of which James warns: "Let no one say when he is tempted, 'I am tempted by God'; for God cannot be tempted with evil and he himself tempts no one" (1:13). In effect, doubt is itself the culmination of those other misreadings or the diseased germ at their core. Occupying the center section of the discourse, doubt represents a paradigm of all misunderstandings rooted in the heart. Perhaps it is time now to turn back in the text to take stock of those other misreadings.

First among them is carelessness (pp. 30–31). Its mode is "unconcern," its representatives are "without knowing," and everything about them bespeaks a blithe mindlessness. Their reading is a slave to fashion, "borne along on the wave of the present." They see no reason to give heed to apostolic warnings ("Do not err," James 1:16). Yet behind their disregard stands doubt; their carelessness proves but the sign of a defection of the heart. More important for our purposes, however, is Kierkegaard's next depiction: the dialectics of sorrow.

SORROW/DEFIANCE

In fact, what Kierkegaard depicts for us are two closely related strategies of temptation. In the one (pp. 31–35), sorrow is the primary disposition issuing secondarily in defiance (p. 33); it begins piously but eventually reveals itself as impious manipulation. In the other (pp. 35–37), defiance is primary, though always presupposing sorrow, but it discards sorrow's pious facade at the outset in order to use impiety as its means of manipulation. In both cases it is God they seek to manipulate ("tempt"), and in both the motive for manipulation is desire. Not surprisingly, we find the two ideas, desire and temptation, twice conjoined in close proximity:

With humble prayers and burning desires you sought, as it were, to tempt God . . .

but the day you desired did not dawn. And still you made every effort, you prayed early and late, more and more fervently, more and more temptingly. (P. 33)

Of course, the connection between temptation and desire was made initially by James. Kierkegaard is only illustrating the relation between 1:13 and its compact elaboration in vv. 14–15:

Let no one say when he is tempted, "I am tempted by God"; for God cannot be tempted with evil and he himself tempts no one; **but each person is tempted when he is lured and enticed by his own desire. Then desire when it has conceived gives birth to sin; and sin when it is full-grown brings forth death.**

The elaboration is pivotal for how Kierkegaard proceeds. His agenda, in other words, remains exegetical. The depictions of sorrow and defiance are not free-form, but the function of a disciplined responsiveness to the biblical text.

As responsive exegete, however, Kierkegaard is also a hermeneutician, which will lead him to see in sorrow a fierce dialectic, a conundrum in the very reading of Scripture. Sorrow becomes both a capacity for understanding and a condition that incapacitates understanding. This bears spelling out.

First, Kierkegaard recognizes sorrow as the condition that James's opening admonition is meant to address: "Count it all joy, my brethren, when you meet various *trials*" (1:2). It is sorrow, of course, not joy, that is the logical emotional accompaniment of trial, and James's assumption that his readers are encountering trials implies that they also know sorrow. This means that they will read the letter *through* their sorrow, and through their sorrow they will find its subject matter fitting, or the subject matter will fit them. In any case, without the sorrow they would hardly know what the letter is talking about. Thus the sorrow marks a capacity, the heart's qualification for a thoughtful and responsive reading (as opposed to a careless one).

And Kierkegaard recognizes how essential a capacity it is for reading the words of James 1:17 appropriately, which is to say appropriatingly, taking them to heart:

These words are so soothing, so comforting, and yet how many were there who really understood how to suck the rich nourishment from them, how to **appropriate** them! Those concerned, those whom life did not permit to grow up and who died as babes, those whom it did not suckle on the milk of prosperity but who were early weaned from it; the **sorrowing,** whose thought attempted to penetrate through the changing to the permanent—those were conscious of the apostle's words and gave attention to them. (P. 31)

Moreover, sorrow parents the humility and patience that James enjoins as necessary attributes of a faith receptive to God's good gifts (1:21, 4:10, 5:7–11). Ultimately, it is the requisite capacity for the repentance—

Be wretched and mourn and weep. Let your laughter be turned to mourning and your joy to dejection. Humble yourselves before the Lord, and he will exalt you. (4:9–10)

—that makes available the exalted, transcendent comfort and joy that the good God gives. That is why James was able to say in the first place, "Count it all *joy* when you meet trials." As in the beatitude, the capacity for mourning is a measure of the capacity for comfort (Matthew 5:4); so sorrow aims at comfort and targets joy as its heart's desire. Sometimes desperately.

And there is the problem. Sorrow is prone to despair, that is, doubt. Often it *is* doubt, Kierkegaard wants us to know, not only by resuming James's wave imagery ("your soul became restive, **tossed about** by the passionate wish . . . ," compare James 1:6) but by drawing out sorrow's train of disillusioned thought, thought that focuses on the disparity between James's comforting words and the sorrower's felt reality, between heaven and earth:

Or is there only a spirit who bears witness in heaven, but no spirit who bears witness on earth! **Heaven only** knows, and the spirit which flees from earth, that God is good; the earthly life knows nothing about it! Is there then no mutual harmony between what happens in heaven and what happens on the earth! Is there joy in heaven, only sorrow on earth, or is it only **said** that there is joy in heaven! Does God in heaven take the good gifts and **hide** them for us in heaven so that we may **some time receive them in the next world!** Perhaps you spoke in this way in your heart's bewilderment. (P. 32f.)

To explain (!) that only God knows that God is good, that good gifts remain hidden, that joy is restricted to heaven, if it exists anywhere—that is doubt talking, under the influence of sorrow.

Hence sorrow is dialectical, necessary on the one hand, corrupt on the other as doubt distorts the sorrowing heart, though subtly enough by transforming its objects. With humility, for example, while James instructs, "Humble yourselves *before the Lord*" (4:10), Kierkegaard shows that sorrow's humility is more likely to have as its object the *world,* life in its inscrutability, than God in his:

So they sat in their quiet sorrow; they did not harden themselves against the consolation of the word; they were **humble** enough to acknowledge that **life** is a dark saying, . . . so were they also slow to speak and slow to wrath. (P. 32)

The form may be right, but surely the inwardness is all misdirected. Similarly, the patience that is willing to wait forever for the granting of *its* "heart's desire" is not the patience James commends that establishes its heart on the ever-imminent coming of the Lord (5:7f.):

Alas, it still did not come to pass! And you gave up, you would dispose your soul to **patience,** you would wait in quiet longing, if only your soul might be assured that eternity would bring you **your** wish, bring you that which was the delight of your eyes and your heart's desire. Alas, that certainty too was denied you. (Pp. 33f.)

The problem is verb deep, for it is the very transitivity of the heart that is injured. The *way* sorrow targets its objects, the manner of its desiring, has been disfigured by the doubt. By desperation, he makes the sorrower's desire into "his *own* desire," as James says, that "gives birth to sin" (1:13f.). All sorrow's children will be tainted.

This must mean even the comfort (the joy) that sorrow seeks. By the self-centered manner of the seeking, it becomes a different sort of comfort from that which God gives. As Kierkegaard suggests ("Alas, that certainty too was denied you"), the comfort desired is that of certainty, a "sign or testimony" as clear evidence of a good gift from God—that is to say, evidence that suits the sorrower's criteria. But the comfort of objective certainty can only be the fearful comfort of bad faith and false confidence and doubt. It is bad faith in which the sorrower's expectation of comfort fails by not being radical enough, by being in fact double minded, wanting comfort from God but not God's comfort, rather that of one's own passionate desiring. "You ask and do not receive, because you ask wrongly, to spend it on your passions—unfaithful creatures!" (James 4:3f.).

But for James and Kierkegaard the gospel renders comfort and the rest of sorrow's family, in a different key: "As an example of suffering and patience, take the prophets who spoke in the name of the Lord [and were often martyred for their pains]. Behold, **we call those happy who were steadfast**" (James 5:10f.). This is a grammatical remark, we say nowadays, a directive for Christians to take comfort *in* their suffering, joy *in* the sorrow, and to receive God in all the minutiae of the mundane. Again, however, sorrow teaches the heart to doubt and in doubt to absolutize the distance between heaven and earth, ideality and actuality, God's Word and human existence. And such a heart can only misinterpret the Word.

In this dialectic of sorrow, then, Kierkegaard demonstrates the conundrum of reading Scripture, for it is in reading as in life. The heart's perfectly natural habit of meeting trial with sorrow, that is, the very condition that the text addresses so as to heal, obstructs the text's purpose, converting the text itself into a trial. James's words are then read sorrowfully, with confidence subverted at the outset in the habituated expectation that life will disappoint the comfort that the words seek to inspire. And the words themselves become the occasion for more sorrow, and doubt.

The precise form of the heart's misinterpretation is to read the words restrictively, though perhaps in the way a surface grammar and an arid scholarship would demand. The statement, "Every good and perfect gift is from above," says to sorrowers in doubt only that some things come from God and some things don't. The good things are from God, but if we cannot see them, the sorrowers reason, then the gifts must be like a "magnificent jewel": reserved for a "festal occasion" that has not yet come (p. 32). But the deeper grammar of the text, its canonical logic, is otherwise. The humility of faith, which receives all things from God's hand in confidence that whatever God gives is good, reads accordingly: *everything* that comes is a good gift from God. But again, such singleminded and comprehensive receptivity is beyond the scope of a heart beside itself with sorrow. Of course, when that heart turns defiant, it becomes utterly hardened.[23] Then it lacks even the interest of a dialectic. In either case, whether in sorrow or defiance, right reading seems impossible.

Hence the leap. Kierkegaard depicts this hell-bent human heart—"impatient and unstable," "hardened and barren" (pp. 34, 36)—as undergoing what by the logic of its own self-disintegrating constitution is an impossible conversion:

But when the busy thoughts had worked themselves weary, when the fruitless wishes had exhausted your soul, then perhaps your being became more quiet, then perhaps your heart, secretly and unnoticed, **had developed in itself the meekness which received the word** which was implanted within you, and which was able to save your soul, that every good and every perfect gift cometh from above. (P. 34)

But, then, **when you humbled yourself under God's** powerful hand and, crushed in spirit, groaned: "My God, my God, great is my sin, greater than can be forgiven," then heaven again opened. . . . (P. 36)

The wonder is how the faithless heart with nothing to work with but diseased tools is able to heal itself. The answer is that it doesn't. Rather, behind the conversion stands the Father of lights, still constant, with whom all things are possible, even creation *ex nihilo:*

Then you acknowledged in all humility that **God had . . . created this faith in your heart;** when instead of the wish, which even if it could do everything, was at most able to give you the whole world, He gave you a faith through which you gained God and overcame the whole world. Then you recognized with humble gladness that God was still the almighty Creator of heaven and earth, who had not only created the world out of nothing, but had done the even more miraculous—**out of your impatient and unstable heart He had created the incorruptible essence of a quiet spirit.** (P. 34)

[T]hen heaven again opened, then did God, as a prophet writes, look down upon you from the window of heaven and say: Yet a little while; yet a little while and I will renew the forms of the earth—and lo, your form was renewed, and **God's merciful grace had produced in your barren heart the meekness which receives the word.** (P. 36)

The development of the undeveloped heart is miraculous, as is the accompanying resolution of sorrow's dialectic and misreading's conundrum. Neither happens naturally. The miracle is that the good gift given in every moment is God, if only one is willing to receive God, as well as receive the faith by which one does the receiving and goes on to read God's words aright. This being the case with doubt's deputies, sorrow and defiance, will it be any less so with the thing itself? We return to Kierkegaard's answer to doubt.

GRATITUDE AND THE CANON

Theological exegesis is like sin: sooner or later it probes that deep layer of understanding where our decisions about what defines reason, what counts as a fact, and where we stand are formed. And it is especially when it confronts sin that it must probe that layer.[24] For sin is its ultimate antagonist, the largest obstacle in its ground-clearing task of allowing the Word of God to be heard as such. But because sin is a spiritual condition, it remains highly resistant, unamenable to exegetical argument and information. That is, sin can take the argument, appropriate its reason, and marshal the information all to its own purpose and in its own spirit. In fact, in the face of sin exegesis itself is utterly impotent; it cannot guarantee the sense it makes. There is a critical point where all it can do is to reaffirm *its* guiding spirit and reinvoke it. That is what Kierkegaard does.

In effect, Kierkegaard has defined sin as doubt, and having shown us doubt's course (from the supposedly naive question, "How is it possible for the words to mean so?" to the direct assault, "God does tempt a man") along with doubt's comprehensive, self-stultifying logic, he simply reinvokes and reaffirms the counter Spirit. In the face of doubt's subversion of apostolicity, Kierkegaard cites the apostle Paul. In the face of doubt's impugning God's goodness and the meaningfulness of God's Word, he reasserts the fullest theological claim that the words can be construed as making:

The apostle Paul says: "All of God's creation is good, if it is received with thankfulness." . . . Would not the same hold true of every man's relation to God, that every gift is a good and perfect gift when it is received with thanksgiving? (P. 41)

What follows in his next two paragraphs (pp. 41–43) can only be called a hermeneutic of thanksgiving. As always, the principle is that reading follows form of life. Understanding James Christianly, Kierkegaard says, requires giving thanks in all circumstances. That is what it means to "obey" the statement made in 1:17 (that is, to take it as applying normatively to oneself, to appropriate it), and that is what it takes to understand it. And that is what it takes to overcome doubt. Such continual gratitude will not be speculative and abstract, like doubt, because it will be confidently focused on the concrete specific, the gift itself, the character of which comes into focus by virtue of the gratitude with which one addresses its Giver:

You did not anxiously ask what it is which comes from God. You said gladly and confidently: *this* for which I thank God. You did not concern your mind with reflections on what constitutes a good and a perfect gift; for you said confidently, I know it is that for which I thank God, and therefore I thank Him for it. (P. 42)

The obvious circularity of this or any hermeneutic is not to be avoided, particularly here, given the quality of gratitude's reality and self-constituting potency. Gratitude is constitutive of the good. For in a sense it is the gratitude that (re)constitutes the gift as good, whereas in doubt's hands it turns sour even though it had been given good by God. And it is not just the gift that is defined by the mode of reception. When Kierkegaard appends to the above statement this one, "You interpreted the apostolic word," he is making a grammatical remark about what constitutes both Christian interpretation and the apostolic word. The life of gratitude effects an interpretation, a demonstration of the meaning of the words. And by interpreting the word with gratitude, one interprets it apostolically, in conformity to the apostolic intention and model; the word *becomes* apostolic (in contrast, say, to confusing or demonic), is *actualized* as the apostolic word, by having been read and interpreted through gratitude.[25] We should add that the grammatical remark further elaborates the rule of faith: Along with the expectation of comfort, gratitude is one of the rule's key components.

Lastly, then, the gratitude constitutes the self, thankfully for the better. Whereas carelessness, sorrow, and defiance diminish the heart, the practice of gratitude develops it, capacitating it for yet clearer purpose and stronger exertions—and for a still deeper grasp of Scripture:

You interpreted the apostolic word; **as your heart developed,** you did not ask to learn much from life; you wished only to learn one thing: always to thank God, and thereby learn to understand one thing: that all things serve for good to those that love God [Romans 8:28]. (P. 42)

Eventually, the heart's capacity is developed even to the point where it can sustain offense without taking offense, covering the sin, as it were, with the gratitude by which it receives it, transforming even sin into "a good and perfect gift":

And when men did you wrong and offended you, have you thanked God? . . . [H]ave you referred the wrong and offense to God, and by your thanksgiving received it from Him as a good and perfect gift?

For emphasis we have then repeated the same grammatical remark as before, twice this time:

Then surely you have worthily interpreted the apostolic word to the honor of God, to your own salvation. . . . Then have you worthily interpreted that apostolic word, more gloriously than if all the angels had spoken in glowing tongues [compare I Corinthians 13:1]. (P. 43)

The emphasis is significant. So is the allusion to Paul's paean to *agape,* which reinforces the earlier reference to Romans 8:28 ("all things serve for good for those that love God"). Kierkegaard is connecting the hermeneutic of thanksgiving (so **self**-constituting is it that it works "to your own salvation") with the rule of faith classically formulated in terms of the law of love. In Augustinian form the rule has it that everything in Scripture and the world is only properly read in the love of God and points to the love of God when properly read.[26] Kierkegaard gives full play to it in the *Works of Love,* particularly where he speaks of "the art of interpretation . . . in the service of love" (*WL,* p. 272). Now in "Every Good and Perfect Gift" he is observing the obvious fact that gratitude and love are deeply wedded emotions and that they are indispensably edifying (constructive) ones: With their application or atrophy, the world waxes or wanes as a whole.

In all of this the hermeneutic circle clearly remains unbroken. But this raises the problem of how one breaks into it. It is the same problem we saw with respect to sorrow and defiance, now raised with doubt itself. Whence this love and gratitude by which the undeveloped, indeed eviscerated heart now begins to read? Kierkegaard raises the question himself, in the very next sentence: "Still, who had such courage and such faith, who loved God in this way?" (p. 43).

It is as if every logical priority suggests yet another mystery; the rule of faith seems to traffic in infinite regress. Certainly, courage would be required to receive everything as a good gift of God and thus to love God as the Good Giver, since such receiving means giving up all proprietary claims on our supposed possessions, our reality definitions, our very selves—things to which we cling as props in a doubt-cum-dread-driven compulsion to secure our dubious existence. But then, whence this courage that Kierkegaard assures us we "will now and then gain to be thankful . . ., to understand that every good and every perfect gift is from above, [and] to explain it in love . . ." (p. 44)? To "gain" it must be to receive it "from above," "for it, too, is a good and a perfect gift." But then so also the *"faith* to accept this courage": even the spirit of receptivity must be received. Everything is received, including our recognition of the imperfection of the faith, courage, gratitude, and love by which we do our receiving. Yet even *this,* the imperfection (is it, too, a gift?), can point to the crucial and all-sufficient fact: The regress has a limit; in fact at every point it has a limit, though not a natural one. For at every point it is God who breaks through the circle of imperfection, who defines and constitutes the real reality, who does the giving, even the loving for and by which we thank him:

Was it not this way, my hearer? You always wished to thank God, but even this thanks was so imperfect. Then you understood that God is the one who does everything for you, and then grants you the childish joy of having him regard your thanksgiving as a gift from you. This joy He grants you, if you did not fear the pain of remorse, nor the deep sorrow in which a man becomes joyful as a child in God; if you did not fear to understand that this is love, not that we love God, but that God loves us [I John 4:10]. (P. 46)

For a third time Kierkegaard has climaxed a point with a biblical reference to love.[27] A deeper penetration of the mysterious dynamics of the rule of faith would be hard to come by. Just as rare is his rigor in traversing the hermeneutic circle. That the discourse does not in fact end with this cadence but makes still another circuit through yet one more misreading (that of one "who in repentance will **only** suffer punishment") suggests that the circle is as hard to break out of as into. There is a misreading for every moment, for every stage along life's way; and the pattern—of misunderstanding, (re)discovering our incapacity, being thrown back upon the love of God, renewed thanksgiving, and understanding anew that every good gift is from God—is a continuous process without systematic conclusion. It takes its shape from our imperfect lives and only concludes when life does.

Toward a conclusion, two aspects of that threefold scriptural invocation of the law of love merit attention, its essential fidelity to James and its profoundly canonical character. As indicated, Kierkegaard uses the citations to underscore the identity of the law of love and the rule of faith as a reading strategy. To make Christian sense of Scripture one must live as well as read in the expectation of (a discomforting) comfort, in courage, and in gratitude—that is to say, in faith and love, the greatest of these being well known. It turns out that James had worked the same hermeneutic in a not dissimilar way. In his insistence that hearing the word entails doing it, "doing it" was summed up in 2:8 as "fulfil[ling] the royal law according to the Scripture: 'You shall love your neighbor as yourself,' " a citation of Leviticus 19:18b. James follows the citation with five more verbal and thematic allusions to its immediate context, the commands of Leviticus 19:12–18a, which he clearly regards as the appropriate biblical explication of the demands of love.[28] Taken with other statements relevant to the theme of love ("ask God who gives to all generously and without reproaching" [1:5], "Yet mercy triumphs over judgment" [2:13], "But God gives more grace . . . gives grace to the humble" [4:6], and "how the Lord is compassionate and merciful" [5:11]), and understood within Christological perspective, the web of allusions to the law of love bears the burden of the letter's argument. As Kierkegaard correctly saw, and induces us to see, the Letter of James rests entirely on the gospel of grace.[29]

One does not have to show that Kierkegaard was aware of James's "halachic midrash" to argue that he rightly discerned the letter's kerygmatic center of gravity. Nevertheless, it is striking how like James he, too, sought an "appropriate *biblical* explication" of the material he was presenting. As James went to Leviticus to explicate "the faith of our glorious Lord Jesus Christ" (2:1), Kierkegaard went to Romans, First Corinthians, and First John to interpret "every good gift. . . ." They both used Scripture to interpret Christ-faith, the difference being that James's formulation of his gospel material had itself become Scripture in the meantime whereas Kierkegaard's remains exegetical only. But what they shared was the conviction that Scripture was deeply congruent with their subject matter because in every case (Old Testament or New, the life of the early Church or nineteenth century Copenhagen) the subject matter was the work/Word of God. Accordingly, their practice of interpreting a given reality through Scripture can be seen as another operation of the rule of faith. It is a singularly theological procedure and a thoroughly canonical one.[30]

The question is, is there an alternative procedure, say, a nontheological, nonbiblical one? I do not believe so: not for talking about restoring a person's life, not if the purpose and hope are to go beyond talk toward actually cultivating a humble and confident heart, and not if the procedure is to be Christian. A form of life marked by the resiliency of courage, incessant gratitude, and love such as James and Kierkegaard depict, specifically the Christian life, once again does not happen naturally. Kierkegaard can write so as to prompt a yearning for such resiliency, and surely it is a quality our world is desperate for, but in desperation we do not achieve it. As Kierkegaard has shown, the doubt that comes naturally to us can only subvert it. And that is a fix unamenable to solutions afraid of naming and addressing God, since only thereby are we able to name the poison and take the cure. Now, as the canonical witness of faith, the Bible remains the Christian paradigm for that naming and healing process.

What Kierkegaard has done is to direct me back to the Bible, back time and again into Scripture where the lineaments of the confident heart are diagrammed and where the heart's Creator and Sustainer is praised as its *sina qua non*. For it will be in life as in reading. Without the text my life won't know its lines. Of course, it is not just *that* I read but *how* I read that matters, with infinite suspicion of myself and utter confidence in God and the faith to be not just a reader but a doer, since it will be in reading as in life.

I take it that it will be so even in life as a professional reader, a would-be teacher who "shall be judged with greater strictness" (James 3:1). Here, too, among a cloud of witnesses, Kierkegaard is a guide, bold as he is to appeal to Paul and John in order to interpret James, to hear the different voices of the canonical ensemble, but to hear the harmony among them as well. For doubt not to invalidate the appeal, the miracle of faith would have to be at work here, too, and at every level, for ultimately the appeal is only plausible in the context of a community of the mysteriously confident heart. The canonical harmony Kierkegaard hears among the biblical witnesses regarding the hermeneutic excellence of love is one that comes by virtue of the witnesses' shared experience and the shared interests, expectations, and purposes that such experience was able to generate among them. More specifically, it comes by their having devoted themselves to what they attest to be one and the same subject matter: the God of Israel and of Israel's Scripture and of Jesus of Nazareth and of the Church. And it comes by their having already been so shaped by Israel's Scripture and its Author as to warrant their experience's being called a *shared* one. Likewise, that Kierkegaard *finds* the harmony suggests that he, too, has tasted something of that experience and undergone a similar shaping by the Church's canon. He belongs with those whose hearts have been developed by referring all things to God in gratitude. For my part, to be persuaded by Kierkegaard's reading so as to come to understand James's words similarly would in some measure be to enter into that same community. On the other hand, to fail to appropriate the words would mark an estrangement.

The concern is not to draw invidious distinctions between insiders and outsiders, only to learn what it means to read and live seriously. In that vein, however, it merits asking if the undervaluation of Kierkegaard's exegesis, even more the long-standing scholarly impression of the banality of James's Christianity and its lack of conceptual coherence, but most of all the Church's neglect of Scripture, are not a self-indictment, a cultural witness to our collective heart failure. For if we fail to see or care how the concepts cohere—like confidence and humility, gratitude, receptivity, courage, and love—it may be because in life and in reading they have fallen out of use with us. If we remain unimpressed with Kierkegaard's understanding of James, perhaps it is because we have lost the tools to see what impedes our own.

Not that being impressed proves me to have mastered the words. All talk of mastery is out of place. For life darkens, the words become hard again, the interpretation even more so. I wonder if the man who could believe that everything that comes is a good gift from God is quite sane, or just hopelessly naive. Perhaps then I shall remember that in the same year the same man published *Fear and Trembling*.

NOTES

1. Søren Kierkegaard, "The Mirror of the Word," in *For Self-Examination and Judge for Yourselves!* (hereafter *FSE*), trans. Walter Lowrie (Princeton: Princeton University Press, 1974), p. 49. Emphasis Kierkegaard's, hereafter mine.
2. Søren Kierkegaard, "Every Good and Every Perfect Gift Is from Above," *Edifying Discourses: A Selection*, ed. Paul L. Homer, trans. David and Lillian Swenson (New York: Harper & Row, 1958), p. 39. Subsequent citations will be given in the body of the essay.
3. The particular line of thinking about canon to be pursued is that of Brevard Childs, perhaps most clearly formulated in *The New Testament as Canon: An*

Introduction (Philadelphia: Fortress Press, 1984). In addition, and especially well suited to describing Kierkegaard's exegetical practice, is Charles M. Wood's *The Formation of Christian Understanding: An Essay in Theological Hermeneutics* (Philadelphia: Westminster Press, 1981), chap. 4 in particular, "The Canon of Christian Understanding," pp. 82–105.

Briefly, the idea is that there is no understanding of a text apart from the commitments and purposes that inform the text's uses. A canonical understanding would be one congruent with the normative uses for which the biblical text was intended and to which it has for centuries been put by the communities who receive it as Scripture. Put another way, it would be an understanding regulated by the exegetical-homiletical, liturgical, and ethical witness of the church. This regulating principle, in turn, is what is meant by the "rule of faith," the church's *regula fidei:* it is by the rule of faith that the church defines both the text itself and the context (of beliefs, attitudes, and practices) in which the text is to be read. As we shall see, the circularity that on the one hand the rule of faith determines what a "normative" use of the text is while on the other the church claims to draw the rule itself from the text is inescapable.

In any case, my contention is that Kierkegaard's understanding of James is a model of canonical understanding. Moreover, his estimation of the means by which that understanding is to be obtained and the maieutic art by which he induces the reader to recognize both the means and the meaning provide a case study in the operation of the rule of faith.

4. See especially the two works by Luke Timothy Johnson upon which the exegetical sketches in this paper are based: "The Use of Leviticus 19 in the Letter of James," *Journal of Biblical Literature* 101 (1982): pp. 391–401; and "James 3:13–4:10 and the *Topos peri phthonou,*" *Novum Testamentum* 25 (1983): pp. 327–47.

5. Sophie Laws, *A Commentary on the Epistle of James* (San Francisco: Harper & Row, 1980), pp. 3, 38.

6. J. L. Houlden, *Ethics and the New Testament* (Harmondsworth: Penguin, 1973), p. 66, as quoted by Laws, *Commentary,* p. 28.

7. Laws, *Commentary,* p. 7.

8. Martin Dibelius, *A Commentary on the Epistle of James,* 11th ed. by Heinrich Greeven, trans. Michael Williams (Philadelphia: Fortress Press, 1975), pp. 7–11, 69, 71, 77, 80, and throughout.

9. Ibid., p. 80.

10. The notorious crux of 4:5 has perhaps best been translated, "Or do you think that Scripture speaks to no effect? Does the spirit which he made to dwell in us long enviously?" See Laws, *Commentary,* p. 167, and Johnson, "James 3:13–4:10," pp. 330f.

11. Søren Kierkegaard, *Concluding Unscientific Postscript,* trans. Swenson (Princeton: Princeton University Press, 1968), pp. 165f.

12. Ludwig Wittgenstein, *Philosophical Investigations,* trans. G. E. M. Anscombe, 3d ed. (New York: Macmillan, 1958), pp. 48–51.

13. The Journals (1847), as quoted in Walter Lowrie, *A Short Life of Kierkegaard* (Princeton: Princeton University Press, 1942), p. 122.

14. Wittgenstein, *Philosophical Investigations,* pp. 19, 51.

15. On apprehension as a fundamental component of knowledge and the role of activity in its acquisition, see Charles M. Wood, "The Knowledge Born of Obedience," *Anglican Theological Review* 61 (1979): 331–40.

16. See, for example, the prophets Hosea and Jeremiah where "forgetting God" is thematic and disobedience is instrumental to it: Jeremiah 5:25, "Your sins have put far the good from you."

17. Wood, "Obedience," p. 336.

18. The phrase belongs to Tocqueville but has been borrowed by Robert Bellah and company as the title for their impressive study on community and the concept of the self. They seek to adjust the American ideology of individualism by relocating the concept of the self in the matrix of social as well as private behaviors by which our identities are constituted. Their use of the metaphor of the heart in this context is illuminating. See *Habits of the Heart: Individualism and Commitment in American Life* (New York: Harper & Row, 1985), pp. 36–37 and throughout.

19. The way this issue intersects with Kierkegaard's own authorship, pseudonymous and "direct," is intriguing, to say the least, and sufficiently multilayered not to touch here.

20. So as not to reify the concept excessively, we should remember that doubt is its own possibility; it is a manner of reception. It is we who doubt. Suspicious of authorship, we read doubtingly.

21. The phrase "not reading God's Word" and its variants recur refrain-like on every page from 53 to 58. Kierkegaard calls on the serious reader to "make a distinction between reading and reading" (*FSE*, p. 52), for the different readings produce different texts. Obviously, for Kierkegaard the "Word of God" is not a static concept, not a property of the ink on the page.

22. The answer is clearly "Yes," assuming that the reader's purpose would be to put the words to *Christian* use, to interpret them "Christianly." Interpretation requires and implies a context of conventions, shared aims and purposes and practices, in a word, a use. The subjective thinker Kierkegaard, like the canonical interpreter and the literary deconstructionist (for example, B. S. Childs and Stanley Fish, respectively), recognizes that there are no a-contextual norms of "right" interpretation. His context was consistently, if sometimes only implicitly, the Christian faith. Right interpretation in this context is interpretation that conforms to the rule of faith; or as Kierkegaard says, it is interpretation that works "to the honor of God" (p. 43).

23. "God *does* tempt a man" (p. 36), concludes defiance in frustration at James's words, for the words seem only to mock its inability to receive from God what *it* desires as good. Thus it hurls this Job-like accusation by which it tries to browbeat God into submission, tempting God to yield to its own hard-heartedness. But "God cannot be tempted with evil" (James 1:13), and "the anger of man does not work the righteousness of God" (1:20).

24. It must, that is, if it intends to explicate what it is the words want to say. It must to some extent enter into their subject matter and wrestle with the difficulties that such matter involves—again, if it is to be faithful to the intent of the words. Of course, its perception of the intent of the words is a function of the pre-understanding, the faith, it brings to the text. This is to say that theological exegesis, like *any* reading, necessarily entails a faith stance (even if that faith happens to be one of "Religiousness A" or outright nonbelief). Theological exegesis, in other words, will be as much a constructive as a descriptive enterprise in which the traditional boundary between exegesis and exposition will blur.

25. The point is boldly made in the *Works of Love:* "As we say, clothes make the man. Likewise one can truly say that the explanation makes the object of the

explanation what it is." Hereafter *WL* (trans. Howard and Edna Hong [New York: Harper & Row, 1962], p. 271). Kierkegaard's view anticipates the sociological definition of the objectivating, world-constructing force of language. See for example, Peter Berger, *The Sacred Canopy: Elements of a Sociological Theory of Religion* (Garden City, N.Y.: Doubleday, 1969), pp. 8–14.

26. Saint Augustine, *On Christian Doctrine*, trans. J. F. Shaw (Chicago: Encyclopedia Britannica, 1955).

27. The previous two references are to Romans 8:28 and I Corinthians 13:1 on pp. 42–43 of the discourse (see above, in this essay).

28. As listed by Johnson ("The Use of Leviticus 19," p. 399), the six passages with their allusions are James 2:9 (Leviticus 19:15), 4:11 (Leviticus 19:16), 5:4 (Leviticus 19:13), 5:9 (Leviticus 19:18a), 5:12 (Leviticus 19:12), and 5:20 (Leviticus 19:17b).

29. Johnson ("The Use of Leviticus 19") is careful to point out how precisely these allusions are framed by explicit Christological references. James's perspective on the Leviticus text, in Johnson's words, "is provided by the understanding of life and law given by the experience of Jesus Christ" (pp. 400–401). Thus, Kierkegaard's way of speaking about love as the love of God and the quintessential good gift is not of a fundamentally different structure from James's emphasis on loving the neighbor. Christ is the middle term by which the two forms of love are mediated and the two perspectives equated, however absent from Kierkegaard specific mention of Christ may be. (But while nowhere visible, Christ is of course everywhere present.)

30. To what extent the theological character of this procedure may account for the long scholarly neglect of Kierkegaard's exegetical work, one can only guess. The procedure seems almost to flout historical-critical conventions, celebrating a harmony among diverse historical traditions where the modern critic would be compulsively precise. Indeed, Kierkegaard signals virtually no awareness of the diversity at all. To the "newer science," the theo-logic (it is not a tradition history) that he follows from James to Paul to John would seem peculiar at best, more likely utterly naive.

   Yet Kierkegaard's harmonization is hardly the sort favored by much of Protestant orthodoxy, that of "correcting" James to Paul according to a "canon within the canon"—ironically, an approach shared by numerous historical critics as well. On the contrary, Kierkegaard is perfectly adamant in seeing that James's distinctive voice is registered. For example, there is no compromising the charge that hearing without doing is self-deception. Kierkegaard's is a "canonical harmony" that does not seek to obliterate the different voices in the ensemble but rather wants to hear the full range and penetrate to that grasp of the subject matter that allows it all to cohere.

14. Forming the Heart: The Role of Love in Kierkegaard's Thought

SYLVIA I. WALSH

It is said of certain plants that they must form hearts; the same must be said of a human being's love: if it is really to bear fruit and consequently to be recognizable by its fruit, it must first *form a heart.* Love, to be sure, proceeds from the heart, but let us not in our haste about this forget the eternal truth that love forms the heart.[1]

Love is rooted in that innermost part of our being that we figuratively call the heart. Signifying far more than a vital organ of the body, the heart is a metaphor for inwardness, the passionate, subjective realm of the human spirit. Although love is a passion that comes from the heart, it is Kierkegaard's contention that love plays a formative role in shaping the human heart or inwardness. If, therefore, we look to Kierkegaard for an understanding of the grammar or morphology of the heart, we shall see that in his thought this grammar is construed fundamentally in terms of a grammar of love.

The role of love in forming the heart is probed by Kierkegaard primarily in *Works of Love,* a volume of Christian discourses written at the midpoint of his authorship and published under his own name as author. This work is perhaps the most deeply reflected of all Kierkegaard's writings and surely one of the most profound meditations on love ever written, yet it is a work that still is not well known or much studied.[2] This misfortune is due in part to the fact that attention has been focused primarily on Kierkegaard's early pseudonymous authorship rather than on his later religious writings, but it may also reflect a general lack of interest in the subject of love among thinkers of the present century. In a history of the nature of love in Western philosophical and religious thought from Plato to modern times, Irving Singer points out that "in the last sixty years or so the analysis of love has been neglected more than almost any other subject in philosophy."[3] Thinkers such as Santayana, Peirce, Scheler, Buber, Sartre, and Simone de Beauvoir have incorporated some reflection on love in their philosophies, but to a large extent the analysis of love has been left to the field of psychology. In theology, too, we have seen the development of the neoorthodox theologies of faith, the theology of hope, the theology of play, process theology, black theology, feminist theology, metaphorical theology, and lately the birth of deconstructionist "a/theology," but very little on the theology of love.[4]

This state of affairs reveals how out of touch much of contemporary philosophy and theology is with one of the primary concerns of the human heart, where the experience of love has always been important and constitutes for many the ultimate value in life. Certainly, if the grammar of the heart is to be addressed in contemporary thought, attention needs to be given to the analysis of love. With the recent rise of interest in virtue ethics and the logic of the emotions, it is particularly timely that such an analysis be carried out. I cannot possibly do justice to that task in the present essay, but I shall try to sketch the contours of the grammar and language of love, using Kierkegaard's understanding of these as a model and guide for stimulating our own reflection on and schooling in the grammar of love and the heart.

THE GRAMMAR OF LOVE

Love is often thought to be a vague, elusive, undefinable passion that does not conform to the dictates of reason. But love has a logic, a structure, a "grammar" if you will, of its own by which it is understood and known. For Kierkegaard this grammar is informed by Christian love, which in his view constitutes the only true or genuine love and is the love that properly forms the heart. As he sees it, Christian love does not exist as a separate type of love in contradistinction to other types (pp. 77, 144, 146). It is not a "higher love" that is affirmed alongside of or in addition to other forms of love such as erotic love and friendship (pp. 59, 70). Rather, Christianity recognizes only one kind of love—spiritual love—and insists that it "lie at the base of and be present in every other expression of love" (pp. 144, 146). Spiritual or Christian love is characterized by Kierkegaard as a transcendent, transforming, inclusive, edifying, abiding, and spontaneous love that expresses itself in an indirect, inverse form and fashion. To master the grammar of that love, we must gain an understanding of its distinguishing features. In this section, therefore, the primary terms by which Christian love may be identified will be sketched and scrutinized.

TRANSCENDENT

Kierkegaard recognizes that human beings have a need both to love and to be loved and that this need for community in love is rooted in the hidden, "most inward depths" of their being, where it is grounded even more deeply and mysteriously in divine love (pp. 26–27, 78, 153). All human love thus has a transcendent matrix in the eternal, whether that is acknowledged or not, but Christian love is distinguished by the fact that it is love that has become *consciously* grounded upon the eternal or God through a command to love. Central to the possibility of Christian love is the requirement that we explicitly relate ourselves to the eternal and allow God to penetrate and become a third or "middle term" in our relations to others (pp. 70, 112–13, 117, 123). Ordinarily we think of love relationships as dyadic in nature; "three is a crowd" we are accustomed to say when a third party becomes involved. But God is not like other third parties. What might it mean to give our love relations a triadic structure by including God? Kierkegaard means something more, I think, than the divine sanction commonly sought and given in the saying of marriage vows, although that is an important aspect of coming to refer conjugal love to God. What the presence of a God-relationship within human love relations means is that God—or love, since for Kierkegaard love is God and God is love (pp. 124, 247)—becomes the object of love; that is, love itself, rather than either lover in the relation, becomes the focus of the relation.

Now this is a very profound but deeply disturbing idea, for it seems to deflect love away from concrete others as well as ourselves to an abstract principle or transcendent reality that binds us. Who wants to love love? Love for love's sake, like art for art's sake, may be a noble idea, but it does not satisfy our deep human need to love and to be loved by other human beings. Moreover, within the context of the stages of life that Kierkegaard describes in his authorship, it even appears to be aesthetic in nature—a romantic flight from entering into real relations with others.[5] But that is not the intent or desired effect of Kierkegaard's view. On the contrary, love forms the proper object of love relations precisely by putting the focus of those relations on helping one another learn *to love rather than seek to be loved* in and through the relation. In other words, the ultimate goal of a love relation should be to assist both parties in learning to love themselves, each other, and other persons in a proper manner. That is what it means to love God. Kierkegaard writes:

For to love God is to love oneself in truth; to help another human being to love God is to love another person; to be helped by another human being to love God is to be loved. (P. 113)

This conception of self-love, love of others, and love of God is quite different from the usual understanding of these and requires a fundamental transformation of both the mind and the heart in order to understand and to love ourselves, others, and God in this way. It brings us, therefore, to the second term in the grammar of love.

TRANSFORMING

Fundamental to Kierkegaard's understanding of Christian love is the claim that it brings about an alteration in love—a "change of heart" we could say—by requiring our natural expressions of love to undergo "the transformation of the eternal" so as to eradicate the element of selfishness in them. We are all well acquainted with the problem of selfishness in human existence, especially as it is manifested in ourselves. There is nothing novel in the idea that we need to overcome narcissism. But Kierkegaard extends the charge of selfishness beyond self-love as we normally experience and understand it to cover also those forms of love, namely friendship and erotic love, wherein we seek naturally to overcome, or at least to modify, the expression of selfishness in ourselves. The problem, as Kierkegaard sees it, is not merely that we continue to act selfishly in obvious ways in our erotic relations and friendships, but that these relations are themselves a form of self-love and a means of perpetuating selfishness. The friend or beloved is an "other-I" with whom we selfishly unite to create a "new selfish self" modeled on our common likenesses and differences from others (pp. 68–69). Friends and lovers are chosen on the basis of our passionate preferences, and although we are (or are expected to be) concerned with their desires and needs in the relation, we expect them to satisfy ours in return. Reciprocity and mutuality in love are essential to friendship and erotic love, but in Kierkegaard's view these qualities are precisely what makes these forms of love selfish in character. Kierkegaard is relentless in his exposé of selfishness in them. Even boundless devotion—an expression of erotic love stereotypically associated with and culturally encouraged in women's relations to men—is revealed as self-love in the "tremendous wilfulness" with which it makes the beloved mean "everything" to the lover (pp. 67–68).

Unmasked at every attempt to masquerade as unselfishness and shown to be self-centered in their very makeup, can friendship and erotic love be saved? In Kierkegaard's opinion, Christianity is opposed to these forms of love only insofar as they are characterized by selfishness. Thus it does not stand *simply* opposed to them but seeks instead to purify, sanctify, and make them new through self-renunciation, or more properly speaking, through the renunciation of selfishness in them. This transformation is envisaged by Kierkegaard as being entirely internal in nature, except for certain marks (to which we shall return later) that may serve to elicit the possibility of offense on the part of the world (pp. 145–46). Thus the outward forms of erotic relations and friendships remain the same, though infinitely changed within, where love becomes, like other affairs of the heart, a matter of conscience (p. 139).

This insistence on the totally inward character of Christian transformation has brought strong criticism of Kierkegaard, in particular the stinging charge that he lacked a social ethic. Although he was in many ways an astute and penetrating social critic of his time, I think we can see something of the limitation of his view as it applies to sexual equality. In *Works of Love* he writes:

Outwardly in a way the old remains—for the man shall be the woman's master and she shall be submissive to him, but in inwardness everything is transformed, transformed with the aid of this little question to the woman, whether she has deliberated with her conscience about having this man—for a master, for otherwise she does not get him. Yet the question of conscience about a matter of conscience makes her in inwardness before God absolutely equal with the man. (P. 139)

On a spiritual level we have in the last sentence the beginnings of a theological underpinning for a doctrine of equality between the sexes, but unfortunately no corresponding call for a change in social structures to make them commensurate with that doctrine. In the present century we have to some extent gone beyond Kierkegaard in recognizing that a change of external structures is needed to give outward expression to the ideals of sexual equality that we espouse. We have learned, too, that such changes, even when forced upon us by law, may actually facilitate the inner transformation of minds and hearts. In the area of personal relations, however, outward change cannot be legislated to any great degree, and we still live largely in the patriarchal structure of male-female relations to which Kierkegaard subscribes. To the extent that is true, many of us are no further along than he and perhaps not as far. This is not to say that Christian love cannot be expressed within a patriarchal structure, but such a pattern of relations, I would contend, is structurally incompatible with Christian love and equality. Certainly it is not an ideal structure for expressing them.[6]

A second issue that arises with respect to Kierkegaard's conception of transformation is whether the "erotic" element can be preserved in the metamorphosis of erotic love into spiritual love. Are we left with the mere skeleton of an erotic form, stripped of its distinguishing characteristics of sensuous desire, passionate preference, and reciprocity in love? Has Kierkegaard so identified the erotic with selfishness, or selfishness with the erotic, that it cannot be saved? Kierkegaard explicitly says in *Works of Love* that Christianity is not opposed to the sensuous as a physical drive and he distinguishes it from sensuality that is an expression of selfishness and egocentric self-love (p. 65). Selfishness is thus to be understood as the *willful* and *demanding* assertion of our passionate preferences in relation to others and is not to be equated with our natural inclinations, needs, and desires themselves. Presumably, then, the sensuous can be taken up into Christian love, just as Judge William in *Either/Or* envisages its preservation in marriage, and given expression in the form of what I have described elsewhere as "spiritual sensuousness."[7] But is this sufficient to save the erotic? Do not erotic relations, as well as friendships, continue to be expressions of passionate preference and thus remain fundamentally selfish in nature? To address this question in the context of the grammar of love as Kierkegaard understands it, we need to consider the next term of that grammar, which introduces the decisive category of "the neighbor."

INCLUSIVE

Central to the Christian concept of love is the requirement that we love others as neighbors. In Kierkegaard's view, neighbor reflects "eternity's mark" on every person; it is the "common mark," "the eternal likeness" or that which is shared by all persons (pp. 96–97). Neighbor is an expression for human being or the fact that being a human being is the fundamental characteristic of all human beings. It further expresses our absolute equality before God. To love others as neighbors means to love them first of all on the basis of our common humanity, as fellow human beings, rather than on the basis of personal preference. Secondly, it means to exercise an eternal equality in loving by existing on an essentially equal basis for every person. Christian love, more specifically identified as neighbor love, is thus inclusive in nature and has as its task the love of all human beings, although one person is sufficient, Kierkegaard claims, to test our ability to love others in this manner (p. 37). Only when others are loved as neighbors are they truly loved as an other, that is, as an "other-you" rather than an "other-I," for in love of neighbor the selfish desires and demands that we customarily exact in our relations to others are turned back and placed on us instead.

In Kierkegaard's opinion, the inclusiveness of neighbor love does not require the doing away with distinctions between persons nor the leveling of them to a classless society. In an apparent allusion to socialist views becoming prominent on the European continent at that time, he makes the point through a play on words that earthly likeness [*Lighed*] is not synonymous with Christian equality [*Ligelighed*] (p. 82). Rather, we are to lift ourselves above distinctions and let them "hang loosely," so as to be able to perceive the "essential person" or fundamental humanity of others (pp. 82–84, 96). Neither does neighbor love prohibit us from entering into or continuing in special relationships with one or more individuals. But the friend or beloved should be loved first and foremost, like others, as a neighbor. The Christian view, Kierkegaard claims, is that "what is eternally basic must also be the basis of every expression of what is special" (p. 141). Thus, while we certainly love persons in our special relations differently from the way we love others, this difference is not essential, since we love them fundamentally as we love others, that is, as a neighbor, and do not exclude love of others in addition to those relations. This seems to be for Kierkegaard the decisive factor in the transformation of erotic love that rids it of selfish exclusivity and establishes equality in love while preserving special relations. If neighbor love is present in erotic love and friendship, then the relative distinctions of passionate preference are allowed to stand. Thus, while we may admire our loved ones for their intellect, wit, sexual attractiveness, and many other fine features, were they to lose any or all of these in the course of life, Christianly we should still love and respect them as human beings.

While such a view of love relations might appear (somewhat oddly, in the case of Kierkegaard) to undermine the particularity of others, Kierkegaard also stresses that persons are to be loved as they are, not as we want them to be, and each in his or her own individuality (pp. 252–53). Although we should seek in our relations to strive against imperfections and to conquer deficiencies, the emphasis should lie on loving the persons we see, whether we see imperfections or perfections in them. The task is to find others lovable as given, no matter how they may change (pp. 157–58, 164, 169). Kierkegaard puts it even more strongly by characterizing the neighbor as "the ugly," in relation to whom the task is not to love the beautiful, but to love the unlovable, or rather, to find the unlovable in a person to be lovable (pp. 342–43). In this way Christian love becomes edifying, or love which "builds up."

EDIFYING

Kierkegaard devotes the whole second part of *Works of Love* to the many ways Christian love is edifying or upbuilding. We can only take note of some of them here. First of all, Christian love believes in love on the part of others and seeks to bring out the good in them. Kierkegaard denies that any person can implant or create love in the heart of another. Only God can do that. Thus we must presuppose love in others and seek to "love forth love" in them—a beautiful expression that Kierkegaard first used in a note to his fiancée Regina Olsen and that reveals the fundamentally *reciprocal* nature of Christian as well as erotic love, even though Kierkegaard insists in other passages of *Works of Love* that reciprocity cannot be required or demanded (pp. 206, 226–27).[8]

Christian love also hopes in the possibility of the future for ourselves and for others; it hopes not simply in the manifold of possibilities that we long for in life but more specifically in the possibility of the good, which is the eternal. Love seeks as well to build up others by searching for a "mitigating explanation" of their sins and hiding them in silence and forgiveness (pp. 261–78). Most of all, it seeks to help others become authentic persons in their own right by encouraging them to become independent, to stand on their own as individuals before God. That is, Kierkegaard claims, "the greatest, the only benefaction one human being can accomplish for another" (pp. 258–59). There are many other ways love can be mutually supportive in special relations and upbuilding of others in general. One of these is through the language of love, which we shall examine in the second part of this essay.

ABIDING

One of the crowning virtues of Christian love is that it abides. Merely human or natural love, as we are well aware, is transient, perishable, and subject to change even if it does not change. For this reason merely temporal love is always uncertain and requires continual reaffirmation of its existence between lovers. Its continuance is dependent on the test of time. Christian love, by contrast, is like "sterling silver," which one knows in advance and without testing will endure (p. 47). It is secured by the commandment to love and thus is love that has been made a duty. When love is a duty, Kierkegaard maintains, it is forever decided that one shall love and that love shall abide (p. 49). In love that has undergone the transformation of the eternal by becoming duty, therefore, there is no question of "falling out of love" or of breaking off relations with others, only of "falling away from love," which makes the ones who do it guilty. Here we can see the advantage of understanding love relationships in terms of three parties instead of two, for if one person forsakes another, the relation still is not broken, since the injured party may continue to hold onto the love that binds them and be strengthened by it. Although Kierkegaard entertains this as a possibility in Christian love of the utmost seriousness, since it involves not only breaking with another but also falling away from love or God, he nevertheless maintains that "the true lover never falls away from love" (p. 283). The true lover never allows matters to reach the breaking point and continues to abide in love. Even if, in an external sense, a break does occur, the true lover still abides in love and turns the break into a possibility of reconciliation in the future.

There is another side of this notion of abiding love that Kierkegaard does not articulate but that is implied, I think, by his viewpoint. As we have seen, even when love is referred to God and recognized as a duty, there is no guarantee that we shall abide in love for others, for we may still fall away from love. But even then, a Christian standpoint would hold, I think, that love abides, for even if we fail in love, the love of God abides in us, with us, and for us. We may fall away but are not cast away from that love. It continues to be extended to us in the form of forgiveness, for God, too, hides a multitude of sins and seeks a mitigating explanation for them. If that is not so, then love does not abide.

Spontaneous

If Christian love abides, does it also preserve the spontaneity of erotic love? In our natural human experience there is nothing quite so exhilarating, so heady, so heartwarming, so rejuvenating and enlivening as falling in love. At no time of our lives does the spirit of Dionysius overtake us more than in the early days of erotic love, whether we experience it in our youth, in middle age, or in later years. Then, as time begins to take its toll with the weight of responsibilities to family, work, and other commitments in life, our loves become routine, a matter of habit, and perhaps troubled as we discover and fail to tolerate the human limitations of our loved ones. If we manage to abide in love, much, if not all, of the early spontaneity of that love is gone out of it. What happens to love to cause it to lose that quality of its youth? Is spontaneity merely a romantic illusion that quickly disappears in reality? Can spontaneity be retained in love? Indeed, is not love itself a spontaneous passion, a free and autonomous feeling or inclination, so that when the spontaneity is gone, love has gone out of our relations, too? The problem of spontaneity is seemingly intensified if we hold, with Kierkegaard, that love is a duty, for that is, he admits, "an apparent contradiction" (p. 40). Commanded love, it would seem, stands in irreconcilable tension with the spontaneity and freedom generally associated with love and the desires of the heart. Even if spontaneity does not die of its own accord in our love relations, has not Christianity set itself against spontaneous love in such a way as to substitute duty for feeling and inclination?

On the contrary, in Kierkegaard's view, duty and inclination, law and love coincide in Christian love in such a way as to enable us to preserve or to regain the spontaneity of love and keep it from becoming subject to "the lukewarmness and indifference of habit" (p. 50). Unlike Kant, who would control and repress inclination for the sake of duty, Kierkegaard envisions in the transformation of love a change of heart that makes it one with duty so that what the law requires, love freely gives. A corresponding viewpoint can be found in *Either/Or*, where Judge William defines duty as "to love truly with the inward movement of the heart."[9] Although love is changed by having become duty, it remains a passion, that is, a form of immediacy. But by virtue of being consciously related to the eternal, it becomes a new form of immediacy, a "second immediacy" or a "spontaneity after reflection."

These expressions are not used by Kierkegaard in *Works of Love*, nor do they receive much explicit mention elsewhere in his writings and journals, yet the notion of second immediacy underlies the understanding of love, and faith as well, in several of his major works. In *Either/Or*, for example, Judge William argues that love does not lose its immediacy in marriage, and he defines that state as an "immediacy which has mediacy in itself."[10] Similarly, in *Stages On Life's Way* Quidam maintains that married love is a "later immediacy" and that "whereas in all other cases the destroying angel of reflection goes about shouting death to immediacy, there is yet one immediacy it suffers to stand, that of love, which is a miracle."[11] Moreover, he goes on to claim that "religion is a new immediacy, it has reflection betwixt it and the first immediacy."[12] Immediacy, he contends, is not devoid of reflection but precisely through "infinite reflection" relates itself to itself in the idea or God-relationship.[13]

So too, in *Works of Love,* we have seen that Christian love is viewed as love that is consciously based on the eternal and that has undergone the transformation of the eternal. For that very reason it is able to preserve the spontaneity of love. Love that has *not* undergone this transformation is subject to another kind of change: it can become habit and lose "its ardour, its joy, its desire, its originative power, its living freshness," in other words, its spontaneity (p. 50). In a graphic description of how habit overtakes us, Kierkegaard likens it to a preying vampire that cunningly sneaks up on a person unawares, lulls him to sleep, and then drinks the blood out of his life. When at last he awakens and becomes aware of the change that has taken place in his life, it may be too late. Kierkegaard writes:

he wants to make up for it, but he does not know where he can go to buy new oil to rekindle his love. Then he becomes despondent, annoyed, weary of himself, weary of his love, weary of its being as paltry as it is, weary of not being able to get it transformed—alas, for he had not heeded the transformation of the eternal in time, and now he has lost the capacity to endure the cure. (P. 51)

However fixed and seemingly intransigent habit is, it is never the unchangeable but is precisely that which should and can be changed. In Kierkegaard's view, however, only the "You shall" of duty can bring this about, for it introduces into love that which is the truly unchangeable, namely the eternal, which "never becomes old and never becomes habit" (p. 52).

Kierkegaard does not elaborate on exactly how the eternal enables us to avoid or overcome habit in love. But we may find an important clue, I think, in the conclusion of *Works of Love* where Kierkegaard, speaking in the guise of the beloved apostle, makes the following statement:

the commandment is that you *shall* love, but when you understand life and yourself, then it is as if you should not need to be commanded, because to love human beings is still the only thing worth living for; without this love you really do not live; to love human beings is also the only salutary consolation for both time and eternity, and to love human beings is the only true sign that you are a Christian—truly, a profession of faith is not enough. (P. 344)

Here we have, I believe, the apotheosis of Kierkegaard's thought, the final insight that unites duty and inclination, passion and reflection, law and love in his understanding of the Christian life. Nothing brings home to us more clearly the rationale for love than the reminder that it is, after all, the only thing really worth living for. In the busyness and the many responsibilities and distractions that crowd our everyday life, it is very easy to lose or never attain the insight that love is the ultimate value of life. Too often we realize or remember that too late, like the pathetic person who awakens to find himself overtaken by habit. But if we keep that insight uppermost in our minds and hearts and center our lives in it, then love can never become habit. It will remain fresh, joyful, vital, and spontaneous, as in the days of our youth, by virtue of having become a second immediacy, seasoned with the wisdom that comes with reflection and self-understanding in life.

INDIRECT AND INVERSE

For all its fine features, there is, Kierkegaard claims, an indirectness and a "strange, chilling upside-downness" about Christian love which requires a "prior transformation of mind and thought" corresponding to the transformation of love in order to be able to perceive its logic, its inner coherence (pp. 141, 173). This indirect and inverse character of Christian love is manifested in a number of ways. Love itself is hidden and must reveal itself "in another form," that is, in an outwardness that reduplicates its hidden inner form. Just as thought is hidden and speech is its manifestation, so love that is hidden reveals itself in words and works of love. It differs, therefore, from other forms of "hidden inwardness" in that it is made recognizable by these fruits. Yet there is always an uncertain and ambiguous character about them. No declaration or act is ever unconditionally a demonstration of love, even those deeds and statements that are commonly recognized as demonstrations, such as charitable acts or the oft spoken words "I love you." In the grammar of love, everything depends on *how* a thing is said and done and meant rather than by the *what* of a declaration or act or intent. And even then, Kierkegaard points out, we must continue to believe in love, for nothing can finally prove the existence of love. Thus no one has the right to claim to know love or to judge others. Only by abiding in love ourselves do we recognize it in one another, for epistemologically the principle holds in relation to love as in other matters that "like is known only by like" (p. 33).

In Kierkegaard's perspective, the ambiguity of love is intensified in Christian love by the fact that love is understood in an opposite manner from the way it is generally understood in the world (pp. 62, 115, 118, 310–11). What the world regards as love is, from a Christian standpoint, self-love, and, conversely, what Christianity calls love is self-love from a merely human standpoint. In their natural forms, erotic love and friendship are really expressions of selfishness, for in them we love others on the basis of personal preference and seek reciprocity and exclusivity in love. Conversely, Christian love may appear to be a form of self-love, even hate, when the one who expresses it is unwilling to understand and practice love as others do. A collision is thus provoked between the two conceptions of love, bringing about the "double danger" of eliciting the possibility of offense from others as well as from within oneself (pp. 83, 86, 90–91, 185–89). So essential is the mark of double danger to Christian love and self-renunciation that Kierkegaard claims "as soon as the double-mark is missing the self-renunciation is not Christian self-renunciation" (p. 189).

What is the double danger in the grammar of Christian love described here? Is Christian love really so different from our ordinary conception of love? And are our natural expressions of love as narcissistic and self-serving as Kierkegaard suggests? Kierkegaard seems to have caught us coming and going here, for if we disagree with the conception of Christian love which he presents, that may only reflect a merely human mentality that wishes to define Christian love in worldly terms. Our disagreements would then be a form of offense and serve only to confirm, rather than to deny, the validity of his conception. But if we agree that his view is essentially correct, yet decline to embrace it, that too is offense. And if we do embrace it, then we are faced with the difficulty of reduplicating this ideal in our lives. Taking these risks in stride, let us pause here for some assessment of Kierkegaard's understanding of the grammar of love beyond what has already been made. What insights does he offer that provide a base from which reflection on love may be carried forward? And what aspects of his thought need to be more adequately addressed?

Beginning with the latter question first, we can detect several weaknesses in his conception of the grammar of love. First of all, there appears to be a certain ambivalence toward natural love in Kierkegaard's thought. He says that Christianity is not opposed to natural inclination as such, only to the selfishness in it, yet he does not seem to recognize any ability on the part of natural love to love unselfishly. But if all love is rooted in the divine, there must be some natural tendency or desire within us to love others in an unselfish manner. Indeed, our lived experience, I believe, bears this out in many instances. Second, while Kierkegaard presupposes love in others and would seek to elicit love from the other in response, he also manifests an ambivalence toward reciprocity in love. Yet surely reciprocity would be the ideal in Christian love, even if it cannot be demanded. Related to this is a third dimension that I think is not adequately addressed by Kierkegaard, namely our human need to *be* loved as well as to love. Although Kierkegaard recognizes that we have such a need and that it is deeply rooted and God-given, Christian love for him is essentially sacrificial. He acknowledges that Christ, who made the ultimate sacrifice in love, felt the need to be loved (p. 154), but this theme is not developed in his thought.

The positive contributions and potential of Kierkegaard's thought for further development, however, far outweigh its limitations. By interpreting Christian love as a spiritual quality that is brought to our normal love relations rather than as a separate form of love, Kierkegaard shows us a way of affirming the unity of love and of overcoming the dichotomy between *eros* and *agape*, human and divine love, sensuous and spiritual love, that has been fostered by much of classical thought as well as by such recent thinkers as Anders Nygren. Kierkegaard thus provides a perspective that avoids or points beyond the untenable oppositions to which previous thinkers were led. In calling for the grounding of love relations in God and assigning them an ethical task, he shows us also how we may give deeper meaning to love than romantic admiration of others and personal satisfaction for ourselves. His interpretation of love or God as the object of love is one that gives Christian love a concrete, personal focus that is lacking in other views that make God or love the object of love.[14] Indeed, Kierkegaard makes sense of this notion in a way that is potentially quite meaningful for contemporary thought. For he takes seriously the identity of God as the transcendent ground of love, thus opening the way for the working out of a relational rather than a substantive understanding of the divine.

Although Kierkegaard does not altogether solve the problem of personal preference in special relations, he shows us a way also of affirming both universal love and special relations in love of the neighbor. In addition, his view of the neighbor as a true other opens up a path for going beyond a Sartrean conflict model of human relations, allowing the other to appear not as a stranger standing in opposition and fundamental hostility to the self but as a co-lover in the exercise of freedom in love. In particular, Kierkegaard's emphasis on our common humanity and equality of being as neighbors provides an essential theological standpoint for moving beyond a Sartrean as well as patriarchal framework of relations between the sexes. For as a neighbor, woman can no longer be viewed as an other or object over against man but must be regarded as his friend and beloved companion. Likewise, man may not be identified by her as being essentially and intransigently willful in his domination over her but capable of undergoing the transformation of love in relation to her. While Kierkegaard leaves much to be desired in terms of envisioning an outward change of male-female relations, that may be seen as an inconsistency in his doctrine of equality as well as with his emphasis on the "outward direction" that love takes in reduplicating itself in the works of love. Toward the end of his life, Kierkegaard became more cognizant of and sensitive to the external dimensions of the Christian life and reluctantly assumed the mantle for initiating social change. To us is passed on the responsibility for seeing it through, even in some ways he perhaps would not approve.

These are but a few of the ways Kierkegaard's thought sets an agenda for contemporary reflection on love. Clearly, there is much to be done. There is one other aspect to which I would call attention as well, namely, the language of love, which may also be illumined through a consideration of Kierkegaard's views on it in

Works of Love. From the grammar of love, therefore, let us turn to the language of love.

THE LANGUAGE OF LOVE

Lovers versed in the grammar of love speak the language of love. Spoken in the context of special relations, the language of love is not discourse about love but the communication of love in "heart to heart" talk between lovers. In this section we shall consider two forms of language through which love may be communicated: ordinary language and poetic language. From a Kierkegaardian standpoint, both of these may be regarded as metaphorical language when used in the communication of love. In *Works of Love,* Kierkegaard states that "all human language about the spiritual, yes, even the divine language of Holy Scriptures, is essentially transferred or metaphorical language" (p. 199). As he sees it, however, religious language is not a special language but rather is the same as ordinary language or what he calls "the language already at hand" (p. 199). Yet there is an infinite difference between the two. The spiritual person uses the same words as those who live solely within sensuous-psychic categories of being but means something entirely different by them. Like the "twilight language" of Buddhist and Hindu tantras, the language of the spirit is secret in character. Its secrecy consists in the fact that it uses ordinary language in a transferred manner, so that the difference between them is never directly apparent. The indirect character of religious language is thus commensurate with the inward, invisible, and transformed character of the life of love. Just as love itself is made new but retains the outward forms of erotic love and friendship, so the language of love uses the sensuous-psychic language of natural love.

In *Works of Love* Kierkegaard applies this understanding of spiritual language to the biblical expression "to edify" or "to build up." In its ordinary meaning, "to build up" means "to construct something from the ground up"; in its transferred usage it refers to anything that gives expression to love, for "spiritually understood love is the deepest ground of the life of the spirit" (p. 201).[15] "Building up," Kierkegaard claims, "is exclusively characteristic of love" because it is self-giving (p. 202). Just as there is no word or work that unambiguously expresses love, so there is none that cannot be edifying. Even opposite words and actions, when spoken or done out of love, may be equally upbuilding in different persons. "Wherever there is building up, love is present, and wherever love is, there is building up" (p. 204). The two correspond perfectly. In fact, one might even say that they are the epistemological criterion of one another.[16]

If we now extend these insights about the language of love and apply them to our special love relations, new yet old modes of expression may be opened to us. Just as Regina loved forth love in Søren and elicited from him passionate expressions of love both spoken and written to her, the language of lovers everywhere may be seen as the reciprocal response of love brought forth by love and used in a transferred manner to express the spiritual quality of their love. Although love is never adequately "said" through word, lovers are ever searching for new means of saying their love to one another. Oral declarations of love, love letters, love poems, love notes—these are the conventional forms of verbal communication in erotic love, at least for a time. As lovers settle into marriage, domesticity, extended presence, and the passing of the years, the language of love, like the spontaneity of love, tapers off and frequently disappears altogether as relations degenerate into conflict and end in boredom or divorce. Is there a way, we ask almost in desperation, of giving continuity to love through language? Continuity, to recall Kierkegaard's conception of it, is not merely the continuance of a love relation but the assurance that love, secured by the duty to love through having undergone the transformation of the eternal, will endure and remain unchanged amid change. If love is to remain fresh, vital, and spontaneous as in the days of its youth, it is part of the duty to love, I would suggest, to sustain the language of love and to find and exploit new as well as old figures in trying to say that love. For that task, we need to generate what I shall call, to borrow a phrase from Wittgenstein, "language games" of love, that is, verbal forms for expressing and celebrating the reality of love in our lives, in much the same way as sex and other acts of love give expression to that passion. In love games, ordinary language, even the explicit language of sex, can be used in a transferred or metaphorical manner to allude to the spiritual character of love. Bawdy lines on the lips

252 / SYLVIA I. WALSH

of devoted lovers may be just as indicative of the purity of their love as words reflecting sexual reserve and moral propriety. Lovers possessing wit and ingenuity may bring added enjoyment and spontaneity to their love by inventing and playing word games with puns, alliteration, rhyme, or inversions of ordinary language to celebrate and perpetuate the vitality of their love.

Along with the playfulness of love, we need to preserve also in the language of love the upbuilding features of memory and hope, gratitude and appreciation, confession and forgiveness, mutual support and acceptance, honesty and trust. Even silence may be cultivated as an unspoken language of love between lovers as long as it is consciously used in a transferred manner as a means of quietly being together or of allowing the other some privacy rather than signifying a separation or alienation between them. Finally, if love is grounded in a third, which is love or God, then the language of love needs to refer consciously as well as implicitly to God and the neighbor as the object of love. In giving voice to that which respects the fundamental humanity and not merely the special features of the beloved, the neighbor is included in the language of lovers to one another, but if they are to avoid being egotistically and exclusively turned in upon themselves, they must extend words of love to others as well. Those words will not be erotic in form, as that is appropriate only to special relations, but they will be metaphorical in the sense of being upbuilding of others.

Besides ordinary language, poetry is another form of metaphorical language that may be used as the language of love. In the romantic tradition love is regarded as the absolute subject of poetry, and the poet is the priest of love. In *Works of Love,* however, there is a running diatribe against the poet. "Christianity knows far better than any poet what love is and what it is to love," Kierkegaard claims; in fact, he thinks they explain things in opposite ways (pp. 36, 63). The poet *celebrates* love and makes the friend or beloved the object of love; Christianity *commands* love and directs it toward the neighbor. The poet sings of loving the beloved above all others; Christianity teaches us to love all humankind. The poet tries to secure love through pledging and swearing by love itself; in Christianity God or the eternal is the one by whom lovers swear and secure their love. The poet understands love and friendship as good fortune for which one is grateful; Christianity understands them as containing an ethical task.

These are but a few of the ways, in Kierkegaard's view, Christianity and the poet differ in the understanding of love. If one were to read only *Works of Love,* one would surely conclude that Kierkegaard takes a negative attitude toward poetry and does not regard it as an appropriate medium for the communication of spiritual love. But there is a positive conception of poetry and the poet to be found in his authorship.[17] Kierkegaard regarded himself as a poet of the religious and his specifically religious writings as a form of "poet-communication" in the service of Christianity. His task, as he understood it, was to portray, like an artist, the "ideal picture" of a Christian. There is, then, a legitimate kind of poet and an appropriate place for poetry in the Christian life. Even in *Works of Love,* if we read it carefully enough, we can see that Kierkegaard makes a distinction between the godly or religious poet and the ordinary or secular poet (p. 60). Of godly poets he writes:

These do not celebrate erotic love and friendship; their songs are to the glory of God, songs of faith and hope and love. Nor do these poets sing of love in the sense a poet sings of erotic love, for love to one's neighbor is not to be sung about—it is to be fulfilled in reality. Even if there were nothing else to hinder the poet from artistically celebrating love to one's neighbor in song, it is quite enough that with invisible letters behind every word in Holy Scriptures a disturbing notice confronts him—for there it reads: go and do likewise. Does this sound like an artistic challenge, inviting him to sing? (P. 60)

Qua poet, the religious poet, like the secular poet, stands in tension with the ethical task of love but is distinguished from the secular poet by the fact that he or she is related to the Christian ideal of love as one who is striving toward it. This seems to be the decisive factor distinguishing the two kinds of poets as Kierkegaard reflects on them in his journals.[18]

What then of the ordinary poet and of poetic celebrations of love? Shall the poets, as Plato would have it, be banished and erotic poems of love no longer be recited? Kierkegaard concludes in *Works of Love* that it would do little good to rid the world of poets as long as people continue to understand existence as they do. Neither does he admonish Christians to shun poetry. A good poet may still be read and admired, but one must know how to relate oneself properly to the poet, that is, be aware of the differences between the Christian and poetic lifeviews.

It would seem, too, that the poetry of erotic love might well be employed metaphorically by lovers as a means of expressing and communicating the "deeper erotic" or spiritual quality of their love. For if erotic love has undergone the transformation of the eternal in such a way as to preserve and sanctify the erotic element, then it ought to be possible to retain and affirm that element in the poetry of love, too. Thus the poetry of love may become the language of love and give powerful expression to it. It may be, however, that new, more explicitly religious love poems will need to be composed by lovers to express the specifically Christian qualities of their love. But such poetry should come *out of* and *in the midst of* the life of love as a mode of expressing and celebrating the actuality of that love. In an early, undated letter to Regina, Kierkegaard observes that "the poetical precedes the actual, which is not to say that the poetical ceases where the actual begins, but that the former is older than the latter and delimits the latter as the eternal always delimits the temporal."[19] What I am suggesting here is that the poetical may and should continue *in* the actual, that in becoming true or genuine lovers we may also become poets of love, giving verbal expression to the ideality as well as to the suffering of Christian love in our lives. That does not mean that we should all "try our hands" at poetry writing. The ideality of love can be expressed poetically in many ways, and best of all by living it. Nor will such poetry as is written need to qualify as "great poetry" as measured by the standards of literary critics. What is requisite for the poetry of love is the passion of love. As one of Kierkegaard's pseudonyms puts it: "without passion, no poet."[20] Those of us who are more gifted in writing may give poetic expression to that passion for the rest of us, as the great poets have always done. Although the poetry of love, like other forms of speaking in the language of love, is never a sure mark of love, we should not for that reason refrain from writing and saying it. For as Kierkegaard eloquently reminds us in *Works of Love:*

Your friend, your beloved, your child, or whoever is the object of your love, has a claim upon its expression also in words when it really moves you inwardly. The emotion is not your possession but the other's. The expression of it is his due, since in the emotion you belong to him who moves you and makes you conscious of belonging to him. When the heart is full you should not grudgingly and loftily, shortchanging the other, injure him by pressing your lips together in silence; you should let the mouth speak out of the abundance of the heart. (p. 29)

The heart formed by love thus will speak out in the language of love and offer that, along with its works of love, as the fruit of love by which it may be recognized, received, and returned by the beloved in reciprocal gestures of love.

NOTES

1. Søren Kierkegaard, *Works of Love,* trans. Howard Hong and Edna Hong (New York: Harper & Row, 1962), p. 29. Future references to this work will be given in the text in parentheses.
2. For recent studies focusing wholly or in part on *Works of Love* see L. Brøndum, "S. Kierkegaard om 'Kjerlighedens Gjerninger,' " *Dansk Teologisk Tidskrift* 20 (1957): pp. 242–51; Linell E. Cady, *The Conceptions of Love and the Self in the Thought of Søren Kierkegaard and Josiah Royce* (Ph.D. dissertation, Harvard University, 1981); Claude Edward Deyton, *The Idea of Love in the Work of Søren Kierkegaard* (Ph.D. dissertation, Drew University, 1981); Hans Friemond, *Existenz in Liebe nach Sören Kierkegaard* (Müchen: Anton Puslet, 1965); Leonard L. Hohbein, *Kierkegaard's Understanding of Love, Particularly as Presented in 'Works of Love'* (Ph.D. dissertation, Depaul University, 1979); Valter Lindström, "A Contribution to the Interpretation of Kierkegaard's Book 'The Works of Love,' " *Studia Theologica* 6 (1953): pp. 1–29, and "Eros och agape i Kierkegaards äskadning," *Kierkegaardiana* 1: pp. 102–112; Paul Müller, *Kristendom, Etik og Majeutik i Søren Kierkegaard's "Kjerlighedens Gjerninger"* (Copenhagen: Kobenhavns Universitet Institute for Religionhistorie, 1976); Gene Outka, "Equality and Individuality: Thoughts on Two Themes in Kierkegaard," *Journal of Religious Ethics* 10 (1982): pp. 171–203; Mark C. Taylor, "Love and Forms of Spirit: Kierkegaard vs. Hegel," *Kierkegaardiana* 10 (1977): pp. 95–116. The author of the present study is indebted to the National Endowment for the Humanities for support of a NEH summer seminar for college teachers that she directed in 1985 on the topic of "Kierkegaard on Sexuality, Love, and Personal Identity." She is especially indebted to the participants in that seminar, who stimulated her thinking on many points developed in this essay.
3. Irving Singer, *The Nature of Love,* 2 vols. (Chicago: University of Chicago Press, 1984), vol. 1, p. xi.
4. Most notable among twentieth-century scholarship on the theology of love are Anders Nygren, *Agape and Eros,* trans. Philip S. Watson (New York: Harper & Row, 1969), and Gene Outka, *Agape: An Ethical Analysis* (New Haven: Yale University Press, 1972).
5. For aesthetic interpretations of love as the object of love compare Roland Barthes, *A Lover's Discourse: Fragments,* trans. Richard Howard (New York: Hill

and Wang, 1978), pp. 31–32, and Denis de Rougemont, *Love in the Western World*, trans. Montgomery Belgion (New York: Fawcett World Library, 1969), p. 52.

6. Kierkegaard himself explores the possibility of a nonhierarchical model for the divine-human relation, and thus by implication also for human relations, in the parable of the king and the maiden in *Philosophical Fragments*, ed. and trans. Howard V. Hong and Edna H. Hong (Princeton: Princeton University Press, 1985), where the two are made equal in love (pp. 26–30). On this point see my essay, "On 'Feminine' and 'Masculine' Despair," in *International Kierkegaard Commentary: The Sickness Unto Death*, ed. Robert L. Perkins (Macon: Mercer University Press, 1987).

7. See Sylvia Walsh Utterback, "Don Juan and the Representation of Spiritual Sensuousness," *Journal of the American Academy of Religion* 47 (1979): pp. 627–44.

8. Søren Kierkegaard, *Søren Kierkegaard's Journals and Papers*, 7 vols., trans. and ed. Howard V. Hong and Edna H. Hong (Bloomington: Indiana University Press, 1967–78), vol. 5, no. 5526.

9. Søren Kierkegaard, *Either/Or*, 2 vols., trans. David F. Swenson and Lillian Marvin Swenson (vol. 1) and Walter Lowrie (vol. 2) and rev. Howard A. Johnson (Princeton: Princeton University Press, 1972), vol. 2, p. 151.

10. Ibid., vol. 2, p. 96.

11. Søren Kierkegaard, *Stages On Life's Way*, trans. Walter Lowrie (New York: Schocken Books, 1967), pp. 147, 155.

12. Ibid., p. 159; see also p. 364.

13. Ibid., p. 376.

14. See Singer, *The Nature of Love* and Gilbert C. Meilaender, *Friendship: A Study in Theological Ethics* (Notre Dame, Ind.: University of Notre Dame Press, 1981) for treatments of this issue in Plato, Augustine, and other Christian thinkers.

15. It is interesting to note that Martin Heidegger, in *Poetry, Language, Thought*, trans. Albert Hofstadter (New York: Harper & Row, 1971), also employs the notion of building in his analysis of human Being in the world, and like Kierkegaard he goes back to the etymology of the word to reveal its fundamental meaning. But whereas Heidegger defines building in terms of the cultivation and construction of things for dwelling in the world, Kierkegaard makes a distinction between building and building up: "Everyone who *builds up* also *builds;* but not everyone *builds up* who *builds*" (p. 200).

16. On this point I am indebted to Robert L. Perkins, "Kierkegaard: A Kind of Epistemologist," a paper presented at the conference on "Kierkegaard and Contemporary Philosophy" at St. Olaf College, 1985.

17. See Utterback, "Don Juan and the Representation of Spiritual Sensuousness"; and Sylvia I. Walsh, "The Subjective Thinker as Artist," a paper presented at the conference on "Kierkegaard and Contemporary Philosophy" at St. Olaf College, 1985 (including references to other studies).

18. Kierkegaard, *Journals and Papers*, vol. 6, no. 6528.

19. Kierkegaard, *Kierkegaard: Letters and Documents*, trans. Henrik Rosenmeier (Princeton: Princeton University Press, 1978), p. 74, no. 28.

20. Kierkegaard, *Stages On Life's Way*, p. 369.

Notes on Contributors

Richard H. Bell is Frank Halliday Ferris Professor of Philosophy, The College of Wooster, Wooster, Ohio. In 1978, with Ronald E. Hustwit, he coedited *Essays on Kierkegaard & Wittgenstein: On Understanding the Self,* published by The College of Wooster. He is also editor of a six-book series published by the Westminster Press, 1984, "Spirituality and the Christian Life," including his book *Sensing The Spirit.* Bell has published several articles on Wittgenstein and religion, including "Wittgenstein's Anthropology: Self-understanding & Understanding Other Cultures," *Philosophical Investigations* 7, no. 4 (October 1984).

Jens Glebe-Møller is professor, the Institute for Systematic Theology, University of Copenhagen, Denmark. He has written the following books: *A Political Dogmatic,* trans. Thor Hall (Fortress Press, 1987), *Jesus og Teologien: Kritic af en tradition* (Kobenhavn: Gad, 1984), *Marx og Kristendommen* (Kobenhavn: Gad, 1971), and *Wittgenstein og Religionen* (Kobenhavn: Gad, 1969).

Paul L. Holmer retired as Noah Porter Professor of Philosophical Theology, Yale University, in May 1987, and is now Distinguished Service Professor at Augsburg College in Minneapolis, Minnesota. Among his many publications are *Making Christian Sense* (Westminster Press, 1984), *The Grammar of Faith* (Harper & Row, 1978), and *C. S. Lewis: The Shape of His Faith and Thought* (Harper & Row, 1976). Holmer has been a major translator and interpreter of Kierkegaard's writings for over forty years.

Ronald E. Hustwit is professor of philosophy, The College of Wooster. He is coeditor with J. L. Craft of the papers of O. K. Bouwsma: *Toward a New Sensibility: Essays of O. K. Bouwsma* (University of Nebraska Press, 1982), *Without Proof or Evidence: Essays of O. K. Bouwsma* (University of Nebraska Press, 1984), O. K. Bouwsma, *Wittgenstein Conversations, 1949–1951* (Hackett Publishing Co., 1986). Hustwit also coedited with R. H. Bell, *Essays on Kierkegaard and Wittgenstein,* (The College of Wooster, 1978) and has written several articles on Kierkegaard.

H. E. Mason is professor of philosophy, University of Minnesota, Minneapolis. He has two recent articles of interest to these essays: "Realistic Interpretation of Moral Questions," *Midwest Studies in Philosophy,* (1987) and "Wittgenstein's Treatment of the Will," *Philosophical Investigations,* forthcoming.

H. A. Nielsen is professor of philosophy, University of Windsor, Windsor, Ontario. His most recent books are *The Bible—As If for the First Time* (Westminster Press, 1984) and *Where the Passion Is: A Reading of Kierkegaard's Philosophical Fragments* (University Presses of Florida, 1983). Nielsen has written numerous articles on the philosophy of language and the philosophy of religion.

Timothy Polk is assistant professor, the department of religion, Hamline University, St. Paul, Minnesota. He has recently published *The Prophetic Persona: Jeremiah and the Language of the Self* (University of Sheffield, Sheffield, England: JSOT Press, 1984).

D. Z. Phillips is professor of philosophy, University College, Swansea, University of Wales. Among his recent books are three dealing with religious themes in philosophy and literature: *Religion and Voices from Twentieth Century Literature,* forthcoming, *R. S. Thomas as Poet of the Hidden God* (Pickwick Press, 1986), and *Through a Darkening Glass* (University of Notre Dame Press, 1982). Phillips is editor of the journal *Philosophical Investigations* and is one of Britain's leading interpreters of Wittgenstein.

Robert C. Roberts is professor of philosophy and psychological studies, Wheaton College, Wheaton, Illinois. Among Roberts's books are *Faith, Reason, and History: A Reading of Kierkegaard's Fragments* (Mercer University Press, 1986), *The Strengths of a Christian* (Westminster Press, 1984), and *Spirituality and Human Emotion* (Wm. B. Eerdmans Publishing Co., 1982). He has recently coedited with Robert B. Kruschwitz, *The Virtues: Contemporary Essays on Moral Character* (Wadsworth Publishing Co., 1986).

Don E. Saliers is professor of theology and liturgics, Emory University, Atlanta, Georgia. Among his recent works are *Worship and Spirituality* (Westminster Press, 1984), *From Hope to Joy: Services of*

Worship & Additional Resources (Abingdon, 1984), and *The Soul in Paraphrase: Prayer and the Religious Affections* (Seabury Press, 1980). He has recently served a term as president of the North American Academy of Liturgy.

Patrick Sherry is lecturer in religious studies, University of Lancaster, Lancaster, England. He has written *Spirit, Saints and Immortality* (Macmillan Press, 1984), and *Religion, Truth and Language Games* (Barnes and Noble, 1977). He recently coedited with Ninian Smart, John Clayton, and Steven T. Katz *Nineteenth Century Religious Thought in the West,* 3 volumes (Cambridge University Press, 1986).

Sylvia I. Walsh is associate professor, department of religion and philosophy, Clark College, Atlanta, Georgia. Walsh directed a National Endowment for the Humanities seminar for college teachers in the summer of 1985 on the subject "Kierkegaard: Sexuality, Love, and Personal Identity." Recent articles include "On 'Feminine' and 'Masculine' Despair," in the *International Kierkegaard Commentary: The Sickness Unto Death* (Mercer University Press, 1987) and "Women in Love," *Soundings* 65, no. 3 (Fall 1982).

John H. Whittaker is professor of philosophy and religious studies, Louisiana State University, Baton Rouge, Louisiana. He is author of *Matter of Faith and Matter of Principle: Religious Truth Claims and Their Logic* (Trinity University Press, 1981). Whittaker has written a number of articles on both Kierkegaard and Wittgenstein and is currently undertaking several writing projects with a National Endowment for the Humanities fellowship.

Rowan Williams is Lady Margaret Professor of Divinity and canon of Christ Church, Oxford University. He has written widely in patristic studies, orthodox theology, and contemporary theology. Among his recent books are: *Arius: Heresy and Tradition* (Darton, Longman & Todd, 1987), *Truce of God* (Pilgrim Press, 1983), *Resurrection* (Darton, Longman & Todd; Pilgrim Press, 1982), and *The Wound of Knowledge* (Darton, Longman & Todd, 1979). A recent article of importance is his "Religious Realism," *Modern Theology* (1984).